# NATURAL APPROACHES
# TO
# READING AND WRITING

**Patricia Antonacci**
**Carolyn Hedley**

*Fordham University*


and


**Robin Alinkofsky**
**Anthony Baratta**
**Regis Bernhardt**
**David Berg**
**Christine Bluestein**
**Sally Costa**
**Patricia Chaplin**
**Patricia Chiarelli Elfant**
**Florence Musiello**

**ABLEX PUBLISHING CORPORATION**
**NORWOOD, NEW JERSEY**

Printed in the United States of America

**Library of Congress Cataloging-in-Publication Data**

Antonacci, Patricia.
    Natural approaches to reading and writing / by Patricia Antonacci,
Carolyn Hedley [et al.].
        p.  cm.
    Includes bibliographical references and index.
    ISBN 0-89391-750-8. -- ISBN 0-89391-922-5 (pbk.)
    1. Children--Language.   2. Children--Books and reading.
3. Literacy.   I. Hedley, Carolyn N.   II. Title.
    LB1139.L3A58  1994
372.6--dc20                                                          93-45365
                                                                           CIP

Ablex Publishing Corporation
355 Chestnut Street
Norwood, New Jersey 07648

# Table of Contents

# The Authors

*Robin Alinkofsky* is a professor at Long Island University's School of Education in Brooklyn, New York, where she teaches reading and special education. She is active in the Brooklyn and Manhattan Reading Councils, New York State Reading Association, and the College Reading Association. She earned her doctoral degree at Yeshiva University.

*Patricia Antonacci* is president of the Westchester (New York) Reading Association and is active in the New York State Reading Association. She teaches in the Westchester Schools and at Fordham University at Lincoln Center and at Tarrytown. She has developed several reading programs and is active in the development of assessment techniques in the Yonkers Public School System. Dr. Antonacci has authored chapters in the book, *Whole Language and the Bilingual Learner* and *Reading and the Special Learner;* she is widely published in reading journals.

*Anthony Baratta* is a professor at Fordham University's Graduate School of Education. Currently, he is chairman of the Division of Curriculum and Teaching and director of the Human Resources and Adult Education Program. Dr. Baratta is co-editor of the books *Contexts of Reading* and *Cognition, Curriculum, and Literacy,* in addition to many other publications. He has been a public school teacher and principal; currently he is on the Board of Education of the Nutley, New Jersey public school system.

*David Berg* is President of the Manhattan Reading Council, delegate to the New York State Reading Association, and member of the Early Childhood Committee in that organization. He is an assistant principal in the New York City Public Schools, District 18, Brooklyn, and has developed materials and handbooks for parenting workshops, for curriculum development, and for a second language program, prekindergarten through grade 5.

*Regis Bernhardt* is Dean of the Graduate School of Education, Fordham University. He is a former teacher and counselor in the public schools and a former Associate Dean of the Graduate School of Education. He has long been interested in shared decision making at the schools level, and writes the chapter in this book from his own experiences in administration.

**v**

*Christine Bluestein* is a kindergarten teacher in P.S. 199 in Manhattan. She is an excellent master teacher who has fostered whole language practice at P.S. 199 in District 3, Manhattan, and at Fordham, where she works with student teachers. She has a strong interest in improving education with a meaning-centered curriculum, and she gives staff training in whole language reading and hands-on math.

*Patricia Chaplin* is a first-grade teacher in DeRuyter, New York. She is a member of the Assembly of Delegates of the New York State Reading Association and conducts workshops for teachers throughout the state.

*Sally Costa* is a reading specialist in the Clarkstown Schools, New York. She is active in the Rockland Reading Council and the New York State Readng Association, where she is on the Early Childhood and Reading Committee. Currently, she is completing her doctorate at Fordham University. She has published articles in *The Connection*, a newsletter for parents and home educational programs.

*Patricia Chiarelli Elfant* is a curriculum specialist in the North Rockland Schools, namely the Haverstraw-Stony Point Schools. Additionally, she is an adjunct at Fordham University teaching courses in reading and linguistics. She earned her doctorate at Fordham University: Her dissertation research was done on the metacognitive processes of first graders.

*Carolyn Hedley* a co-director of the annual Reading Institute and professor of reading at Fordham University's Graduate School of Education, is active in the New York State Association and is vice president of the Westchester Reading Council. Dr. Hedley is co-editor and author of the books, *Contexts of Reading, Home and School: Early Language and Reading; Reading and the Special Learner; Cognition, Curriculum, and Literacy;* and *Whole Language and the Bilingual Learner.*

*Florence Musiello* is a teacher of fifth graders in the Ardsley Public Schools. In addition, she is adjunct professor at Fordham University, where she received her doctoral degree. She runs workshops on whole language in the Westchester schools.

# Acknowledgments

The learners in our classes participated in creating demonstrations of literacy, and we wish to thank them for helping us to learn more about natural language processes. Their quips, their verbal protocols, their readings, their writings, and the portfolios that followed are the stuff of this book. Second, as the other half of this language learning process, we are grateful to one another as teaching professionals for keeping the faith and expending the effort for producing this collective work based on our schooling experiences.

Further, we wish to thank the New York State Reading Association, particularly the Assembly of Delegates, for providing the impetus for our meetings, our workshops, and the resulting publications. Their support was essential to our effort.

We thank Barbara Bernstein for encouraging us and for being the perfect editor, sensitive to her authors, trusting us when we needed to be trusted, and upbraiding us when necessary. Fordham University is good about providing support for the final typing of the manuscript, as they did in this case; we thank Fordham administrators for their enlightened position in these matters. As usual, we thank Anne Goldstein for her superb manuscript and for being there when needed. Finally, we wish to acknowledge those meaningful others who support us through these periods of composing and make the whole project worthwhile.

The Authors, Spring 1991

# Preface

Most of the authors of this volume have yet to become aware of the factor that has made this book most possible: the collaborations involved in composing and the professional friendships that grow from such transactions. The author-contributors to this volume have been professional colleagues and friends for years. Nearly all of us are members of the New York State Reading Association (NYSRA) and serve on the Early Childhood Committee for that organization. Together we devised the *Position Paper on Early Literacy* for NYSRA long before we conceived of this book. From these professional relationships, we decided to put together a two-day presentation workshop on *Early Reading and Writing: Natural Approaches* at the New York State Reading Association's Annual Conference (1989) at Kiamesha Lake. Prior to our presentation, we met several times to draw our presentation together; we also phoned one another regularly as the presentation deadline neared. Finally, we met for one whole morning sharing materials, developing audiovisual presentations, sharpening our speeches, and working out hands-on techniques. Thankful that we were well received at the preconvention session, we thought what we had presented was just too good to simply let lie. As a result of our discussion, we approached Barbara Bernstein at Ablex Publishing with the notion of creating a book. She agreed to let us go forward based on a prospectus for our work. Consequently, we have spent the last six months developing our chapters in this book. The point is, almost all of our production has been quite a lot of fun.

When one sits down to the blank word processor screen with the notion of producing a book, the task is nearly overwhelming. But we had been through our organizational outline and our respective chapters in so many forms before we wrote them that the actual culmination of the book was not very daunting. Had we worked in isolation, the book never would have come about. It was delightful to work with task-oriented others. So we celebrate one another before we begin to introduce what we have said. Particularly we celebrate Pat Antonacci who was our guiding light, and who filled in the chapters that needed doing to provide a balanced production. We have decided that we are all authors, and we asked to be listed as such, even though some are first among equals. We are still colleagues and friends!

An overview of the book is presented in Chapter 1. The book begins with the sources of literacy. Carolyn Hedley provides the three leading theories supporting natural language development—Piagetian, Vygotskian, and cognitive or information processing. In fact, these theories embody what is most accepted in cognitive psychology today. They are not viewed as antithetic, but as different presentations of a rather complete theory of cognitive processing.

Following the theoretical basis for natural language processes, in Chapter 2, Pat Antonacci asks (and answers) "How do young children acquire such rapid growth in oral language without direct instruction?" Infants are social and they need to satisfy their social needs through mastery of the culturally based symbol system. Dr. Antonacci has developed this theme deeply and well, as she moves to discuss the highly essential adult role in the language acquisition.

David Berg, in Chapter 3, indicates the universality of play in language learning; he notes that play empowers children, that they live out their roles, their own socialization and, to some extent, their fears and inhibitions in the play process. Not only do children command their own learning and restraints during play, these play structures are nearly always conducted through symbolism and language. Thus, play becomes a powerful means for learning language.

Chapter 4, the last chapter in this section (developed by Pat Antonacci), is on portfolio assessment. Although there is movement in this country away from the use of standardized tests in the early grades, there is a greater emphasis on "kid-watching" and on portfolios with accompanying techniques and checklists to ascertain what young children, highly knowledgeable and very individual, know about print reading and print creation. Dr. Antonacci does a magnificent job of providing the teacher with everything one needs to put in a portfolio. It is probably the development of such informal assessment techniques, along with Barbara Bush and her TV demonstrations, that is currently fostering an almost obsessive movement to read with one's children and grandchildren. We applaud!

In the second part of the book, we develop specific approaches for developing literacy. It was here that we felt most comfortable, since many of our presentations were strongest in this area. Pat Antonacci begins this section with chapter 5 on the development of preschool early writing; many of us feel that writing, at least pictures and scribbles, occurs with or even before reading. As fortunate as the read-aloud experience is and as early as it can begin (infancy), writing is developing concurrently with the child's understanding and telling of story in both oral and written presentation. Dr. Antonacci discusses the characteristics of emergent writing as it develops naturally in the home. She provides a description of the informal means and materials that children use to create written communication in the nonschool and school setting. Finally she describes the use of techniques for developing emergent and formal writing in school.

In Chapter 6, Dr. Antonacci continues her good work with the writing process by providing in-school techniques for developing effective, joyous, collaborative writing experiences. She describes the writing process classroom, its stages and programs, formats, and settings for supporting such processes. Her work grows from her experiences in her own classroom and the applicational aspects are abundantly clear.

Christine Bluestein parallels Dr. Antonacci's chapters in her treatment of emergent reading in Chapter 7. She develops her position from her work with kindergarten children and from the research in the field, supporting such ideas as creating and facilitating literacy classrooms. She develops notions of the shared reading experience and continues with strong recommendations as to the kind of books children will want to read or have read, finally developing a list of teaching techniques that will foster children's reading.

Sally Costa develops Chapter 8 on the topic of children's literature. What kind of books do we want children to read? What are the criteria for selecting books? What concepts should we try to develop through literature? What feelings and social and emotional skills are fostered through stories? A recommended list of tried-and-true books is provided that meet the needs for the developing conceptualizatioan of young children; the various genre of books are explored. Then appropriate activities growing from literature are developed, with a fine appendix full of recommendations for story book reading.

In Chapter 9, Patricia Chiarelli Elfant develops an important but ignored aspect of the reading process, the presence and development of metacognition in the reading process. Does the young child know what he knows? Can he predict the outcomes of a story? Can he monitor his own progress? Can he evaluate it and rectify some of his procedures for learning to read? Dr. Elfant sees such metacognitive strategies as critical to becoming a good reader and she has found a great deal of evidence of such development in young children. Dr. Elfant suggests what teachers can do to develop metacognitive strategies in a natural approach to teaching reading. A fascinating chapter on an underdeveloped and critical aspect of reading!

Finally, in Chapter 10 of this section, Pat Chaplin develops the notion of the theme unit through literature. Ms. Chaplin advocates teaching literacy across the curriculum and provides easy strategies for developing theme units from single stories or from literary genre. She calls her technique for integrating literature into the subject area *literacy webbing*.

The last section of the book discusses support for literacy development. In Chapter 11, Florence Musiello indicates the psychophilosophical perspectives for classroom practice—including Piaget, Vygotsky, Britton, and others—as a basis for her developmental model for teaching. She discusses natural language environments and their implications for school-based literacy. In a very concrete manner, she discusses what the natural language learning classroom would be, how it would look, and what practices would apply. Following Dr. Musiello's work, Regis Bernhardt and Anthony Baratta in Chapter 12 discuss how teachers can become empowered to implement natural language programs. These two administrators write that the schools must be restructured to include students, parents, and teachers in a more participatory process and structure. Line and staff relationships must be reconceptualized; if it is true that the unit of measure for school success is the individual school, most strongly influenced by the particular style of the principal, then greater empowerment of teachers, and greater participation and interaction of students and parents, must occur under the aegis of the principal. The authors conclude with a discussion of how changes in teacher governance can occur. Finally, a fine appendix of Family Resources is provided by Robin Alinkofsky.

So there we have it. We've already begun to empower teachers, since it was they who wrote this book. We wanted to support the current trend of acknowledging that experiences counts, and that teachers should be recognized for the profound contributions that they make, in this case, authoring a book. Thus, we are all *authors*—and comrades in arms for the promotion of literacy.

Carolyn N. Hedley

# Part I

# The Development of Literacy

# Chapter 1

# Theories of Natural Language*

## Carolyn N. Hedley

Theory provides the rationalization for practice, for the reasoned behaviors that give teaching balance and direction. Without theory, teachers become baseless romantics, who know they "do well" in the classroom without understanding how they are accomplishing their work with children so effectively. Educators will have little to say to critics, who may feel they are sentimentalizing curriculum practice, unless teachers understand the hard-headed rationale for motivating students to higher thought and continued learning. When a parent asks a teacher why she is using these "library books instead of basals to teach reading," it is not a rhetorical question; the teacher had better have some sound reasons for teaching as she does. In our use of natural language approaches for implementing holistic instruction, we find ourselves emotional, defensive, and polarized proponents of methods we may not fully understand. Supported by philosophical and psychological theory, natural approaches to learning language become sound teaching based on firm policies, rather than a sentimental journey.

## WHY LITERATURE?

We need to practice natural and whole-language instruction in our classrooms, not because we are following a fad, but because the use of literature-based programs (a) allows students to participate in the aggregated

---

* Excerpts for this chapter were taken from the chapter by C.N. Hedley, 1991, "Theories for Whole Language Teaching: A Cross Cultural Perspective," in A. Carrasquillo and C.N. Hedley, *Whole Language and the Bilingual Learner*, Norwood, NJ: Ablex.

wisdom of civilization, (b) motivates them to embark on a personal journey of exploration of their own during which their experiences and knowledges are valued, (c) helps them to make connections between their own lives and literature, (d) demonstrates how to make connections among literary pieces, (e) aids them to observe and practice effective reading and writing strategies, and (f) shows them how to observe and reflect on the ways in which fellow students understand literature (Flood, 1990). If one can give the above explanation to parents or to nonadvocates of natural language practice, then one need only know how to augment such a program to gain their support.

## WHAT WE KNOW ABOUT NATURAL LANGUAGE

Before we begin a discussion of the theories underlying natural language practice, basic principles and applications of natural language are presented , thus providing learning outcomes supported by theory.

### Basic Principles of Natural Language Instruction

- Language is social and learned in social settings. Young children learn by observing demonstrations or by modeling others' behavior; they are encouraged to participate actively, to practice independently and gradually, to become competent and confident in their use of language.
- We learn language and reading in the process of using language, a social requisite for enduring in the culture. Language users learn new perspectives, and shift psychological and social perspectives during literacy events. Literacy events include any social or introspective aspect of communication: speaking, listening, reading, writing, thinking, and/or paralinguistic activity.
- Practices include: reading to children; children seeing a reading model; the availability of a wide variety of books and materials; involvement with writing; and positive, quality, interactive responses with the child (Routman, 1988).
- Functional and social reading and writing encourage learners to discover the regularities and rule-governed nature of language, revealed by such productions as invented speech, invented readings, and invented spellings. Gradually and realistically, the student learns the mechanics of language use from the need to keep faith with other readers and writers. That is, such abilities as using phonics, word attack skills, and editing are learned from the need to share meaning effectively.

- The learner searches for meaning from print in a context or setting. The negotiation of meaning occurs between all of the users in a literary event. The author of a literary piece is one of the participants in this event. The way that a student interprets a particular literacy experience is dependent upon transactions which occur in a particular context.
- Teachers try to avoid the "cute" curriculum, teaching reading as thinking and living as reflection and decision making. We don't dwell on teaching what makes children happy, or is fun, soft, or cute, necessarily, but on teaching what is sound (Harste, Woodward, & Burke, 1984).
- Approaches to assessment view the students as the best informant of what he knows about language. Thus, the student is not an observer of his own experience, nor a performer to be measured by a standardized test. Though these measures may be used, portfolio approaches to assessment and evaluation are preferred for the young learner.
- Teachers use literature and practical life materials to teach reading. Literature allows meaning to dominate, concentrating on the development of reflective readers rather than on the development of skills. Literature promotes positive self-concepts in beginning readers, promotes fluent reading, deals with human emotions, and involves the reader in a variety of genres. Literature uses the best illustrations and literary forms (Routman, 1988).
- Skills evolve from reading meaningful text. Phonological awareness and structural analysis grow from reading literature and discovering one's need to understand the underlying principles of language.

These principles are well demonstrated in Cambourne's Model of the Conditions for Learning (see Figure 1.1).

In Cambourne's Model for Learning, children are *immersed* in literature and experiences; they best become engaged in literacy events when convinced that they are potential learners—that is, they feel they can succeed in activities that will further their life goals (literacy events include activities that have a second life in the culture around them). Further, students need to know they will not be penalized for making errors, especially intelligent errors, when they are learning; thus, they may take risks or hazard a best guess.

*Demonstrations* are important. Children learn from adult models or advanced peers. Demonstration is defined as a display of how something is done; children need behavioral, affective, and contextualized language demonstrations that are coordinated and consistent. Learners need to see how reading and writing are done, and they need to see that language *has* a system or *is* a system. They need to know what is wanted and expected; finally, children should feel that language is its own experience (Harste, Woodward, & Burke, 1984).

## Figure 1.1. The conditions of learning.

(A schematic representation of Brian Cambourne's model of learning as they apply to literacy learning)

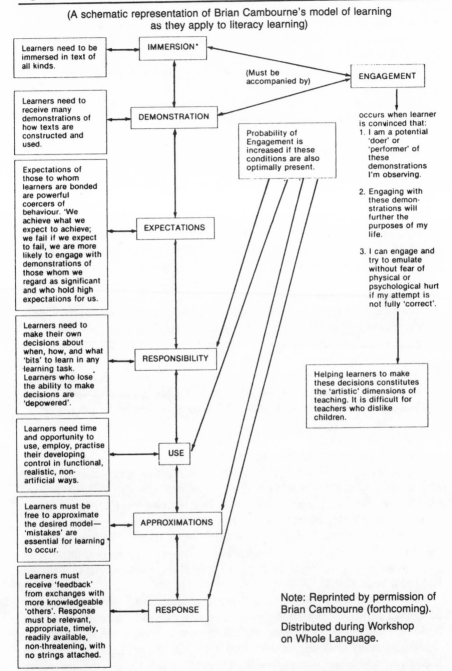

IMMERSION*

Learners need to be immersed in text of all kinds.

(Must be accompanied by)

ENGAGEMENT

DEMONSTRATION

Learners need to receive many demonstrations of how texts are constructed and used.

Probability of Engagement is increased if these conditions are also optimally present.

occurs when learner is convinced that:

1. I am a potential 'doer' or 'performer' of these demonstrations I'm observing.

2. Engaging with these demonstrations will further the purposes of my life.

3. I can engage and try to emulate without fear of physical or psychological hurt if my attempt is not fully 'correct'.

EXPECTATIONS

Expectations of those to whom learners are bonded are powerful coercers of behaviour. 'We achieve what we expect to achieve; we fail if we expect to fail, we are more likely to engage with demonstrations of those whom we regard as significant and who hold high expectations for us.

RESPONSIBILITY

Learners need to make their own decisions about when, how, and what 'bits' to learn in any learning task. Learners who lose the ability to make decisions are 'depowered'.

Helping learners to make these decisions constitutes the 'artistic' dimensions of teaching. It is difficult for teachers who dislike children.

USE

Learners need time and opportunity to use, employ, practise their developing control in functional, realistic, non-artificial ways.

APPROXIMATIONS

Learners must be free to approximate the desired model— 'mistakes' are essential for learning to occur.

RESPONSE

Learners must receive 'feedback' from exchanges with more knowledgeable 'others'. Response must be relevant, appropriate, timely, readily available, non-threatening, with no strings attached.

Note: Reprinted by permission of Brian Cambourne (forthcoming).

Distributed during Workshop on Whole Language.

'Immersion' means that prior to this retelling, the children have, through various experiences (being read to, reading themselves, discussion, various writing/sharing activities), been given the opportunity to become familiar with the concepts, language, structure, etc. of the retelling theme. Thus if it is a myth being retold, they have been immersed in other myths prior to this one being retold. If the topic is rainforests, the concepts inherent therein have been presented through other texts, experiences, prior to the retelling text being used.

Children need to know that we believe in them, that our *expectations* are high, but realistic. They need to feel that they will not be depreciated if they do well. Teachers may feel threatened by students who are beginning to trust their own judgment and logic, who are becoming autonomous. We need to show we know they can succeed mightily; it only reflects well on the class and the culture when such achievement occurs.

Growing from expectation is a sense of student *responsibility* which is a natural outcome. Students should become reflective, engaging in higher level thought, problem solving, and decision making. Over time, learners become the owners of their own academic progress. They need to feel empowered and enabled to act on their own behalf and on the behalf of others.

The *use* or practice of knowledge, the outcomes of reflection and decision making, are validated in the continued control of learning functional and realistic activities. When learners are at least becoming empowered and independent, they will find they no longer need the model to follow, but will work out their own approximations of how to achieve creatively, how to approach problems, and how to arrive at resolutions. This separation from adult models means that they will begin with *approximations* or novel ways of learning; during the process, students make mistakes; they may even experience failure in the process of learning independence.

Finally, according to Cambourne's Model of the Conditions for Learning, student need feedback or *responses* from knowlegdeable and supportive others. These responses need to be consistent, relevant, appropriate, timely, and readily available, with no strings attached.

It is worth noting that Cambourne's Model for the Conditions for Learning most closely parallels Vygotsky's thinking and we will develop the theory that supports Cambourne's model in the following section.

### Theories for Natural Language Practices

What learning theories support natural language and what practices can we take from them to do what we do better? The three theories that are presented in this work are: Piagetian, Vygotskian, and information processing. Among these three theories of cognition, we deal first with Piagetian theory as it applies to language development, then Vygotskian theory, and last, information processing theory. All three theoretical bases are viewed by cognitive psychologists as being integrated as various presentations of cognition that tend to support, rather than refute one another; thus, these three theories will be presented as complementary. Piaget, Vygotsky, and the information processing theorists are presented as offering different perspectives of the languaging process, thus avoiding fruitless and exasperating controversies that obscure the value of each viewpoint. A cohesive rationale provides natural and whole-language practitioners with a program base that is neither faddish nor soft-headed about what children need to learn. The natural, whole-language teacher espouses a content-rich classroom, filled with literacy experiences and activities that provide students with meaningful transactions; these applications should derive from a sound theoretical perspective.

The theory that has the greatest number of propositions for the support of natural language teaching is that of the Russian psychologist, Lev Vygotsky. However, much of his theory is based on Piaget. He was fascinated by Piaget and translated his work into the Russian language. But he came to disagree with much of what Piaget said, and finally developed his own comprehensive theory of language learning. Nevertheless, we cannot discuss Vygotsky adequately without beginning with a discussion of Piaget.

*Piaget and the Classroom Teacher of Natural Language.* Gardner (1990) makes the statement: "Jean Piaget, the great developmental psychologist, believed that he was studying all intelligence, but I believe he was studying the development of logical-mathematical intelligence." Gardner supports a theory of multiple intelligence, defining at least seven kinds of intelligence. Piaget, who focuses on scientific intelligence, is not primarily concerned with linguistic intelligence, which is certainly where language theory should begin. Much of Piaget's work has little to say to the language philosopher, precisely because Piaget really never deals with language development per se as he develops his stages of cognitive development. Therefore, an interpretation of Piaget as his theory applies to language progression must be provided. Piaget's four stages of cognitive development allow for language development, though he is not clear how these stages relate to language. Piaget's cognitive stages are presented below with their implications for language development:

*Sensorimotor stage.* From birth to age 2 approximately is a highly sensory stage of cognitive development. The child notes objects in his universe rather skillfully. He receives experiences and information from the world around him through his senses. Language, itself, forms part of this information base. This stage is considered to be the preverbal stage, toward the end of which egocentric behavior emerges, whereby the child is at the center of his own world, cognitively speaking.

*Preoperational or preconceptual.* From 2 to 7 years of age, the child begins to have a stable internal image of external events and actions. He engages in imaginative play; language develops rapidly. He knows a great deal about the nature of objects, but he cannot handle conservation concepts yet. He has begun to use "egocentric speech," collective monologues, and words that name things; he creates compound sentences; the child is considered perceptually egocentric, but can act upon objects; his thoughts exist in action.

*Concrete operational.* Between the ages of about 7 or 8 to the ages of 11 or 12, the child learns to do the following: combinativity ($a+b=c$), associativity ($a+(b+c)=(b+c)+a$), identity (the negation of an operation annuls it), and reversability (each operation implies its converse). The child has achieved mastery of the symbol. In terms of language, the child has learned socialized speech, conservation, and thought with concrete objects.

*Formal operational.* After age 11 or 12, the learner develops the capacity for formal, logical, abstract thought; he can cope with the past, the future, and the imagination of possible ideas. Socialized speech continues to develop along with abstract language and thought. The learner thinks about thought, he hypothesizes and generalizes; now thinking occurs without the need for external objects as a basis for it.

Major concepts in Piaget's theory are, first, the *stages of development* which tend to be age-related and somewhat rigid; there is a progression from one to the other with almost no possibility of reaching a new stage without having passed through the last one. Later, Piagetians modified this view, which was criticized for its inflexibility. In the discussion of Vygotsky's theory that follows, we find another view of cognitive development.

A second major concept of Piaget is the notion of *egocentrism*, not in the pejorative sense, but in the sense that the young child views himself at the center of activity. Perceptually, for the child, the world about functions as if he were at its center; in his perception, things and others exist to support his existence. It takes time for him to learn that he is part of a larger whole, that others have needs and feelings, to imagine himself in someone else's shoes, taking their point of view. According to Piaget, the learner outgrows this egocentric view.

A third major concept in Piaget's theory is that of *equilibrium-disequilibrium*, which provides the dynamic for learning. When the learner feels uncomfortable, or unable to solve problems effectively, he is driven to learn new forms and behaviors. He must change in order to adapt to cultural demands. Thus, disequilibrium or a vague sense of not-knowing is what moves the learner. If the sense of frustration and stress becomes too high, the learner may become dysfunctional. However, low but tolerable stress causes learning to occur, a rather negative and punitive interpretation of how learning takes place, in the view of this writer.

Adaptation to problematic situations for the learner occurs through *accommodation and assimilation.* Thus, the learner assimilates new knowledge incrementally, it would seem, until the schema (knowledge framework in memory) of a concept no longer accommodates new and incoming information. In this case, the learner must adjust or modify his schema (plural = schemata) to accommodate new information. In other words, the learner changes some of his perceptions about incoming information to include new knowledge and information. Piaget and the information-processing theorists come to agreement with regard to his notions of schema (prior knowledge, background experience, knowledge frameworks) and the adaptation processes of assimilation and accommodation. The role that language plays in such processes is less clear; for that we move to Vygotsky's theory regarding thinking and language.

*Vygotsky's Social Theory of Language Development.* Vygotsky builds much of his theory as a refutation of some of Piaget's thoughts. Vygotsky does not support the notion that language is developmental based on the number of years that the child has developed. Vygotsky finds that instruction precedes development and that the learner can learn some aspects of cognition through demonstration and experience, provided his development and maturity are taken into account. The learner must be given abstraction tasks and higher level thought problems as part of his experience. Vygotsky views the language and experience provided by the society as a primary source of developmental thought.

> For Vygotsky, unlike Piaget, there is no "stage" but only a *progressive unfolding of the meaning* inherent in language through the interaction of speech and thought....The discussion of the role of the dialogue in the shaping of thought and imagination has today an even higher place on the agenda of contemporary debate in literary theory and psychology. (Bruner, in Rieber & Carton, 1987, p. 11)

In some ways Vygotsky rejects the notion of egocentrism, though he retains the term. The child may have perceptions that are nonegocentric at very young ages; the egocentric monologue that Piaget finds inevitable, Vygotsky describes as *inner speech.* Thus, the child's early egocentric speech, when the child seems unable to separate the external world from his own experiences, as described by Piaget, is the beginning of inner speech, according to Vygotsky, whereby the child is internalizing language forms as a way to develop thought. Writes Vygotsky:

> It is on the basis of this egocentric speech, a form of speech derived directly from social speech, that the child's inner speech begins to develop. And it should be emphasized that the phenomenon of inner speech is fundamental to both autistic (self oriented) and logical forms of thinking. (Vygotsky, in Rieber & Carton, 1987, p. 75)

For Vygotsky, inner speech, a kind of dialogue with one's self relating language and thought, continues throughout one's life, as a means for realizing thought; conversely, one's thinking is realized through language production.

The idea of equilibrium and disequilibrium as the dynamic for the development of cognition describes the learner as restive or uneasy (disequilibrium) with his lack of insight and information (he knows he has a problem). Thus, the learner, finding himself in disequilibrium, is driven to learn in order to reestablish a sense of equilibrium. This notion of equilibrium-disequilibrium is rejected by Vygotsky as the dynamic for cognitive development. Instead Vygotsky provides the concept of the *dialogue* as the dynamic that promotes cognitive growth, a conceptualization that seems both more powerful and more positive. The learner is social in a socially stimulating environment, interacting with knowledgeable adults or advanced peers. The stimulation provided by transaction and interaction, later internalized through inner speech (that continues throughout cognitive development) is a major force in developing thought. The notion that some of this dialogue may be provocative or may induce problems for the learner is not negated by Vygotsky, but it is only a partial aspect of dynamic, socially constructive dialogue.

Vygotsky never discusses the primacy of thought or language—they develop separately, in his view; he does not indicate that one precedes the other (Vygotsky, in Rieber & Carton, 1987). Though Vygotsky *never* equates speech and thought as being the same, he believes that transactional speech fosters cognitive development and that thinking, which does not have the same forms as speech, is realized in speech, particularly written speech. Speech and thought develop separately with points of interface realized largely through inner speech (a speech for one's self; not whispering, but verbally constructing cognitive reality). Speech and thought do not accurately reflect one another, but each is realized in the other.

In his discussion of the *zone of proximal development*, Vygotsky provides the rationale for the adult models and advanced peers as the providers of growth experiences and developing thought of the learner. Vygotsky finds that *instruction precedes development.*

> The development of the psychological bases of school instruction does not predate instruction; they develop in an unbroken internal connection with it. Research has shown that instruction always moves ahead of development. The child becomes proficient in certain skills before he learns to apply them consciously and volitionally (intentionally). There is always a divergence between school instruction and the development of the corresponding functions. These processes never run parallel. (Vygotsky, in Rieber & Carton, 1987, p. 206)

Thus, the learner is developing both thought and speech but he has a kind of learning potential (zone of proximal development) based on this development and realized in transaction with an adult. "Research indicates that the zone of proximal development has more significance for the dynamics of intellectual development and for the success of instruction than does the actual level of development" (Vygotsky, in Rieber & Carton, 1987, p. 209). In other words, we, as teachers or knowledgeable adults, assist the learner through tasks (demonstrations) that are beyond him, a phenomenon which Vygotsky sees as more important than the actual level of development. Thus, we see that Vygotsky believes that children do not have fixed intelligence, nor are they confined to stages of cognitive development, given stimulating environments and knowledgeable adults, with whom to work in the mastery of scientific language (school-like language) and everyday communication alike. In his work, Vygotsky extols the role of teachers, since it is schooling that moves the learner from everyday functional language to scientific language. Much of this development of rational language is brought about by models demonstrating the learning acts of reading, writing, and oral language.

Vygotsky particularly praises the school for *valuing writing*. In this, he claims more for written speech than some of the advocates of process writing who are in no way diminished by Vygotsky's thinking.

> Research indicates that the development of written speech does not reproduce that of oral speech. Any similarity that exists between the two processes is external and symptomatic rather than essential. Written speech is more than the translation of oral speech into the written sign....Written speech is an entirely unique speech function....Even the most minimal level of development of written speech requires a high degree of abstraction....Written speech is speech in thought, in representations. (Vygotsky, in Reiber & Carton, 1987, p. 202)

He goes on to make the point that primarily inner speech occurs as predicate-oriented, using verb forms, or action. Supplying the contexts for speech communication requires a high level, abstract, complex grammar. Thus, writing is the highest form of verbalization and occurs as a result of instruction.

We return here to Cambourne's Model of the Conditions of Learning (Figure 1.1) and we see that Cambourne's ideas of immersion in literary events, guided by demonstrations of advanced learners, with high expectations for learners parallel in practice what Vygotsky says in theory. Additionally, the notion of delegated responsibility is accompanied by the use and practice of the concepts learned. Such responsibility allows the learner to make mistakes—while providing feedback on his progress—fit a dialectic that Vygotsky could approve. All of the above would be implemented through natural classroom dialogue.

Using Vygotsky's principles to develop classroom practice, the educator would:

- Develop content-rich and content-deep learning environments, through demonstrations with content, for children to experience.
- Develop the notion of patterned learning, providing models of learning and problem solving for children to follow. Role playing and demonstrations by adults, teachers, and advanced peers would provide models for scholarship, reading, and writing.
- Provide for dialogue and interaction with the persons listed above.

- Become mediators of learning, avoiding a return to the standup lecture mode as a usual method of presenting information. A period of adjustment for teachers and learners alike should be allowed for this departure.
- Insist the learner become engaged in his/her own learning, that one is responsible for much of what one knows. Thus, the learner is respected and empowered.
- Help students become independent learners, empowered with competencies and strategies for practicing higher-level thought, attempting new experiences that create other expressions of thinking and speech.
- Realize at personal levels that learning and creating are at root social, that language, dialogue, and social interaction are a means of developing mind in society.
- Have positive expectations for students, believing that they learn through interaction. Create classroom environments that suggest that the learner need not be mildly anxious and frustrated in order to learn and create.
- Understand that social dialogue involves approximations and risk-taking; that one may not always evolve the most felicitous solution, but that attempting a resolution to a problem is more important (and more socially valuable) than being a passive observer.
- Come to terms with the notion that dialogue in the classroom must have constraints for learning to occur. Students must remain task-oriented and learn to participate effectively during group work.
- Provide learners with feedback to improve performance. Others with more knowledge make suggestions as part of the dialogue, but these suggestions should not be made as a correction, but as a means for improving personal and group outcomes.
- Realize the importance of formal education and the school for developing scientific speech (rationalization of experience). Vygotsky views the school as most important for developing higher-level thought, particularly through language in its written forms.
- Use assessment and measures of intelligence, ability, and achievement as a point of departure for instruction. Educators should not endorse evaluation that describes fixed qualities to categorize learners. Scores exist to be modified by instruction.
- Understand that reading and writing help formulate abstract speech; that they preserve thought (and memory) and may be considered the highest forms of language, in that one realizes a high level of abstraction and elaboration of speech in its written forms (John-Steiner, in Hedley, Houtz, & Baratta, 1990).

*Information-processing theory.* A final theory for the teacher of natural language is information-processing theory. The origins of information processing theory may cause some educational resistance to it. Cognitive processing derives in part from the notion that the human mind in action resembles the operations of the computer; the parallels are obvious: immediate memory, long-term memory, sensory input, buffers, processing, retrieval, long-term store, schema, and so on. The currency of such a notion developed from the premise that if man could invent the computer, then the computer must in some way replicate man's own mind as an information processor—ordering, storing, and extending information systems.

Information-processing theory implements and reinforces much of the thinking of Piaget and Vygotsky, in the view of this writer. In much the same way that Vygotsky finds Piaget highly perceptive, useful, and accurate—providing a springboard for much of his own and others' thinking—cognitive processing theory—coming as it does from the modern form of computer technology—uses many of the terms and ideas of Piaget particularly, but also those of Vygotsky. In spite of its origins, the cognitive processing view of the mind is not mechanistic, but human. In those many aspects where the mind surpasses and/or negates computer formats, the information processing theorist is quick to say that no computer can devise a means for this kind of thinking.

In this section, we describe briefly information-processing theory, demonstrate some of its useful aspects for the natural learning of whole language, and point out some of the parallels between Piagetian and Vygotskian constructs.

Information-processing theory is useful for the natural language learning practitioner. The theory helps explain the more neurophysiological functions of the brain, as well as some of the higher-level thought processes. At its basic levels, information-processing theory tells us how the mind may work with regard to receiving information and storing it in memory, at least at a physiological level. One reason this writer is reluctant to discard cognitive-processing theory is that some medical research reveals that neurobiological processes are being discovered that seem to correspond to these basic sensory processes of cognitive processing.

At a more cognitive level of explanation, the theory offers an explanation as to how we process cognitive and affective knowledge, using such notions as schema, retrieval of information, rehearsal, elaboration, restructuring schemata, the use of metacognitive strategies, and methods for understanding metaphoric and analogic forms.

As we can see from the model above, information is received through the senses, while the learner is almost simultaneously selecting and processing information in working memory (short-term memory). Immediate working memory, that functioning of the mind of which one is consciously aware, is considered the bottleneck for receiving and processing

**Figure 1.2.   Memory as information processor.**

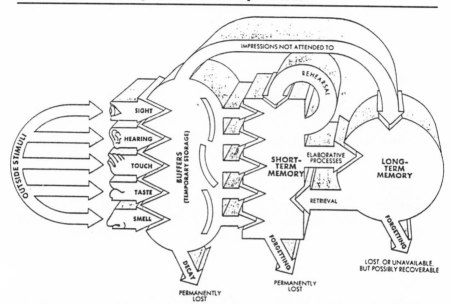

**MEMORY AS INFORMATION PROCESSOR:** *This conceptual model shows how some cognitive scientists believe memory works. The senses send information to a temporary storage, or "buffer" zone, where the mind selects what to notice. Some selections move into short-term memory, where, after "rehearsal" (repetition), they are used and soon forgotten. A few impressions go directly into long-term memory, but most of what is remembered must undergo "elaborative processes" that classify and link new information with previously stored material.*

Model courtesy of the New York Times
New York Magazine Section, 1984.

information, since we can only focus on a few ideas at a time. Thus, the learner is acquiring information from contextualized experience and combining new elements into his cognitive schemata. What the learner selects to remember is based on prior knowledge (schemata in long-term story) and what he understands is that information which is integrated into the prior knowledge (schemata, knowledge structures, frameworks, and/or scripts). Concept-driven knowledge (prior knowledge) and data-driven knowledges (new concepts from the environment, not well internalized) are both essential in the learning process. Learners gain information from both top-down strategies (an outcome of prior knowledge) and data-driven processes. The deeper that one processes information, that is, summarizes it, embellishes it, clarifies it, predicts from it, makes inferences about it, and relates these processes to one's own purposes, the more likely one is to remember it (McNeil, 1987).

Schemata (knowledge frameworks, scripts, etc.) include the concepts, expectations, processes, and beliefs—that is, all prior knowledge that helps the learner to make sense of incoming events and actions. These schemata serve the function of providing slots for new information; of helping the learner to be selective, to see what's important; of guiding the development of inferential information; and of providing a kind of summary of experience aiding in memory recollection. Much of this kind of schematic knowledge is not represented in computer-like replications of the mind, but is acquired through semantic networking that includes the affective dimensions of thought in the development of cognition.

The contexts of communication influence what will be retained, recalled, or retrieved from deep memory. One learns better through the development of strategies for learning—that is, a conscious awareness (metacognition) of one's own needs and predispositions for learning, including the procedures needed for achievement. Metacognitive knowledges are commonly described as knowledges about self, task, and procedures for gaining new knowledge. Much of this discussion seems to derive from concepts initiated by both Piaget and Vygotsky.

For the teacher the rather simplistic concepts underlying human information processing suggest practices that are useful in teaching and learning:

- The teacher needs to encourage the child to attend to task, by means of motivation, exhortation, affective strategies, group dynamics, or other effective means. Attention is mandatory for learning.
- Instruction should be based on activating prior knowledge of the learner.
- Top-down approaches are more effective in terms of activating such knowledge. Therefore the reconciled lesson that reverses the instructional process, beginning with enrichment activities or the language arts activities at the end of each lesson and working backward from these more integral social activities to reading the selection in text, and finally, attending to the knowledge of grammars, written forms, phonics, and usage is a more appropriate way of using manuals of instruction. In a top-down approach, teaching vocabulary and testing students is an ineffective way of approaching knowledge, since it does not build on the experience of the learner, activating prior knowledge.
- Scaffolding should be provided for the learner. That is, the student will gain schema more rapidly when an adult models the behavior that is appropriate. Visible demonstrations are a powerful means for learning and remembering.

- Word meanings should be linked to prior knowledge. One means for accomplishing this linkage is through the development of semantic mapping strategies and diagrams of word meaning relationships with students.
- Teachers should use direct instruction combined with the dialogue and discussion to present knowledge.
- Finally, the student is considered the best reporter of his own progress and experience. The self-report must be used as a best way to evaluate the learner's progress; moreover, these self-reports should include not only cognitive reactions to information, but insight into why learning is taking place, including feelings about learning, about one's self, about human relationships and group dynamics, and about strategies that work best and why. Students may keep journals on themselves as learners.

It is evident that these principles support natural whole-language practice in very basic ways. The parallels in the practices of information processing and the outcomes of Piagetian and Vygotskian theory are equally evident.

## SUMMARY

For the teacher of whole natural language, such a theoretical foundation of the most recent theory combined with sound practice gives real authority to the practices for natural language teaching. These notions support a rigorous curriculum, implemented by dynamics that are both humane and efficacious. Indeed, more could be written on the research that is being carried forward using the cognitive processing as its basis, research that tells us we are dealing with the best conceptions of learning for our time. Our direction for changing the classroom modestly, but effectively, is enormously right. We cannot give in to our own past practice if we are to prepare students for living in the year 2000 and beyond.

## REFERENCES

Flood, J. (1990, May). *Unifying the integrating the language arts: Part myth, part mirth, part merriment.* Distributed at the meeting of the Westchester Reading Council, Tarrytown, NY.

Gardner, H. (1990). Developing the spectrum of human intelligences. In C.N. Hedley, J. Houtz, & A.N. Baratta (Eds.), *Cognition, curriculum, and literacy* (pp. 11–19). Norwood, NJ: Ablex.

Harste, J., Woodward, V.A., & Burke, C.L. (1984). *Language stories and literacy lessons.* Portsmouth, NH: Heinemann.

Hedley, C.N., Houtz, J., & Baratta, A.N. (Eds.). (1990). *Cognition, curriculum, and literacy.* Norwood, NJ: Ablex.

McNeil, J. (1987). *Reading comprehension.* Glenview, IL: Scott Forsman.

Rieber, R.W., & Carton, A.S. (1987). *The collected works of L.S. Vygotsky.* New York: Plenum Press.

Routman, R. (1988). *Transitions, from literature to literacy.* Portsmouth, NH: Heinemann.

# Chapter 2

# Oral Language Development

## Patricia A. Antonacci

Children born into our society enter into a communicative environment, a place where talk plays a central role. It is no wonder that by the time the child reaches his second birthday, he is communicating with ease, and by the time he enters school, he maintains some linguistic competence. How do young children acquire such rapid growth in oral language without direct instruction?

The intent of this chapter is to answer this question through a discussion of selected concepts that are the basis of adult–child interaction that promote language development in the early years. A set of suggestions for prompting interactive language within the classroom setting along with approaches that facilitate the language development of the young child conclude this discussion.

No matter how many opportunities we may have to track the language of a young child, we will still be amazed at the rapid growth of his oral language development. It is not so much the number of words in his vocabulary that is the cause of astonishment, but it is the child's interactions with his mother, father, or caregiver. He is communicating, and with language, he is certainly trying to make sense of his environment; he is using what he already knows to attach meaning to novel experiences and objects in the environment. How can such a young child make these achievements within a natural home enviroinment?

### INFANTS ARE SOCIAL

In his research on how children learn language, Wells (1986) attributes such major gains of the infant to his inherent sociability; babies show preferences to the faces of their caregivers, even distinguishing their human voices. "They seem to want to communicate" (p. 34). Between the infant and the caregiver a relationship of mutual attention is developed. Very early, parents have a special way of treating their infants: They communicate with their infants and they respond to the intentions that they believe their children express. Wells notes that the parents' recognition and interpretation of their infant's intentions are fundamental to communicative behavior. It is this behavior during parent/child interaction that fosters language development. It is through these expressive dialogues, although wordless, that the infant learns to be a conversational partner.

## THE DEVELOPMENT OF INTERSUBJECTIVITY

Another important achievement in oral language development related to communicative competence is *intersubjectivity* (Bruner, 1975; Trevarthan, 1980). This fundamental concept in language development provides the basis for negotiation of meaning between parent and child. Not only does the child act intentionally but he now begins to develop an awareness of the intentions of others. Now there is a growing pattern of mutual intention with respect to conversing. Wells (1986) explains how the child's world is drawn into the conversation or into the relationship of intersubjectivity.

The infant has a need to interact with others and he is also equipped with a developing mental model that enables him to construct meaning from his environment. The relationship that he develops with his parent/caregiver and their joint focus of attention play a fundamental role in the development of communication. Not only is the young infant learning how to take turns in a conversation, but he sees how certain utterances are associated with a sequence of actions. He is learning a set of spoken phrases within a familiar context (Wells, 1986).

## CHILDREN NEED TO LEARN LANGUAGE: THE FUNCTIONS OF LANGUAGE

Language is *functional* (Halliday, 1975). That is, language is for our use: We use language to communicate our needs; we use language to make sense of the environment in which we live; we use language to maintain social relationships. When we think of how people in society—more specifically, in our culture—use language, it is not formidable to understand the rapidity in which language is learned by the infant. Language is for use!

According to Halliday (1975), the first communications of children are full of meaning. Prelinguistic children have acquired a range of possible meanings along with the functions of language; this is *before* they can speak. So by the time we first hear the young child utter his first words, he knows why language is used, that is, how language functions in human interaction.

As children continue to interact with others, their language expands; they become more competent linguistically. It is easy to understand that when children use language for a specific need or function, they become more competent in that language function. Thus, if we expect young children to continue to develop competencies in oral language, they must be given the opportunities to use language. Further, if we also expect young children to express themselves effectively for different purposes and functions, then they need to engage in oral language for a variety of functions and purposes.

What are these functions of language? Halliday (1975) aptly categorized the reasons we use language in the set of seven function categories listed below:

*Instrumental Language.* We use instrumental language when we want to get something; we are expressing a need or a want; we wish to fulfill or satisfy a certain desire. The earliest stages of instrumental language are demonstrated by requests to fulfill a specific need: "Milk, please!" "May I have another cookie?" The latter stages represent a more sophisticated use of this function. It may appear in a lengthy newspaper editorial categorized as persuasive. Throughout the day, we can listen to children speak, and we will hear this function of language dominate their conversation.

*Regulatory Language.* When we use language to regulate and to control behavior, to tell others what to do, we are using regulatory language function. Parents and teachers use this language very often in speaking to their children. This language function is also used by children in playing games, in small group activities, in social play. As language develops, controlling and regulating the behavior through speech can become subtle when that type of control is necessary.

*Interactional Language.* This very important function of language enables the user to maintain relationships. Whenever we hear children speaking to others to encourage, to ask their friends or teacher how they feel, to negotiate, to express words of friendship, or to tell a joke, they are using interactional language. Their purpose is to maintain a friendship or a certain position in a group. The importance of this language function cannot be overlooked: It is this language use that fosters harmony in personal relationships and allows individuals to work co-operatively in larger group settings.

*Personal Language.* Personal language is used to express our personality and individuality. When we express an opinion or a strong feeling, we use personal language. While this is not considered appropriate within the traditional classroom setting, it is important; because it is through this language function that the speaker builds confidence and self-esteem, establishes a sense of identity, and relates his own prior knowledge to the concepts that are being learned in class.

*Imaginative Language.* We often hear teachers say to older children during a creative writing class, "Use your imagination!" This is what the teacher of the young child must do within her class to encourage children to use their imaginations: Engage the children in imaginative language. With this language function, the child will create a world of his own and will utilize fantasy in poetry, storytelling, dramatic play, social play. If the teacher of the young child fails to encourage imaginative language, it will be lost. Its continued use throughout the grades will foster its growth.

*Heuristic Language.* When we allow children to find things out on their own, when we confront children with real problems to solve, when children wonder why things happen as they do, they use heuristic language. The purpose of this language is to learn. One might say that this is school language. Unfortunately, in too many instances, it is not. If the teacher tells the child, and the child no longer needs to investigate nor explore to find out, then he has no need for this language function.

*Informative Language.* When children convey information, they are engaged in the use of informative language. After a child has found out ideas and reports back to the group, he is using language for this function. Too often, it is the teacher who dominates this language use when she becomes the one who does the telling.

Extending classroom interaction to utilize all functions of language is an important way that teachers can ensure language development. To become competent language users, children should be competent in all language functions. Therefore, this means that a classroom that supports language development is one where language is used by the students for a variety of purposes.

## THE CONTEXT OF LANGUAGE LEARNING

No learning takes place in a vacuum; neither does language learning. A thoughtful, creative, knowledgeable teacher understands that all facets of the curriculum need to support language growth. Designing a curriculum with a language foundation demands an architect who understands how language is learned—one who knows that the basis of language acquisition is use, that language occurs for a variety of purposes, and that language develops in social contexts. In other words, if the child is to keep the momentum of his language growth and progress, then spoken language must be an out-growth of a variety of natural and spontaneous experiences.

While the social context in which the child learns language within school cannot, and probably should not, be a duplicate of the home, it can be an extension of it. Therefore, in considering the context of language learning, the following factors should be accounted for: the language context, the environment, and the school and classroom climate. In addition, the listener(s) and the speaker, along with their knowledge backgrounds and their expectations, need consideration. This is because the "function of language is intimately bound up with the speakers' and listeners' mental intentions, the ideas speakers want to convey, and the listeners' current knowledge" (Clark & Clark, 1972, p. 25). Thus because these factors must be considered in promoting oral language development, teachers can utilize content area as a means of providing the context for language learning.

## THE NATURE OF LANGUAGE LEARNING

What is the process of language acquisition by the young child? The nature of children learning their primary language is best described by Lindfors (1985):

Language acquisition is:

- a continuous, dynamic evolving process
- a meaning-focused process
- an interactive process
- an active process of creative construction. (pp. 54–55)

As we observe, listen, and monitor the child's language, we hear a language user who is not imitating but trying out the word meanings he heard his parent/adult caregiver use, we hear the overgeneralizations of word forms ("gooder"). By these we know that the young child is learning the language through its use. The focus on language use is always *meaning*.

The child is learning the critical concept of why language is used in society. Through interaction with others, within real and natural contexts, the child learns how language works by "observing, comprehending, producing, questioning." He does not learn through direct instruction; rather through his active engagement in constructing meaning, he forms hypotheses about how to use his language. The child who is constantly creating meaning makes, tests, and revises his hypotheses of how his language works. Through interaction with others, his hypotheses are either confirmed or rejected. In summary, the young child is an active participant in learning language which occurs through interaction with others, in natural contexts, and for real purposes.

## THE ROLE OF THE TEACHER
## IN ORAL LANGUAGE DEVELOPMENT

### Scaffolding, Mediation, and Collaboration

If a child actively constructs meaning and if a child makes, tests, and revises his hypotheses about language, what is the adult's role in facilitating oral language development? While the concept of the child as an active participant in his own learning has been emphasized, it does not deny the role that the parent or the caregiver plays in nurturing the language development of the child.

Bruner's (1978) concept of scaffolding, Cochran-Smith's (1988) application of mediation to literacy, and Wells' (1986) discussion of collaboration in language learning all emphasize the importance of the adult's role in the young child's language learning.

*Scaffolding.* In his studies on the role of dialogue between parents and young children on their language acquisition, Bruner (1978) explains the important role that a parent or caregiver plays. Through "scaffolding," the young child is helped by the adult. The adult acts like a support or a scaffold to the child while he is learning a new language concept. When the child becomes more and more competent in a particular language form, he no longer needs the help, or the scaffold, so the old scaffold disappears. Since language learning is a continuous process, the child begins to learn a new language concept that is supported by new scaffolding. This temporary support system that is supplied by the adult enables children to become competent language users.

*Mediation.* To Cochran-Smith (1988), "mediation means that a more experienced language user (teacher, parent, or someone else) fills in some of the gaps that exist between children and" (p. 110) the spoken language that they are attempting to use. While Cochran-Smith (1988) applies the mediation strategy in helping children with their use of print in some way, the mediation strategy can be used in oral language development as well. The teacher (or some adult) who is an experienced language user helps children engage in oral language beyond their current capabilities. Mediation is much like scaffolding, where the teacher is the support and continues in her attempts until the child becomes competent.

An emphasis is made with regard to the use of the mediation strategy and language contexts. Language in context means how, when, where, why, accompanying actions, and by whom the language was spoken. These reference points to the language provide additional meanings to the spoken words. Decontextualized oral language is quite different from contextualized language: In decontextualized language, meaning is independent of the objects and events in the environment as well as of who is speaking. Oral language instruction should never be the context of language. This occurs when we teach language out of context—for example, attempting to teach vocabulary through definition. The role of the teacher should be to be mediator between the child and the language he is using in everyday language experiences. When children are engaged in natural language events, the environmental objects and events as well as the purpose of language use are all familiar and, therefore, bring additional meaning to the language experience. This promotes the child's language growth.

*Collaboration.* According to Wells (1986), the role of the teacher in the children's language development is one of *collaborator.* In his studies on dialogues between parents and young children, Wells (1986) has provided many insights to the teacher of the young child on her role that places her in a collaborative position with the child who is learning language. The collaborative role that the teacher may assume to promote oral language development in the young child is discussed below in the form of suggestions:

*Children Need Feedback.* Because it is emphasized through the literature that children are "largely autonomous constructors of their own representation of language" (Wells, 1986, p. 44), it may appear that the role of the adults in oral language development is minimal. This is far from true! Children need feedback in their attempts to go beyond their linguistic capabilities. When they are learning new language concepts, they test hypotheses. They therefore need an adult who will collaborate with them in accepting, rejecting, or refining the tested hypothesis. That is, they need help from one who knows the language to experience growth.

*Children Need to Be Engaged in Conversation.* Children who experience more conversation will enjoy faster growth in language than those whose experiences are less. The role of the teacher is obvious: The young child must be granted many opportunities to use his language in this format.

*Young Children Need a One-to-One Conversation.* The format of the conversation is a critical factor that can be expected to affect language development. When the child is engaged in a one-to-one conversation, with the adult talking about what interests and concerns the child, linguistic progress is positively affected.

> The reason for this is the fact that, when both child and adult are engaged in a shared activity, the chances are maximized that they will be attending to the same objects and events and interpreting the situation in similar ways. This means that they will each have the best chance of correctly interpreting what the other says or so of being able collaboratively to build up a shared structure of meaning about the topic that is the focus of their intersubjective attention. (Wells, 1986, pp. 44-45)

The role of the teacher is to set aside more time to speak with each child individually. Without the individuality of the child, collaboration cannot be achieved.

*While conversing with the child, understand both the linguistic capabilities of the child as well as his internal model of the world and make adjustments to ensure comprehension.* It is important that the two conversants possess mutual understandings during the conversation. When two adults are speaking, one or the other will ask for clarifications, repetitions, and explanations to keep on the same track. When a young child is engaged in conversation with an adult, there is a mismatch between their linguistic competencies and their background knowledge. It is, therefore, even more important that attention be paid to what the child is saying and then check to determine whether there is a mutual understanding.

The role of the teacher is to be collaborator or mediator. That is, she needs to make adjustments with language structure: Use short and grammatically simple sentences; use exaggerated intonations to hold the child's attention; emphasize key words with the same intonations; limit the topics talked about to things familiar to the child; use frequent repetition and paraphrasing to ensure understanding.

*Adults Need to Be Good Listeners.* In order to stay "on track" with children, who are sometimes difficult to follow in conversation because of their limited resources as speakers, adults need to listen carefully. In being a good listener, therefore, the teacher very often must rely on the contextual clues as well as the individual interest of the child. When the teacher learns how to do this, she can focus on the meaning that the child is intending to communicate to provide appropriate responses.

*Children Need Rich Language Experiences.* Systematic comparisons between home and classroom language experiences show that schools do not create environments with rich language experiences. "For *no* child was the language experience of the classroom richer than that of the home—not even for those believed to be 'linguistically deprived'" (Wells, 1986, p. 87). The role of the teacher is to ascertain the linguistic competencies and interests of each child. The teacher will then extend and develop the language of the child around his/her interests. The teacher collaborates with the individual children in designing a child-centered curriculum.

## A SUMMARY:
## DESIGNING CLASSROOMS
## THAT PROMOTE RICH LANGUAGE EXPERIENCE

To summarize the discussion above, a brief list of suggestions is outlined below to facilitate creating classroom language environments that are interactive and that promote rich language experiences:

Give time to children to use their language. Do not be afraid of a noisy classroom; let the children talk!

Allow for language development in all of the language functions by providing experiences with different language uses.

Allow for language growth and development within the context of rich natural and personal experiences.

Provide opportunities for learning through language.

While communicating with the child, focus on meaning.

Make special efforts to speak to each child one-to-one on a daily basis.

Be a good listener; take the child's efforts seriously by checking to see if "you heard him correctly."

While speaking to the child, adjust your adult language patterns: Use short and grammatically simple sentences; use intonation to hold the child's attention, emphasize key words; use frequent repetition, paraphrase.

# CLASSROOM STRATEGIES
# TO PROMOTE ORAL LANGUAGE DEVELOPMENT

For a teacher who is interested in the language growth and development of the young child, the role has been briefly outlined. What we need to do is to create an environment of natural and interesting experiences to generate interactive communication that can be elicited by strategies that are consistent with current research on how children learn language.

## Dramatic Play

Dramatic play is an excellent opportunity to extend children's language. Young children use language in new and imaginative ways as they act out roles that are part of their life experiences. Role playing enables them to encounter new experiences and try them out by becoming part of them. They use their language and are free to take risks with language forms that they may have just learned. During dramatic play children will imitate, converse with others assuming a variety of roles, and use creative expressions (Fromberg, 1987; Singer, 1986). There are a variety of formats that can be used in dramatic play.

*Spontaneous Drama—The Dress-up Corner.* Dramatic play is encouraged when there are a variety of interesting and appropriate materials and costumes available to the children. The dramatic play of the very young child is solitary and spontaneous (Moffett & Wagner, 1983). With simple toys and materials, they will begin to act out the roles of those who are familiar to them—mother, father, teacher, baby. Later the children will use a variety of props, costumes, and toys to engage in more complex role-playing situations. Therefore, a special corner with appropriate costumes and materials for a variety of roles should be accessible for this language experience. Time and encouragement should be given for the children's engagement in this natural experience.

Another more elaborate way to encourage spontaneous drama is the creation of a grocery store (Glazer, 1989) or a restaurant. The children are familiar with the setting as well as with the roles played by the shoppers and the storekeepers, in the case of a grocery store. The setting of the grocery store also has plenty of contextualized print that the children will encounter. There are numerous opportunities for children to speak about natural experiences that they are quite familiar. Switching roles by children allows for further dialogue.

*Puppetry for Story Drama.* Literature is a wonderful part of a child's life. It is no wonder that children first learn to read through stories. Stories are exciting and fascinating that became for us, as adults, cherished memories that continue to help us through life. The relationship between children's literature and oral language development is undeniable—both act as supports for each other. When we read or listen to good stories, our language develops further; when there is progress and growth in our oral language capabilities, our understanding of stories is further heightened. The rationale for relating literature and storytelling to language experience is quite evident.

Children love to act out stories, and story drama may be spontaneous or formal. After hearing an exciting story, such as Paul Galdone's *Three Billy Goats Gruff*, children may retell the story using simple puppets made from paper plates or brown paper lunch bags that fit over the hand. A sturdy box can be an improvised bridge. Children may want to put the play on for other classes and construct more elaborate props and create their own costumes using life-size story puppets. In any case, these activities offer children an opportunity to engage in rich and interesting natural language experiences.

*Story Drama and Storying.* In another instance children may be encouraged to act out their own stories. Paley's (1986) account of three-year-olds' experiences in social play provides insights into the teacher's role as collaborator with the children in their language development through *storying*. In her dialogues with children during this social drama, she deliberately sees from the child's perspective. She urges children to take on roles and to elaborate their feelings and thoughts. They act out their own stories and she records them. In the format of drama, the young children are telling and writing original stories. These are the natural accounts of life's experiences as seen through the eyes of the young child. Storying—making stories in the mind—is an exciting way to tap the natural and personal experiences of the child. After all, it "is one of the most fundamental means of making meaning" (Wells, 1986, p. 194). It is a natural for promoting oral language growth.

## Small Group Discussions

By the time young children enter school, they are familiar with the structure of a conversation, because through it they have learned to speak. We can bring children from conversation to a small-group discussion format. When discussions focus on natural experiences, they will maintain their efficacy in promoting oral language development. Showing their effectiveness in facilitating language growth, small-group and whole-class discussion have been compared (Fox & Allen, 1983). For the following reasons, keeping the group discussion small fosters language growth:

1. Its small numbers (2–3 children) encourage each child to speak.
2. Its small numbers promote natural language.
3. Its small numbers foster freedom of expression.
4. Its small numbers allow group members to take risks.

Thus, the small-group discussion is suggested, because its format encourages interaction by members who would find it difficult to speak to larger numbers.

### Response to Literature

Literature is a powerful means to promote oral language. Because children's books are interesting and exciting, it is comfortable for children to make spontaneous responses. Immersing children in literature also develops their vocabulary (Ninio, 1980; Ninio & Bruner, 1978). Another source of enjoyment is the rhyme repetitions of verse, and these experiences also provide children with the sound patterns of their language. The following are a few suggestions that may be used to engage children in literature and promote oral language:

1. *Lap reading.* Young children, while being held on the parent's/caregiver's lap, should hear repetitive stories that contain predictive language.

2. *Small-group reading.* When reading to small groups, choose stories that are interesting and encourage participation by the children. Stories with rhyme and short repetitions will inspire children to join in through chanting the short verse.

3. *Rhymes and verse.* Engage children in activities that use poetry and nursery rhymes. One activity is finger plays with rhymes.

4. *Wordless picture books.* Picture books that tell stories are priceless in developing language. Before children learn to read, they can turn the pages of the book and tell a story from the illustrations.

### In Summary

Clearly, children learn to speak naturally in a home environment that is supported by rich language experiences. Both parent and child possess important roles in the language learning event: The child actively constructs hypotheses about the language he is using; the parent collaborates with the child by being an interesting conversational partner, by sharing knowledge of the topics discussed, by providing feedback to the child on his linguistic attempts, and by providing a model of how their language works.

As caregivers and teachers, we need to look to the child as he attempts to learn new language forms that further his development; we need to construct a rich language environment in our classrooms by providing natural experiences that use language for a variety of functions. The teacher can be called collaborator only when she takes the dynamic cues from the parent who helped the child in his initiations with language learning.

## REFERENCES

Bruner, J.S. (1975). From communication to language: A psychological perspective. *Cognition, 3*, 255–287.

Bruner, J.S. (1978). The role of dialogue in language learning. In A. Sinclair, R.J. Jarvella, & W.J.M. Levelt (Eds.), *The child's conception of language*. Berlin: Springer-Verlag.

Clark, H., & Clark, E. (1977). *Psychology and language: An introduction to psycholinguistics*. New York: Harcourt Brace Jovanovich.

Cochran-Smith, M. (1988). Mediating: An important role for the reading teacher. In C.N. Hedley & J.S. Hicks (Eds.), *Reading and the special learner*. Norwood, NJ: Ablex.

Fox, S.E., & Allen, V.G. (1983). *The language arts: An integrated approach*. New York: Holt, Rinehart, & Winston.

Fromberg, D.P. (1987). Play. In C. Seefeldt (Ed.), *The early childhood curriculum*. New York: Teachers College Press.

Glazer, S.M. (1989). Oral language and literacy development. In D.S. Strickland & L.M. Morrow (Eds.), *Emerging literacy: Young children learn to read and write*. Newark, DE: International Reading Association.

Halliday, M.A.K. (1975). *Learning how to mean: Explorations in the development of language*. London: Edward Arnold Ltd.

Lindfors, J.W. (1985). Oral language learning: Understanding the development of language structure. In A. Jagger & M.T. Smith-Burke (Eds.), *Observing the language learner*. Newark: DE: International Reading Association.

Moffett, J., & Wagner, B.J. (1983). *Student centered language arts and reading, K-13: A handbook for teachers*. Boston: Houghton Mifflin.

Ninio, A. (1980). Picture-book reading in mother-infant dyads belonging to two sub-groups in Israel. *Child Development, 51*, 587–590.

Ninio, A., & Bruner, J.S. (1978). The achievement and antecedents of labeling. *Journal of Child Language, 5*, 5–15.

Paley, V.G. (1986). *Mollie is three*. Chicago: The University of Chicago Press.

Pinnell, G.S. (1985). Ways to look at the functions of children's language. In A. Jaggar & M.T. Smith-Burke (Eds.), *Observing the language learner*. Newark, DE: International Reading Association.

Singer, D.G. (1986). Make-believe play and learning. In J.S. McKee (Ed.), *Play: Working partner of growth.* Wheaton, MD: Association of Childhood Education International.

Trevarthan, C. (1980). The foundation of intersubjectivity: Development of interpersonal and cooperative understanding in infants. In D.R. Olson (Ed.), *The social foundations of language and thought.* New York: W.W. Norton.

Wells, G. (1986). *The meaning makers: Children learning language and using language to learn.* Portsmouth, NH: Heinemann.

# Chapter 3

# The Role of Play
# in Literacy Development

## David N. Berg

Play is the work of children. It is how they discover what they need to know about the world, how they cope with their fears and nightmares, how they learn about what physical possibilities they possess, how they deal with separation from those who nurture them, how they learn to socialize with others, how they express their natural curiosities, and how they learn to speak and manipulate language. Play is natural and needed. It is also common to all thinking beings. To some educators, play strikes fear in their hearts that somehow play is not learning. By calling it the work of children we are, in a way, excusing its inclusion in early childhood education by telling the uninformed that it can fit in the Puritan work ethic with legitimacy.

There has been much debate as to whether early childhood classrooms should be developmentally or academically based: whether the activities should be teacher or child initiated. This is an issue that I will ignore in this chapter, for it is known that play is an essential part of any early childhood classroom since it utilizes a natural aptitude of children and may be extended and expanded upon to instruct or to lead the child to make discoveries depending upon the approach used. Play is learning for young children.

Young children engage in many forms of play. Depending upon the age of the child, the play in each of several areas of development changes as the child matures. It has been classified by observation and has revealed a natural and spontaneous progression in normally developing children.

## WHAT IS PLAY?

Bettelheim (1987) defined play in relation to game. He stated:

> Although the words play and game may seem synonymous, they in fact refer to broadly distinguishable stages of development, with play relating to an earlier stage, game to a more mature one. . . . (P)lay refers to the young child's activities characterized by freedom from all but personally imposed rules (which are changed at will), by freewheeling fantasy involvement, and by the absence of any goals outside the activity itself. (p. 37)

As used in this text play is not merely the spontaneous activity of young children; rather it includes this and extensions of play by the teacher to enlarge the child's understandings, reasoning and thinking, language, and/or other skills and abilities, as well as gamelike situations devised by the teacher that are enjoyable and simultaneously instructive such as sociodramas and less formalized, nonwritten instruction, by the teacher.

The Association for Childhood Education International (ACEI), in a position paper, stated that "play . . . is a necessary and integral part of childhood, infancy through adolescence" (Isenberg & Quisenberry, 1988). Harp (1988) reported that "the link between reading and play is the search for meaning." He further states that "sociodramatic play, a form of symbolic play, has the clearest link to reading because it involves both simple and complex uses of imagination and through it a child manipulates reality and time."

Sociodramatic play has a richness of language necessarily integrated into it by the participants. Since it is spontaneous and unrehearsed, it involves creativity, intellectual growth, and social interaction. Smilansky (1971) defined sociodramatic play as "a form of voluntary social play activity in which young children participate." She further defined sociodramatic play:

> In dramatic play, the child takes on a role; he pretends to be somebody else. While doing this he draws from his first or secondhand experience with the other person in different situations. He imitates the person in action and speech with the aid of real or imagined objects.

Dramatic play becomes sociodramatic play if there is collaboration between two or more children. There are two basic components to sociodramatic play: imitation of real-life situations and personae and make-believe enhancements that make the imitative play come closer to reality. These make-believe enhancements are usually rich in verbalizations (Smilansky, 1971).

This use of objects as representations of ideas parallels reading's use of words as representations of ideas. Both use a symbolic encoding to enhance thought. It has been shown that children who use the greatest amount of symbolic play are the ones with the greatest ability to create representations in play and reading (Harp, 1988). Two things seem to be essential to play: self-direction and activity (Cuffaro, 1974).

## LANGUAGE DEVELOPMENT IN YOUNG CHILDREN

Children play with sounds and language almost from birth. Infants make sounds in profusion. When the sounds approximate the words adults use they receive positive feedback, thereby reinforcing the behavior and causing the child to repeat the sounds. This explains why infants in different cultures learn to speak in different languages.
    Garvy (1977) told us that

> almost all the levels of organization of language (phonology, grammar, meaning) and most phenomena of speech and talking, such as expressive noises, variation in time and intensity, the distribution of talk between participants, the objectives of speech (what we try to accomplish by speaking) are potential resources for play.

We have learned much about how children play with language by observational research. This research by Weir has shown that youngsters often play with different rules and forms of language (Johnson et al., 1987). They play with sounds by repeating strings of nonsense syllables; with syntax, by substituting words; and with semantics to make word jokes. This language play helps them to understand the basic structure of our language and to hone their skills in using language (Cazden, 1976). Children go through a logical progression of language development that begins with playing with noises and articulation, then repeating strings of syllables. In the first year of life, infants may engage in successive motor activities which seem to be a form of play. This play includes vocal activities accompanied by a listening to the sounds they produce and experimentation with breath, saliva control, and mouth postures (McFarland, 1971).
    At two to 3 years of age they conventionalize the noises they have learned and make associations between objects and sounds such as ting-a-ling for telephone and bow-bow for dog. They then go through a stage where they play with the linguistic system until that is extended to include using language in social play. This is succeeded by spontaneous rhyming word play, then play with fantasy and nonsense, and finally play with conversation (Garvey, 1977).

At four years of age play no longer just centers around the home. It is extended to include other settings known to the child with roles appropriate to the setting played out by the child. The major issue the child must confront is the management of aggressive impulses. These are acted out in play by creating safety zones or pretending that there are bad guys who are outsiders. There is an exaggeration of role characteristics often enhanced by costumes and props. The child begins to discriminate in playmate selection using gender, color, attire, and so on as the determining factor. The play shows that the 4-year-old has a greater ability to discriminate between reality and fantasy and can transfer aggressive behaviors onto toys or representations of a character. The child still exhibits swings between a dependent and independent self, but can use play as a vehicle to explore what frightens, baffles, or interests him. Nightmares can be dealt with at this stage through play exploration. At four, hiding and burying things supplants peek-a-boo; games and sand or block play become inviting to the child (Curry, 1971b).

The 5-year-old exhibits a wide range of play, many with earlier but yet unsolved themes still being worked upon. Some children at this age are beginning the stage of play where they use games with rules. The 5-year-old can verbalize the difference between realistic and fantasy play. At this age play integrates external stimuli with the child's developmental interests. Aggressive or frightened feelings are sublimated through dramatic play. Play includes role playing with the enacting of real (nurse, teacher, policeman, bride, groom, etc.) and fictional heroic (spacemen, cowboys, Indians, kings, etc.) characterizations. Romance, too, is explored in role playing through play. Sociodramatic play contains realistic elements imitative of adult behaviors; structured dramas such as puppet shows contain biting animals or monsters that kill as deeper feelings are explored. Abstractions now enter the child's concrete world with the use of symbolic props rather than actual representations of the real thing (Curry, 1971a). These abstractions may be the use of a block held in the child's hand or used as an airplane, or the use of a doll to represent a family member rather than another child playing the part.

From 6 to 10 years of age dramatic fantasy play takes the form of staged dramas which include self-made props and improvisations of plot created as the play goes on. It is common for the theme of these plays to remain the same over a period of weeks or longer. Monsters, blood and gore, death, destruction and the like are included in these sociodramas. Included, too, are characters who reveal hidden aspects of their personality. Mild mannered, benign individuals may suddenly be shown to be monsters or traitors leading friends into danger. When romance is a part of the play, it usually is treated with distain. Parents are absent, for the most part, from these sociodramas, with Peter-Pan-like groups of parentless children confronting a villain. Children will often remove themselves from their emotional involvement with the situations that are played out by denying authorship and blaming another child for creating the situations, or calling the scripts bad dreams, or regressing to nonsense speech or immature behavior as if to refute any possible meaning for these fantasies. Actual targets for aggressive behavior enter the play, albeit there is often a respect for fairness. Hostile aggression is expressed through bathroom talk and euphemisms for bathroom fixtures. Denigration of playmates by accusing them of being smelly, dirty, or messy is often observed (Arnaud, 1971). Play at this age usually involves children of both sexes.

By age 8 or 9, play seems to be all-boy or all-girl with impersonations of the opposite sex being used as a vehicle when called for. Boys value physical strength and prowess, while girls extol physical attractiveness.

At 10 children begin to wonder about the future. They become aware of crazy behavior in themselves and others and include it in their play, conversation, art, and clowning.

## PLAY AND LITERACY

Peligrini observed that the degree of sophistication of a child's play was a better predictor of success in reading and writing in grade 1 than either IQ or socioeconomic level. He attributed this to the child's need to consciously assign meaning to symbols in both dramatic play and reading (Harp, 1988). This same connection was noted by Roskos (1988) who urged teachers of young children through kindergarten to enhance this tie between symbolic play and literacy by establishing centers in the classroom that encourage symbolic play that encourages experimentation with literacy. She suggests that teachers observe children's play for signs of emerging literacy and draw upon that play by recording play stories onto experience charts. Ashton-Warner (1963) utilized children's compelling need to learn to read words which were meaningful to their lives. The emotional and developmental need is much the same.

Harp (1988) suggests three implications for the class based upon research on play and its link to literacy. They are that teachers should provide children with the time and materials for sociodramatic and symbolic play in preprimary grades as a way of enhancing background knowledge before children read. Secondly, teachers should create situations whereby they can observe children at play with literacy behavior so that the teacher may better plan future activities to enhance the child's literacy understandings. Finally, teachers must be firm in their conviction that play does not steal instructional time from reading if that play involves manipulation of symbols and/or acts of reading and writing.

Durkin (1982) stressed that the initial reading process is a complex mix of a child's heredity and environmental abilities, experiences, and the type and quality of instruction. She writes that traditional reading readiness tests often are unreliable predictors since results are not consistent in a test/retest situation nor reliable from one test to another. This, she says, is because reading readiness is only assessable by viewing one child at a time vis-à-vis a specific reading task being taught using a specific instructional strategy. In other words, the content of the lesson cannot be viewed apart from the pedagogical methodology. With the advent of earlier and earlier instruction for children, Durkin blames the lack of success on educators' merely transplanting traditional first-grade material and methods into kindergarten classrooms without regard to the child's developmental ability and experiential background.

Katz (1988) underscored this idea in talking about a dynamic versus the traditional, normative view of child development. The normative view is based upon comparing a child's abilities to the "average" child of the same age and quantifying them against some sort of scale. In the normative view, one would speak of such things as developmentally appropriate or being on grade level. The dynamic view also takes into account a far greater implication of instruction. The dynamic dimension looks at the sequence in which human beings change over time and with experience. It looks, too, at how early experiences may impact upon future functioning and the effect of long-term or repeated experiences on the young child. Katz warned that just because a child is able to perform a certain task is not reason enough to have the child do it. We must ask ourselves, "*Should* the child do it?" We must examine the long-term consequences of any activity.

Children are capable of many things. They are always learning. However, if we push them into inappropriate tasks that they will perform to please us, are we then developing undesirable attitudes and behaviors that may only surface in the future? Katz spoke of four learning categories: knowledge, skills, disposition, and feelings. Our charge in the early years, she says, is not to make readers, but rather to inculcate the disposition to read; not to make writers, but to develop the disposition to write. Put another way, we must always keep an eye on that difficult-to-measure domain that Bloom includes in his taxonomy, the affective domain. For this reason, Katz urges that young children be taught through activities that provide for interactive processing, active rather than passive activities, and by interacting with each other, adults, and their environment. Communicative competence is developed when young childen are engaged in conversation rather than when simply exposed passively to language.

Conversation occurs most easily with young children in small groups with or without an adult. Young children's conversation is best fostered by an adult making comments rather than asking questions. This is logical since the adult's aim should be to extend and expand the conversation and thinking rather than diverting it onto another plane. Questions asked during conversation may steer the children off-course due to the nature of a question being extrinsic to the conversation. An adult posing questions is not a participant in that conversation. Communication, expression, and reasoning are all developed through conversation since it requires active processing of language with each participant's contribution contingent upon the others in an orderly sequence.

The traditional early childhood classroom has centers, each of which is based upon a theme. Careful preparation of both materials and setting promote literacy by fostering spontaneous literacy behaviors while the children are engaged at free play. A study has shown that the amount of literacy activity during play increases significantly when reading and writing materials based on a theme in the play area were added to those areas by the teacher (Strickland & Morrow, 1989).

## IMPLICATIONS FOR INSTRUCTION

It is necessary for the teacher to be a part of the child's play in order to enhance it. If one is an outside observer who comes over to look at what the child or children have created during their play sessions, one will, research has shown, accomplish little by posing questions about what was done, even if those questions are thought-provoking or mind-expanding.

Instead, it is necessary for the adult to be with the children as they play so that when a teachable moment arrives, it can be immediately recognized by the teacher and used as the basis for expanding the children's experiences. It is important to note that when the teacher leads the child to arrive at new conclusions or observations, the teacher should always ask questions that include language that makes the adult part of the group. For example, in the block corner, the teacher might ask, "How could we build a longer bridge?" rather than saying, "How could you build a longer bridge?" Even though it is the child who will be led to make the discovery, the language must imply or overtly state that the teacher is included in the play group.

Research has also shown us that when reading and writing materials are appropriately placed in a play center, literacy behaviors of children playing in that center are increased. These literacy activities are best developed if the teacher places materials on a specific theme within each activity center in the room. For example, in the play corner one might place a theme of a fast-food restaurant; it can be developed by creating a dining area, a kitchen, posting a menu, providing order pads for the people behind the counter, recipes for chefs, placemats with activities which can be found in many fast-food places, cash registers, telephones, money, and so on. All of these enhance the play of children and help them to use the props spontaneously to behave like readers and writers. Other possibilities include doctors' offices, veterinarians' offices, supermarkets, or any themes that involve literacy and are related to areas of study in the classroom (Strickland & Morrow, 1989).

Literacy play is not restricted merely to props and play areas. Children love to hear stories read to them over and over again. They soon imitate the reader's tone of voice, phrasing, and general delivery. They imitate the turning of pages and may be seen "reading" the story to other children or playmates. As the story is read to them, they memorize it and develop a love of language in addition to extending their spoken vocabulary. It is not unusual in an early childhood classroom to find a child sitting in the seat usually occupied by the teacher while reading a story to the class, holding a book (sometimes upside down), and reading to another child or toy. Although the child cannot actually read the words on the page, it is not unusual to observe the pages being turned at just the correct time. Clearly this is an indication that children love and spontaneously exhibit behavior related to literacy.

It is in this nonthreatening way that children develop the propensity to read. It is a logical progression from giving an infant a soft-covered book in the crib or playpen and watching the book become more than a toy. The child who later in life imitates reading is moving on to the next step and making logical connections about literacy. The child realizes that the pages of a book contain words and pictures that together give us meaning. The child is also discovering that those lines and curves that we call words look different and are connected to the language that we know and speak to communicate ideas. The child is discovering that there is an order to these lines and that each page has a finite number of them as well as a finite number of words. If we want to continue our story, we must turn the page to uncover more of these marks. The child who is a careful observer may also discover that there is a top and a bottom to a book, and a left-to-right progression in turning those pages and looking at those lines.

In the play area or elsewhere, the child should be encouraged to create his or her own books. After examining books quite on his or her own, the child should be encouraged through the placement of writing materials to create original writing. This writing will only be crayon scribbles, but even more early literacy behaviors will develop through this play. Placement of the scribbles on the page will happen to approximate words. A realization that there are many scribbles, not just long lines, and other literacy discoveries are made during this type of play. It is important to remember that all the communication arts—listening, speaking, reading, and writing—must develop together and support and enhance each other. As the child plays with the creation of a self-made book or piece of writing, the child is also making important discoveries about reading. The teacher should encourage the child to play with writing materials to foster literacy behaviors. However, the child should not be forced to do so. These behaviors should occur spontaneously. We want to develop the desire to read and write, not crush it by forcing a child too early to play with language.

We have heard that a child will seek the foods that are needed by the body and that caregivers should not worry too much about a child having a controlled diet for health. Similarly, the child who is exhibiting emerging literacy behaviors will explore them through play when the child is ready to do so. If we force the child into discoveries before he or she is ready, we not only will not be developing the desired outcome, but may well create a child who is a reluctant reader in later life. The placement of reading and writing materials around the room and in the exploration and play centers will encourage children to move to these prereading and prewriting behaviors when they are ready to do so. Careful observation is necessary, and children who are not as ready as other children may need encouragement and guidance from the teacher to move from the known to the unknown.

Emerging literacy has been rethought and studied more closely during the last few decades as a complex process involving cognition, social and linguistic development, and a psychological aspect. It is thought to begin at even an earlier age than we had previously believed and is, therefore, being looked at not just in school surroundings, but in the home as well. This is especially so since it is thought that emerging literacy behaviors may begin at age 14 months or earlier. Two-year-olds who are able to recognize a favorite item while shopping or the toddler who knows how to recognize a favorite book for reading all demonstrate examples of this theory. This recognition is not merely imitation but an attempt by children to construct their own knowledge through experimentation and exploration. They are searching for patterns and connections in their environment so that they can apply their own logic to arrive at a new sense of understanding (Strickland & Morrow, 1988). If this sounds very much like Piaget's work and description of concept development, it should.

If one analyzes this view of emerging literacy and how it develops, play is a perfect setting for many of these behaviors to be experimented with. Mentioned earlier was the interdependence of listening, speaking, reading, and writing. They are all mutually developed when any one is strengthened since they are all interrelated. However, each must be given an opportunity to be investigated by the child in various activities, in many contexts, and through active involvement.

For the early childhood teacher, this means that children should not be bombarded with naming letters, sound-symbol relationships, visual-perceptual tasks, and the like. Rather, it should be recognized that the child must have had an opportunity to experiment with language in all its aspects, both written and oral, and to develop internal structures to build upon if future instruction is to have a firm foundation. More importantly, at the earlier stages of literacy development, we must allow the child to explore and discover and develop the disposition to be a reader, rather than to learn those behaviors too soon. As the child makes connections and discoveries, we must be there to help celebrate each achievement, to recognize and appreciate, to help the child to develop a sense of self-admiration for moving closer to adult literate behavior.

This is quite a task. How then can we accomplish this? By play alone? Obviously not as the only vehicle for guiding the child to becoming more literate. But play is a powerful testing ground for children to uncover the complexities of their universe. It provides a safe harbor for meaningful exploration with literate behavior. As with any teaching, a great variety of experiences and modalities must be presented to the child to allow him or her to learn in the way that is most effective for that child. This is especially true for young children who come to us with a greater knowledge about written language than we might think, but whose prior experiences differ and whose developmental stages vary more.

It is necessary in planning for an early childhood environment to provide the child with a richness of printed materials ansd supplies to encourage the use of language. In this environment should be a library corner, a writing center, and a profusion of supplies for reading, writing, and oral language. By carefully preparing and placing materials on a specific theme in play areas, spontaneous literacy behaviors are more likely to develop as literacy is promoted during play (Strickland, 1989).

The teacher as organizer of the curriculum and learning environment is essential. It is the teacher who provides the child with the tools of learning and stimulates the desire to learn. It is no easy task to accomplish all of this, but the rewards of the efforts are limitless, and the alternatives of not doing this too devastating to imagine. An environment which permits and encourages experimentation with literacy through play is essential, but the teacher must also provide the child with a print-rich environment laden with books, words, charts, labels, and written records of children's own words; provide appropriate experiences for the child to stimulate discussions about the event; model reading and writing for the child by our own use of it in our own lives; read to the child and have time for the child to reread favorite books alone or with other children; preserve the child's language by recording it in print and having it readily available for future reference; provide the tools of language in the play and activity areas; appreciate invented spellings as the child makes his or her connections between symbol and sound distilled from observation from numerous language experiences that have been provided; interact with the child who is reading scribbles from a childmade book, but demonstrating the child's own connections between print and thoughts.

By providing the child with the tools of literacy in the play area we can meld the child's active explorations with the concept building that occurs from the teaching environment. Children are very astute: one need only consider the vast amount of information processing and assimilation that occurs in the first few years of life. When we support and encourage the child's own natural curiosity about the world and learning, we make our own job easier and simultaneously respect and reinforce the child's learning behaviors.

Children learn best from the people with whom they feel a bond. Parents and teachers are usually among the most important in this group. It is for this reason that children should also see numerous occasions when those whom they trust and respect model using language in its written form as a means to social and intellectual interaction. If a picture is worth a thousand words, then a meaningful demonstration must be worth a tome.

As the child becomes older, the play will become more complex. The teacher is faced with incorporating play into a curriculum that is based more and more on the work ethic as we progress upward in grade level. However, play is still a necessary and should be an integral part of the child's play. There are ways to integrate the two as we look at the classroom of six- to eight-year-old children.

Recognize that with the study of learning styles we have come to realize that choice is something desirable. If we provide children with choices whenever possible, we allow more possibilities for children to learn through play. Although this play now includes much more content due to the child's own acquisition of skills, it is still meaningful and with merit if we think not of the outcome as much as the process and all the learning that may occur during that process.

We also should help children focus on the process rather than the outcome to give them the disposition to learn and to love learning. Think of the child who makes up and tells riddles and jokes, who writes them in a book for his or her friends and then reads them to others. The child's own desire to make play into a reading, writing, and thinking skills activity answers the curriculum's scope. The child's perception of the activity and the teacher's are probably very different, and yet, they are both accomplishing their own desired outcome and at the same time providing for the child's affective love of learning. The secret is that the teacher must ensure that the child is engaging in tasks that are challenging enough and still not too difficult to master (Sawyers & Rodgers, 1988).

## INSTRUCTIONAL ENVIRONMENTS AND ACTIVITIES

As an example of the types of environments and activities that lend themselves to language development through play, I am going to look closely at the block corner, an area where some may feel that there is little opportunity for language to take form. We know that with young children, learning should evolve from an interaction with their environment, a use of learning activities and materials that are concrete, real, and relevant to their lives. The curriculum should be developmentally appropriate so as to provide an integration of all areas of the child's development: physical, emotional, social, and cognitive. We know that there should be a variety of materials and activities that provide for the wide range of abilities, interests, and skills of the young child that allow the child to be challenged further as he or she develops his or her skills and understandings (National Association for the Education of the Young Child, 1986).

There is a definite developmental progression of play with blocks that begins with the child playing with blocks by himself or herself or briefly with others. The next stage is where the child alone or with another plays with the blocks near other children playing with their own blocks. Finally, the children work cooperatively for longer periods of time and often with preplanning of what they will do. However, no matter what the stage of block building, three things occur during this dramatic play: The child creates the context for play; the child translates reality and scale into the medium of the blocks; and the child gradually moves from needing a child to play a family member or a living thing (such as a pet) to being able to use representations of living things for family members, and so on (such as dolls) within the structure. As the child is moving toward using representations of self, the objects built with blocks have more and more detail incorporated into them: The objects built are expressions of the child's information about them based upon prior experiences.

It is the adult who influences the dramatic play by controlling the amount and variety of blocks, the space for play, and the enhancements provided to use with the blocks. These enhancements include dolls or other representations of people, animals, car, trucks, planes, boats, and so on. In some activity centers of the room, such as the housekeeping corner, a sense of structure is provided. The props restrict the child to exploring the world within the context of a kitchen or eating area with activities related to those areas. In the block corner, it is the child's creativity or developmental stage that is the only restriction to dramatic involvement. Initially, the child is mostly involved with the action of the play. A block may be pushed around with the sounds of a train emanating from the child whose hand never leaves the block. As the child develops, blocks are used to create a train. Form and size are of importance. The child interacts within the train. Its details are more specific and represented by the child's creation. The child is no longer as one with the block, no longer melds with the block to give it sound and movement.

As dramatic play with blocks develops, the child is increasingly attentive to scale and detail and moves from direct involvement and egocentricity in play to the ability to participate through a representation of self. This movement away from egocentricity allows for a more objective view of reality. As the child is able to step outside of self and use representations of people to operate within the confines of the structures created, the child can assume the roles of each of the representations and project feelings and actions onto the representations. Being first self, then mother or father, or other person or living thing, the child can explore relationships, practice empathetic understandings of motives and actions, and help bring his or her perceptions of the world into focus with the perceptions of others. It is for this reason that it is not unusual to find that when a child is encountering conflict in his or her world, those conflicts are represented in play. It is important to realize that while play is and should be an important part of every child's world, not every play episode is going to be meaning packed and an exploration of the child's psyche. As with many momentous events in a person's life, one must face up to them, build up to them, rehearse how one will handle them, and then, and only then, is one ready to explore one's innermost feelings. We must trust the child to know when the time is ripe for his or her quantum leap of understanding, and need to rest secure knowing that we are providing the time and opportunity for the child to encounter and deal with whatever is needed to be worked out in the play session (Cuffaro, 1974).

Almost all of these events are expected, developmental, and appropriate. They may be motivated by external or internal needs unrelated to literacy per se. However, they cannot be separated from literacy development. Sociodramas need dialogues, characters, logical thought, events, plot, conflict, resolution—all the elements of literature.

Symbols used in play are the precursors for using abstract ideas, letters, and numbers. As the child experiences prereading activities, it is usually in the block corner that the child will express a need to write messages to indicate the merging of the block play's abstraction and the real world of other children invading the child's own experiments with perceptions of the world.

## SUMMARY

We are learning more and more about young children and how they learn, especially as the areas of language development and literacy are concerned. There are some things that are so apparent that we do know that they are important and correct. The child must be provided with numerous experiences with language, first with making sounds, then words, then sentences, and in discovering the syntax and semantics of the language heard around him or her. Being provided with experiences to hear English correctly modeled is paramount. Providing the child with books, even before he or she is able to read, helps to develop a love of reading for the rest of his or her life. Having someone read a story to a child allows for his love of literature and books to be nurtured and encouraged. The bond of a young child to a parent enhances that experience. Parents should take the time to sit in a chair and read with a child.

However, once the child comes to school, it is the teacher who must also provide these types of experience for the child. A print-rich environment includes not only the books, stories, and poems that the teacher reads to the child, but also the labels on objects, the charts and transcriptions of the children's words, and the materials of literacy in profusion and easy access in the play areas. Teachers can encourage language learning play situations by providing the child with the variety of materials necessary to become actively involved in play. Language is better understood if the child realizes the necessity of using it and is provided the opportunity to imitate the ways it is used around him or her. As the child explores his or her environment and uses dramatic play to recreate what is not understood so that it may be worked through and understood, the availability of the materials of language enhances that exploration and allows the child to make further explorations even more in the area of literacy.

As the child moves from the stage of needing to use play as a solo medium of exploration for understanding, he or she will spontaneously pick up on poems and stories if they are provided in his or her environment. These should be provided so that the child may imitate the adult behavior that is observed and use that model to help develop vocabulary, concept, and an appreciation for the beauty of language on his or her own.

Play implies a lack of rules, or if there are rules, they are nonstatic and set by the child. Games are also a form of play but with prescribed rules that govern how one may behave. As the child is more and more capable, the teacher may use games to help the child develop even more language skills. It should be understood, however, that the teacher's role begins much earlier than when he or she provides games for the child. The teacher influences the child's discoveries by providing verbal interaction to help guide the child's play and by providing the materials and setting for play that will naturally lead the child to make discoveries at his or her own time and pace, in the areas that the teacher hopes to help to child develop. There is no need to rush that pace, nor is it beneficial to pressure the child to rush into working in books. This will occur as a natural outgrowth of what the child is doing, and, more likely, will be initiated by the child.

Child's play is much more than an idle observer would imagine it to be, for the child is setting a pattern of behaviors and dispositions which he or she will carry throughout life. Childhood is a precious time of life full of the wonders of discovery. As adults, we must help the child to make the most of it.

## REFERENCES

Arnaud, S. (1971). The dramatic play of six- to ten-year-olds. In G. Engstom (Ed.), *Play: The child strives toward self-realization* (pp. 11–12). Washington, DC: National Association for the Education of Young Children.

Ashton-Warner, S. (1963). *Teacher.* New York: Simon & Schuster.

Bettelheim, S. (1987). The importance of play. *The Atlantic Monthly, 259*(3), 35–46.

Cazden, C. (1976). Play with language and meta-linguistic awareness: One dimension of language experience. In J.S. Bruner, A. Jolly, & K. Sylva (Eds.), *Play: Its role in development and evolution* (pp. 603–608). New York: Basic Books.

Cuffaro, H. (1974). Dramatic play—The experience of block building. In E.S. Hirsch (Ed.), *The block book* (pp. 69–87). Washington, DC: National Association for the Education of Young Children.

Curry, N. (1971a). Five year old's play. In G. Engstom (Ed.), *Play: The child strives toward self-realization* (pp. 10–11). Washington, DC: National Association for the Education of Young Children.

Curry, N. (1971b). Four year old's play. In G. Engstom (Ed.), *Play: The child strives toward self-realization* (pp. 9–10). Washington, DC: National Association for the Education of Young Children.

Durkin, D. (1982). *Getting reading started.* Boston: Allyn & Bacon.

Garvy, C. (1977). *Play.* Cambridge, MA: Harvard University Press.

Harp, B. (1988). When the principal asks "Doesn't play steal time from reading?" *The Reading Teacher, 42*, 244–245.

Isenberg, J., & Quisenberry, N. (1988). Play: A necessity for all children. *Childhood Education, 64*, 138–145.

Johnson, J., Christie, J., & Yawkey, T. (1987). *Play and early childhood development.* Glenview, IL: Scott Foresman & Company.

Katz, L. (1988). Engaging children's minds: The implications of research for early childhood education. In C. Warner (Ed.), *A resource guide to public school early childhood programs.* Washington, DC: Association for Curriculum Development.

McFarland, M.B. (1971). The first year of life. In G. Engstom (Ed.), *Play: The child strives toward self-realization* (pp. 7–8). Washington, DC: National Association for the Education of Young Children.

National Association for the Education of Young Children. (1986). NAEYC position statement on developmentally appropriate practice in early childhood program serving children from birth to age 8. *Young Children, 41,* 3–20.

New York State Bureau of Child Development and Parent Education. (1982). *Play.* Albany, NY: New York State Education Department.

Roskos, K. (1988). Literacy at work in play. *The Reading Teacher, 42,* 562–566.

Sawyers, J., & Rogers, C. (1988). *Helping young children develop through play.* Washington, DC: National Association for the Education of Young Children.

Smilansky, S. (1971). Can adults facilitate play in children? Theoretical and practical considerations. In G. Engstom (Ed.), *Play: The child strives toward self-realization* (pp. 39–50). Washington, DC: National Association for the Education of Young Children.

Strickland, D., & Morrow, L. (1988). New perspectives on young children learning to read and write. *The Reading Teacher, 42,* 70–71.

Strickland, D., & Morrow, L. (1989). Environment rich in print promote literacy behavior during play. *The Reading Teacher, 43,* 178–179.

## Chapter 4

# A Portfolio Approach
# in Documenting Literacy
# in Young Children

## Patricia A. Antonacci

A major challenge for early childhood is replacing the traditional evaluation programs. There is no argument for the need of literacy assessment at every level in education. The controversy arises over the design of the assessment programs for the young child. Currently, standardized testing in the early years is the prominent feature in programs for assessing literacy abilities in the young child. The limitations of such programs are clear, and the need for substantial change is evident.

Thus the purpose of this chapter is to suggest an alternative approach to the traditional method of standardized testing to evaluate the reading and writing development of young children. A rationale for the use of the portfolio approach will be given, followed by a discussion of natural techniques appropriate for classroom use by the teacher to gather data on students' reading and writing behavior and to document their literacy growth.

### A RATIONALE FOR NATURAL APPROACHES IN ASSESSMENT

#### Testing: A Trend in Educational Assessment

Current trends in educational assessment are consistent with the reading readiness paradigm that has been institutionalized by school districts throughout the United States and other countries as well as by publishing companies. Programs for beginning reading instruction suggest that children can become fluent readers only after they have mastered a set of skills in reading readiness and reading that follow a definite scope and sequence. Further, such published programs imply that formal instruction in reading must begin only after basic skills prerequisite to reading are mastered. Consistent with this philosophy is the assessment program for young children.

Mastery in readiness skills is customarily tested by the administration of a standardized test. In some school districts, standardized testing for basic readiness skills takes place upon entrance to kindergarten (in the form of pretesting) as well as a test of mastery of basic skills (in the form of posttesting). This is also the case in the primary grades where mastery of isolated language skills is determined through a formal testing program. Most unfortunate are the decisions of promotion that are all too often made on the basis of this one test score.

While there is apprehension among educators in using standardized tests with young children, the testing trend is still growing. One professional organization for early childhood education (NAEYC, 1986) has repeatedly expressed concern in the use of paper-and-pencil tests as screening devices for beginning formal instruction in reading. Such concerns are founded on problems with these formal tests along with the use of test results as discussed below.

## Problems with Standardized Tests in Early Education

*Narrowness of Formal Tests.* Since it is true that children starting school enter with varying abilities related to reading and writing (Teale & Sulzby, 1986), teachers and administrators must be sensitive to the developmental differences related to the literacy growth of each child. In light of the current research on language learning, standardized tests are not able to identify numerous literacy abilities that children come to school with due to the tests' focus on a narrow set of isolated language skills.

What are these untestable literacy behaviors children have learned before coming to school? Learning to read and write starts very early in life, as young as 2 years old. Many children at that age can identify contextualized print; that is, they can read and write signs and labels and logos they see in their homes and in their communities (Goodman, 1986). The preschool child is well aware of the functions of literacy (Taylor & Dorsey-Gaines, 1988; Teale, 1986). Watching parents write phone messages, send greeting cards, use recipes to bake cookies along with other literacy activities carried on in the home bring the young child to the relationship that language is not an end in itself; rather literacy is directed toward a goal. That is, each literacy event has a special function. Children also learn book behaviors, such as page turning, direction of print, boundaries of words, and so on from lap reading with their parents. In addition to developing concepts about print and book behaviors, children are developing a schema for story, an important concept for understanding and producing stories (Applebee, 1978). All of the above literacy concepts are not isolated skills; each is a set of complex language learnings resulting from social transactions and interactions with print. These literacy concepts are not only the beginnings of reading and writing but they are prerequisites for formal instruction in reading. However, there is no single formal measure that can determine a child's acquisition of such literacy concepts. Some standardized tests are not sensitive to these literacy behaviors developing in young children.

*Test Items Often Penalize Young Children.* Many children are penalized not by the content of the test but by the tasks that the test demands of them. This happens when the young test takers do not understand the directions of the test. Some youngsters have not been exposed to paper-and-pencil tasks; their unfamiliarity with the task interferes with the content being tested. Performance on a formal test is further affected by the environment created by the test setting. Testing conditions are dramatically different than the classroom environment with which young children are familiar, and to some the anxiety mediates the results.

*Test Results Are Often Used to Make Weighty Decisions.* Testing young children's abilities in language with standardized measures poses significant problems. This is particularly true when the results will be used to make decisions about them and their curricular needs. Children are often promoted or retained on the basis of one test result. Placement in ability groups or special education programs are further abuses of test results. When one considers the nature of the test to determine literacy growth in a "one-shot" situation, quite disparate from real language contexts, the use of test results as a factor in such decisions is quite absurd. Additionally, curricular decisions are governed by test scores. Consider the effects of judging the teaching ability and evaluating school programs through the use of test results. When the effectiveness of instruction is linked to how a group a students score on the standardized test, the consequences are a test-driven curriculum. Instead of tailoring the curriculum to meet individual needs of the students, instruction is designed to raise test scores. Further, instructional programs are often evaluated based on how well students in the program score on tests. If the scores are high, the program is considered effective and, most likely, it will be retained; if the scores are low, the reverse is possible.

In view of the findings of current research on language learning, standardized testing in early childhood programs is simply inappropriate. When assessment and instructional programs for literacy development focus on isolated skills such as letter-sound matching, letter discrimination, and letter names, they are out of step with the nature of the young children as literacy learners (Hiebert & McWhorter, 1987).

What is needed to monitor the literacy growth and development of the early learner is an approach that is compatible with how language is learned most effectively and efficiently. As an alternative to traditional testing, the portfolio approach is proposed as a means to assess and document literacy growth.

## A PORTFOLIO APPROACH
## FOR ASSESSING LITERACY DEVELOPMENT

Artists carry their portfolios to demonstrate to interested people what they have achieved. It is a documentation of their abilities. To each artist, the portfolio is personal, because it graphically describes his interest, his artistic direction, and the efforts he has taken to get where he's at. A portfolio of a student's literacy development is much like the artist's.

The student's literacy portfolio focuses on the individual progress made in reading and writing. It contains descriptive data documenting his growth over an entire school year, and sometimes even longer. When you open the literacy portfolio you find performance samples of reading and writing along with annotations, narratives, and checklists describing literacy behaviors. Rather than a statistical summary of language achievement which the formal test yields, the literacy portfolio furnishes a descriptive analysis of literacy development. It is a portrayal of reading and writing growth over a long period of time. Process strategies that a student uses in constructing meaning from print in a variety of language contexts are included to further refine the portrait of the language learner. To develop such a portfolio, it is necessary to have a systematic plan to gather data on literacy progress and to document it.

### A Plan to Develop a Literacy Portfolio

A literacy portfolio is as useful as the quality of assessment data that it contains. Therefore, a systematic plan of gathering evidence on literacy development and another plan for documenting those literacy behaviors are presented. Gathering evidence on literacy development will come from a variety of sources over a lengthy period of time. One of the most useful techniques is regular observation in a variety of natural language contexts (Goodman, 1985). While observation is not new to the classroom, it is true that its focus has changed dramatically. Effective "kidwatching" is conducted by teachers who are sensitive to the growth and development of children and how children learn language. Further, since we hope to achieve true portraits of our students' growth in language, observation must occur in naturalistic settings where children use language for a variety of purposes.

Additional evidence is gathered through the analysis of students' performance samples. Analyzing the miscues of children's oral reading provide us with insights into the process strategies they use while they are constructing meaning from text. After children have listened to or read a story, they can retell what they remember from that story. Their story retells are demonstrations of their story sense. Other performance samples include their writing. Samples from different parts of their journals, their stories as well as publications, will provide further understanding of their literacy growth.

Documentation is critical to our plan of tracking the students' literacy development. This process is part of describing literacy which suggests that such descriptions be recorded. No matter how elaborate and insightful the information may be, without efficient techniques for recording the data that have been gathered, it cannot be used effectively, since most of the data will be lost or generalized, given the nature of our memories.

Depending upon our resources, our plan of documentation may be elaborate be modest. Some techniques that may be used are journals, logs, checklists, and anecdotal records. In any case, the procedures employed to document children's language behaviors should facilitate and validate the process of collecting data. Therefore, it is important that the plan of documentation be compatible with the plan of gathering data. Below is a detailed description of the procedures to gather data and the techniques employed to document the data.

**Procedures to Gather Data**

*Observation* provides a powerful database in securing diverse information (Chittendon & Courtney, 1989). The potential of naturalistic observation is derived from the observer, because the underlying effectiveness of "kidwatching" is filtered through the philosophy of the observer. That is, the teacher's focus of observation is directed by her knowledge of child development as well as the understanding of how children learn language. The following basic principles will help to give a broader perspective of this important technique in gathering data:

1. Children learn language in a variety of natural contexts; they come to school knowing how to speak and to listen which they did not learn in formal settings. Our assessment program should include all contexts of language learning. Since learning language happens most effectively in natural ways, informal observation yields information that is most compatible with effective learning.

2. Language serves several functions (Halliday, 1977)—that is, people use language for several reasons. Children have demonstrated their understanding of the functional use of print (Teale, 1986). Just as they need many opportunities to use print for the different communicative aspects of language, we need to observe them using print for different reasons. If we observe children reading for one function, our data are limited and restricted.

3. The question of when observation should begin is often raised. As an integral part of the curriculum, assessment is an ongoing process. Determining the abilities, attitudes, and interests of each child allows for immediate curriculum revision and modification. Therefore, as an ongoing process, observation should begin immediately and be part of the instructional process in both formal, where direct teaching is involved, and informal settings. The teacher studies the interactions of the child with his learning environment, not to evaluate to make judgments and then stop. Rather observational data will be utilized to reconstruct the curriculum to build a more powerful learning environment.

4. All forms of language support literacy development. Atwell (1980) demonstrates that young children read and reread what they have read. Further, children learn about the craft of writing from reading (Smith, 1983). Since reading and writing develop together, and since all forms of language support each other, observation of reading and writing may often occur together.

5. Language serves different functions and occurs in a variety of contexts; therefore, observations should be equally diverse. Many literacy events are self-initiated, and the proficient observer will profit from an observable moment, capturing much knowledge from the child's unplanned language engagement. Other informal observations will be supported by planning and purpose. An example of such an observation is one that occurs during journal writing determining students' interest in such writing. Not all observations are as unobtrusive (Rhodes & Dudley-Marling, 1988) as these informal ones. In small-group reading, the teacher becomes a participant-observer with an agenda to determine specific language behaviors of the readers in the group.

Each child is an individual, bringing with him experiences gathered from this print environment as well as interests and attitudes cultivated from diverse interactions with family and friends that are quite different from their peers. To reduce a student's unique background to a single statistic derived from a test is worthless in facilitating his language learning. Through careful observation, a portrait of a language learner may be developed, helping to facilitate the instructional decisions that we make for him.

### Analysis of Performance Samples

A second naturalistic method of obtaining data on literacy development is the analysis of the students' performance samples. Discussed below are oral miscue analysis, retellings of stories, and writing samples.

*Oral Miscue Analysis.* Observing the reader provides the teacher with a valuable source of information with regard to how the reader handles the book in different situations. As suggested above, insightful observations rest on the teacher's knowledge of the learner and the process. Since we view reading as an interactive process and as a constructive process, our observations must consider the reader as he interacts with the text. More specifically, the view of reading as a tentative process (Rosenblatt, 1978) directs the observer to focus on the reader as he transacts with text. Questions that might be raised are the following: Does the reader have adequate background knowledge? Is the book well written, that is, does it have a well-structured story? Is it cohesive? Is it predictable for this reader? Is it conceptually appropriate and interesting?

These questions suggest that we observe readers before, while, and during reading (Watson, 1985). We listen to readers tell about their perceptions of their reading abilities, their interests, and the troubles they encounter during reading. While they are reading we observe to determine their reading strategies—their ability to use their own schema to make meaning from the text: Do they use text meaning to self-correct? Do they monitor for meaning, or do they rely on single-word pronunciations? Do they predict? Do they know when they don't know and what to do about it? These are important process strategies that may help to distinguish a mature reader from one who lacks fluency. How the reader behaves after reading provides an additional set of valuable information. Does the reader comment on the meaning and make connections to other texts? Is he able to relate personal experiences to story events? Does the reader show enjoyment in a postreading discussion? Is the reader able to retell the story? Observations of the reader allow us to view his strengths as well as his weaknesses. This indeed makes sense when we need to build on what the learner knows.

*Coding Oral Reading.* A system for studying a reader's diversions from the text was devised by Goodman and Burke (1972) who suggest that such information provides the teacher with an understanding of how the reader uses the cueing system. Patterns of types of mistakes or miscues that are made during oral reading of a passage show whether the reader uses semantic, syntactic, graphic, and phonemic cues in the reading process. In the section on documentation, the coding system for identifying the following miscues is given: word omissions, word insertions, word substitutions, repetitions, corrections, and pauses. According to the interactive view of reading, we use all of the available information to construct meaning from text. Thus miscue analysis demonstrates how the reader uses his own language cues while interacting with the language of the text. (For an extensive interpretation of miscues in oral reading, see Goodman & Burke, 1972, *The Reading Miscue Inventory Manual.*) Figure 4.1 below is an example (Antonacci, 1993) of the coding system applied to a student's oral reading.

*Retelling of Stories.* How we recall a story, how we predict what iscoming next in the story, how we are able to remember specific details from the story are determined by our "story schemata." Developing a sense of story begins at a very early age, as soon as children are exposed to stories through listening to them. More than 15 years of research on story grammar (Applebee, 1978; Kintsch, 1977; Mandler & Johnson, 1977; Rumelhart, 1975; Stein & Glenn, 1979; Thorndyke, 1977), reveal the following about story structure:

- Every good story has a structure that contains all the elements of a story.
- Story schema is used by readers and listeners in understanding and remembering stories.
- Developmental differences exist between younger and older children's story schemas.

The more children are exposed to stories with structure, the more they become competent in using it to construct their own stories. Children who do not have a well-developed story sense may be trained in developing it.

Since a child's sense of story affects his abilities to comprehend and remember a story, it is an important aspect of his literacy development, and therefore it should be part of the literacy portfolio. What is story grammar and how may we use it in literacy assessment? Story grammar

**Figure 4.1  Miscue analysis of oral reading.**

Use the following directions for miscue analysis of reading:
  Select an appropriate book for a student's oral reading, remembering that a book far above or below his reading competence will not yield useful information.
  Give the student a purpose for reading, and read the title to him.
  Allow the student to read a short passage aloud.
  While the student is reading, mark his oral reading errors; a list of useful types of errors and a shorthand for marking them is listed below.
  Categorize the types of errors and interpret these errors to help you understand the reading strategies that the student is using. Analysis and interpretation of miscues demands insights into language learning. An excellent interpretation of reading miscues can be found in Weaver's (1988) Chapter 10 on assessment.

| READING ERRORS | EXAMPLES AND MARKINGS |
| --- | --- |
| Substitution | It is cold. See the snow. |
| | (Write the substitution over the text.) |
| Omission | See the snow come down. |
| | (Circle the omitted word(s).) |
| Insertion | Little Bear said, "Mother Bear." |
| | (Write in the inserted word(s).) |
| Reversal | "I am cold." |
| | (Draw a line indicating the words reversed.) |
| Correction | "See the snow." |
| | (Draw a line under the self-corrected word and write its initial error.) |
| Repetition | "I want something to put on" (Minarik, 1957). |
| | (Draw a line under the repeated word(s).) |

may be described as an "idealized internal representation of the parts of a typical story and the relationship among those parts" (Mandler & Johnson, 1977, p. 111). By using a story grammar procedure, a narrative text may be defined into its elements and their relationships. According to Stein and Glenn (1979), these elements consist of two major parts within the story, the setting, and the episode. The following is a description of those parts:

Setting — This story part introduces the main character, describes the time, place, and the context in the set of events that take place.

Episode — The episode consists of the five following categories:

1. Initiating Event — This event sets the story in motion that causes the main character to respond in some way.

2. Internal Response — This event is the main character's reaction to the initiating event that determines the goal and motivates subsequent behavior.

| 3. Attempt | This event consists of an action or a series of actions that leads to goal achievement. |
|---|---|
| 4. Consequence | This story part notes goal attainment or failure to achieve the story goal. |
| 5. Reaction | This story part describes the main character's response to the consequence. |

While simple stories contain one or two episodes, complex stories are constructed on many interrelated episodes.

Since story schema has been shown to have significant value in comprehending stories, determining students' story sense through the use of their story retells would be insightful for the teacher. Very young children who have not had too many opportunities at retelling a story will find it overwhelming at first. Therefore, the children need demonstrations along with many opportunities to retell stories with which they feel comfortable.

To make a statement about a child's story schema, there should be a standard procedure to follow when assessing the retelling of a story; this will ensure the inclusion of all story elements by the teacher. Below is an adaptation (Antonacci, 1988, pp. 166–167) of the procedure suggested by Marshall (1983) for scoring story retells along with a set of generic questions to prompt responses when the child forgets a story part.

The procedure for evaluating story retellings involves the following steps:

1. Select an appropriate story for retelling by the student. While kindergarteners can retell very short stories that they listen to, children in the upper primary grades will be able to retell longer, more complex stories they have read.

2. After having read or listened to the story, have the child retell it. Make sure you are familiar with the story so that you are able to code the story parts during the student's retelling.

3. Using a grid similar to the one developed by Marshall (1983) and found in the section on documentation, check off each story element as the student retells the story. Follow the code explained in the section on documentation to assess and record students' responses when retelling a story.

The following coding system records students' responses:

| (+) | Use a plus (+) in the box under the story part recalled by the student. |
|---|---|
| (✔) | When a student fails to mention a story part, stop him and give him a cue. The prompt response is given in the form of a question designed for the specific story element that the student |

failed to mention. If he uses the prompt correctly to recall the appropriate story part, place a check (✓) in the appropriate box.

(−) When the student fails to recall the story element, even after the prompt question was given, write a minus (−) in the appropriate box.

Generic questions such as the following are used to develop prompt questions:

*Setting*

| | |
|---|---|
| Character: | Who is the main character(s)? What is he/she/they like? |
| Time: | When does the story take place? |
| Place: | Where does the story take place? |

*Episode*

| | |
|---|---|
| Initiating event: | What happens at the beginning of the story to set it in motion? |
| Internal response: | How does ____ realize he had a problem? |
| Goal: | What is ____'s problem? |
| Attempt: | What does ____ do to solve the problem? |
| Consequence: | How does it work? |
| Reaction: | What happens to ____? |
| | How does ____ feel at the end of the story? |

Use the record form "Record of Story Retellings," Figure 4.2, for recording students' responses of story retell.

*Writing Samples.* Writing samples provide useful data on the development of literacy. It is a tangible way of following the child's writing development over a longer period of time.

The types of writing samples that should be included in the literacy portfolio should represent writing for many purposes as well as different types of text, such as fiction and nonfiction. Examples of writing samples that might be included are the following:

Samples from journals—diaries, response journals, dialogue journals, logs from content areas
Dictated stories
Science and social studies reports
Other samples of writing from across the curriculum areas
Messages, letters, invitations, and greeting cards
Stories, including first drafts and revisions
Poems

**Figure 4.2    Record of story retells.**

| STUDENT'S NAME | | | | | |
|---|---|---|---|---|---|
| | TITLE OF STORY AND DATE OF RETELL | | | | |
| | ' | ' | ' | ' | ' |
| | ' | ' | ' | ' | ' |
| STORY EVENTS | ' | ' | ' | ' | ' |
| Setting | ' | ' | ' | ' | ' |
| Character | ' | ' | ' | ' | ' |
| Place | ' | ' | ' | ' | ' |
| Time | ' | ' | ' | ' | ' |
| Episode | ' | ' | ' | ' | ' |
| Initiating Event | ' | ' | ' | ' | ' |
| Internal Response | ' | ' | ' | ' | ' |
| Goal Attempt | ' | ' | ' | ' | ' |
| Consequence | ' | ' | ' | ' | ' |
| Reaction | ' | ' | ' | ' | ' |

KEY
+   Student described this event with no prompt
±   Student described this event assisted by a prompt
↙   Student failed to describe this event when assisted

Posters to advertise school and community events
Rules for a game
Scripts for drama, puppet plays, and radio broadcasts
Jokes, riddles, and cartoons

While much of the progress that the student makes in writing can be assessed during the writing conference, analysis of performance samples provides a clearer portrait of the language learner. It tracks his progress over a period of time, it enables us to judge strengths and weaknesses from a different perspective, and it will demonstrate the kinds of writing he is best at.

Is there a specific list of writing behaviors that one can expect a young child in kindergarten to exhibit? Since natural approaches to teaching literacy posits that each child will demonstrate those writing behaviors based upon his development, there is no one standard against which we measure the child's growth. Writing for one child may be scribling, then responding by telling a story from his writing; for another child, writing may be writing labels for drawings; another child's writing behaviors may be advanced to the level of writing meaningful text that tells short stories. In any case, we do not expect the child to be in step with a pre-formulated curriculum; rather the curriculum should meet the individual needs of each student.

Therefore, the teacher becomes a researcher, a "kidwatcher" who is willing to learn the literacy growth of each child, recording those writing behaviors she observes. In any case, the teacher-observer analyzes the student's writing behaviors and records them. By using the "Checklist of Writing Behavior" found in the section on documentation, specific writing concept and skills, appropriate to his level, can be evaluated.

## DOCUMENTING LITERACY GROWTH AND PROGRESS

An effective plan of assessment rests upon the quality of data that are gathered and the precision of the records that are kept. Without a systematic plan of documentation, any information that has been collected becomes useless in planning for an appropriate student instructional program.

Documentation allows one to say with credibility that Johnny has experienced dramatic growth in writing, but in the area of revision he needs work in sequencing thoughts. Since we are keeping a literacy portfolio with tangible evidence and descriptive data that delineate literacy behaviors, such statements will be quite authentic. Documentation allows us to say, "See for yourself!"

Chittenden and Courtney (1989) have demonstrated that classroom teachers do experience problems with record keeping. However, our system of documentation should be tailored to our needs, often dictated by the resources available to us. Since a variety of formats for keeping precise records do exist, it is just a matter of selecting those that will do the job well. There are a number of methods suggested (Teale, Hiebert, & Chittenden, 1987) for documenting descriptive data which include the following:

Journals
Checklists and rating scales
Anecdotal records
Literacy folders
Language inventories

The following is a brief description along with a sample of each of the suggested formats for documenting literacy behaviors:

## Journals and Logs

Journals and logs are the constant companions of the "kidwatcher" who is the participant-observer in dynamic learning events. "A teacher/ researcher is an observer, a questioner, a learner, and a more complete teacher" (Bissex, 1987, p. 4). Active inquiry within the context of her own classroom are the data that count, that she depends on to learn each child. She, therefore, needs to record complete descriptions of interactions, relevant context, and learning processes she observes. The journal is the tool that permits such recordings. In a narrative style, the observer is able to write as much of the details of the literacy event that she observed. The wealth of information obtained may then be organized and categorized to make decisions about instruction. Logs like journals allow for written descriptions of observations; however, usually logs are restricted to shorter, more focused entries.

## Checklists and Rating Scales

These types of records facilitate the process of documenting literacy behaviors. By simply checking the behavior(s) or rating the strength of the behavior, documentation is achieved. While this recording system is easy to use, the a priori classification scheme may become quite restrictive. That is, the observer may tend to focus on the literary behaviors listed, missing potentially valuable information. Further, with a checklist, the context as well as the specific literacy will not be described. Below (Figures 4.3 and 4.4) are examples of a checklist for "Selected Reading Behaviors for the First Grade" and a modified sample of the checklist with a rating scale of "Selected Writing Behaviors for the Third Grade" (Antonacci, in press), where each literacy behavior is ranked with a code which allows for varying degrees of performance.

## Anecdotal Records

These records consist of short comments describing the literacy behaviors of students. Unlike the journals and logs that are written in narrative style, anecdotes are short and simple comments comprised of a few words or phrases.

When anecdotal records become part of a rating scale or a checklist, the recorded data become more valuable. In addition to rating a child's performance on a specific literacy concept or skill, the anecdotal record permits notations about specific examples of the child's work and behavior from a given context. Below Figures 4.5 and 4.6 present examples of

**Figure 4.3   Sample checklist form.**

SELECTED READING BEHAVIORS FOR THE FIRST GRADE

STUDENT'S NAME _____ DATE _____

STORY TIME*

.... Student listens attentively to the story
.... Student uses the title to predict what the story will be about
.... Student participates in the story (e.g., saying repetitive words)
.... Student comments on action of the characters
.... Student comments on illustrations
.... Student elaborates on various parts of the story
.... Student answers questions about the story
.... Student requests certain favorite stories to be read
.... Student tries to predict an ending to the story being read
.... Student retells the major parts of the story that was read
.... Student recalls certain details of the story
.... Student explains the illustration and how it adds meaning to text
.... Student requests a rereading of the story
.... Student participates in shared-reading activities
.... Student participates in reading-response activities

INDEPENDENT READING*

.... Student enjoys reading independently
.... Student selects an appropriate book
.... Student knows the beginning of the book
.... Student knows beginning/end of print on a page
.... Student knows page-turning techniques
.... Student knows "next page"
.... Student knows directionality of print
.... Student knows how to read selected book
.... Student tries to retell the story using print and pictures

Place a "+" next to each reading behavior demonstrated by the student.

* These reading behaviors are preselected and do not represent all of the reading behaviors
demonstrated in the first grade.

the annotated record for "Observing Writing Behaviors" and an annotated checklist of "Book Behaviors of the Young Reader."

**Literacy Folders**

The purpose of the literacy folder is to keep track of the reading and the
writing growth of individual students. While some of the teacher's
observations may not be an open record to the student, the literacy

**Figure 4.4    Rating form.**

---

SELECTED WRITING BEHAVIORS FOR THE THIRD GRADE

STUDENT'S NAME _____ DATE _____

TYPES OF WRITING*

____ Student enjoys writing
____ Student engages in narrative writing
____ Student writes poetry
____ Student engages in informational writing
____ Student engages in functional writing
____ Student writes in journal
____ Student writes in science log
____ Student enjoys writing messages to peers
____ Student uses graphics and illustrations with text

PROCESS STRATEGIES*

____ Student is willing to revise work
____ Student deletes information from text
____ Student reorganizes information within text
____ Student collaborates with peers during the revision process
____ Student allows editing from peers and teacher
____ Student is anxious to publish stories
____ Student enjoys reading his/her work from the author's chair

Use the following code to rate the student's writing behaviors:
   0   Does not demonstrate this behavior
   1   Sometimes demonstrates this behavior
   2   Usually demonstrates this behavior
   3   Always demonstrates this behavior

---

* These writing behaviors are preselected and do not represent all of the writing behaviors that may be demonstrated in the third grade.

folder is. For both reading and writing, there are records that show what skills the child has mastered along with the skills over which he does not have complete control. Using the literacy folder, both the teacher and the student consult at least weekly on his progress. This folder helps to determine the direction the student needs to take.

## Language Inventories

A list of reading and writing behaviors may be used by the teacher to guide her in observing the language learner. Language inventories are essential to teachers with no experience who need help in focusing on

**Figure 4.5   Anecdotal record.**

---

ANNOTATED RECORD FOR OBSERVING
WRITING BEHAVIORS IN YOUNG CHILDREN

---

NAME: _____  DATE: _____

---

WRITING BEHAVIORS

---

ENGAGES IN SCRIBBLE WRITING

---

USES SCRIBBLE AND PICTURES

---

USES INVENTED LETTERS

---

USES ALPHABETIC LETTERS

---

COPIES WORDS, LABELS PICTURES

---

TELLS A STORY ABOUT PICTURE

---

WRITES A STORY ABOUT HIS PICTURE
(Uses scribble, invented letters,
alphabetic letters)

---

literacy behaviors. There is the temptation to use language inventories inappropriately: to group language behaviors by grade and priority, to try to place them in a hierarchy, or to use the list as a "curriculum manual" to direct one's teaching. Simply, the purpose of these lists is to help in our observations by showing the "kidwatcher" what to look for and to aid the teacher/researcher in categorizing the data yielded from observations and analysis of performance samples. A partial reading inventory is found below (Figure 4.7).

## SUMMARY

The value of using natural approaches in an assessment program cannot be overemphasized. For one, its compatibility with instructional strategies makes sense since it allows assessment and instruction to occur

**Figure 4.6    Checklist.**

---

ANNOTATED CHECKLIST
OF BOOK BEHAVIORS OF THE YOUNG READER

---

NAME: _____ DATE: _____

---

BOOK BEHAVIORS

---

. . . . . HOLDS BOOK CORRECTLY

---

. . . . . TURNS PAGES, RIGHT TO LEFT

---

. . . . . KNOWS WHERE PRINT BEGINS ON A PAGE

---

. . . . . KNOWS WHERE PRINT ENDS ON A PAGE

---

. . . . . KNOWS THE NEXT PAGE

---

. . . . . DEMONSTRATES DIRECTION OF PRINT

---

. . . . . DEMONSTRATES LINE DIRECTIONALITY

---

. . . . . MAKES MEANINGFUL COMMENTS ABOUT ILLUSTRATIONS

---

. . . . . PRETENDS TO READ THE BOOK, TELLING THE STORY

---

. . . . . LOOKS AT BOOKS INDEPENDENTLY

---

together. Moreover, informal approches acknowledge that assessment is an ongoing process for the purpose of designing, modifying, and revising curriculum for the individual needs of the students.

Since a portfolio approach to assessing literacy growth is an alternative to the current formal program of standardized testing, acceptance of such a novel program depends on its effective implementation. Because this proposed program of assessment may be quite new to teachers, administrators, and parents, it success needs strong leadership committed to the support and advancement of natural approaches in assessing literacy development.

**Figure 4.7   Inventory of reading behaviors.**

Inventory of Reading Behaviors of Young Children
Observed in Natural Contexts

Listening to Stories

Enjoys all types of literature
Responds through participatory actions
Makes predictions when solicited
Retells the story
Recalls specific details from the story
Uses illustrations to help retell the story
Relates story characters and story events to personal experience
Participates in the follow-up activities
Uses a familiar story to create a new one

Book Behaviors

Holds book correctly
Turns pages, right to left
Knows where print begins on a page
Knows where print ends on a page
Knows the next page
Demonstrates the direction of the print, left to right
Demonstrates line directionality
Tries to read words from a familiar book
Tries to read text from a familiar book
Uses illustrations and "reads like a book"
Retells a story, pretending to read, pointing to words and to lines
  of text
Looks at books independently
Identifies favorite books by titles
Asks to have favorite stories reread

Print in the Environment

Reads own name
Reads students' names
Reads labels
Reads signs
Attaches meaning to logos
Reads classroom charts
Reads group journals

## REFERENCES

Antonacci, P. (1988). Comprehension strategies for special learners. In C.N. Hedley & J.S. Hicks (Eds.), *Reading and the special learner.* Norwood, NJ: Ablex.

Antonacci, P. (1993). Natural assessment in whole language classrooms. In C.N. Hedley & A.L. Carrasquillo (Eds.), *Whole language and the bilingual learner.* Norwood, NJ: Ablex.

Applebee, A.N. (1978). *The child's concept of story: Ages 2–17.* Chicago: University of Chicago Press.

Atwell, M.A. (1980). *The evolution of text: The interrelations of reading and writing in the composing process.* Unpublished doctoral dissertation, Indiana University, Bloomington, IN.

Bissex, G.L. (1987). The beginnings of writing. In B. Fillion, C. Hedley, & E. DiMartino (Eds.), *Home and school: Early language and reading.* Norwood, NJ: Ablex.

Chittenden, E., & Courtney, R. (1989). Assessment of young children's reading: Documentation as an alternative to testing. In S. Strickland & L.M. Morrow (Eds.), *Emerging literacy: Young children learn to read and write.* Newark, DE: International Reading Association.

Goodman, Y.M. (1986). Coming to know literacy: Writing and reading. In W.H. Teale & E. Sulzby (Eds.), *Emergent literacy: Writing and reading.* Norwood, NJ: Ablex.

Goodman, Y.M. (1985). Kidwatching: Observing children in the classroom. In A. Jaggar & M.T. Burke-Smith (Eds.), *Observing the language learner.* Newark, DE: International Reading Association.

Goodman, Y.M., & Burke, C. (1972). *Reading miscue inventory manual: Procedures for diagnosis and evaluation.* New York: Richard C. Owen.

Halliday, M. (1977). *Explorations in the functions of language.* New York: Elsevier North-Holland.

Hiebert, E.H., & McWhorter, L. (1987). *The content of kindergarten and readiness books in four basal reading programs.* Paper presented in the annual meeting of the American Educational Research Association, Washington, DC.

Kintsch, W. (1977). On comprehending stories. In J. Just & P. Carpenter (Eds.), *Cognitive processes in comprehension.* Hillsdale, NJ: Lawrence Erlbaum Associates.

Mandler, J.M., & Johnson, N.S. (1977). Remembrance of things parsed: Story structure and recall. *Cognitive Psychology, 9,* 111–151.

Marshall, N. (1983). Using story grammar to assess reading comprehension. *The Reading Teacher, 36,* 616–620.

Minarik, E.H. (1957). *Little bear.* New York: Scholastic.

National Association of Educators of Young Children. (1988). NAEYC position statement on standardized testing of young children 3 through 8 years of age. *Young Children, 43,* 42–47.

Rhodes, L.K., & Dudley-Marling, C. (1988). *Readers and writers with a difference: A holistic approach to teaching learning disabled and remedial students.* Portsmouth, NH: Heinemann.

Rosenblatt, L. (1978). *The reader, the text, and the poem.* Carbondale, IL: Southern Illinois University Press.

Rumelhart, D.E. (1975). Notes on a schema for stories. In D.G. Bobrow & A.M. Collins (Eds.), *Representation and understanding: Studies in cognitive science.* New York: Academic Press.

Smith, F. (1983). Reading like a writer. *Language Arts, 60,* 58–567.

Stein, N., & Glenn, C. (1979). An analysis of story comprehension in elementary children. In R.O. Freedle (Ed.), *Discourse processing: Multi-disciplinary perspective in discourse comprehension.* Norwood, NJ: Ablex.

Teale, W., & Sulzby, E. (1986). Emergent literacy as a perspective for examining how young children become writers and readers. In W. Teale, E. Sulzby (Eds.), *Emergent literacy: Writing and reading.* Norwood, NJ: Ablex.

Taylor, D., & Dorsey-Gaines, C. (1988). *Growing up literate: Learning from inner city families.* Portsmouth, NH: Heinemann.

Teale, W.H. (1986). Home background and young children's literacy learning. In W.H. Teale & E. Sulzby (Eds.), *Emergent literacy: Writing and reading.* Norwood, NJ: Albex.

Teale, W., Hiebert, E.H., & Chittenden, E.A. (1987). Assessing young children's literacy development. *The Reading Teacher, 40,* 772–777.

Thorndyke, P. (1977). Cognitive structures in comprehension and memory of narrative discourse. *Cognitive Psychology, 9,* 77–110.

Watson, D. (1985). Watching and listening to children read. In A. Jaggar & M.T. Smith-Burke (Eds.), *Observing the language learner.* Newark, DE: International Reading Association.

Weaver, C. (1988). *Reading process and practice: From socio-psycholinguistics to whole language.* Portsmouth, NH: Heinemann.

# Part II

# Natural Approaches in Developing Literacy

# Chapter 5

# The Development of Early Writing

## Patricia A. Antonacci

### WHEN DO CHILDREN BEGIN TO WRITE?

Writing plays a prominent role in the development of literacy behaviors in young children (Bissex, 1980; Clay, 1975). For some time researchers and educators began observing literacy behaviors of young children in "print rich homes." Children learn about writing with their first print encounters. They begin to write long before they enter school. Just as a child does not wait until he enters school to learn to speak, neither does writing development wait for formal instruction. Rather writing develops in young children along with other language forms.

The changing definition of writing, with its focus on the construction of meaning, has helped us to realize that young children use what they know about print concepts to express themselves through writing. Ferreiro (1984) differentiates between the figurative and the constructive aspects of children's written productions. When considering the figurative aspects of writing, the focus is on letter formation, tendency to horizontal or vertical movements, speed, spelling, and so on. The constructive aspects of writing, on the other hand, focus on the relation between the strings of letters and the meaning constructed by the child, the strategies employed by the child to communicate meaning from his written text, and so on.

The development of writing or emergent writing is primarily concerned with the constructive aspects of written productions. It is this focus on writing that broadens its definition to include a number of different forms of writing that were once not considered as part of writing development.

The purpose of this chapter is to discuss characteristics of emergent writing that develop at home in natural ways, that is supported in "print-rich" environments. How preschool and kindergarten classrooms may facilitate writing development through natural approaches conclude this discussion.

## EMERGENT WRITING IN A LITERATE ENVIRONMENT

Only a few children who enter our classrooms from a literate environment may know how to read and write, but all children have developed at least some critical concepts about the written forms of language. Further, there are distinct differences between children and what they know about the print forms of language, and this is highly dependent on their literacy experiences (Ferreiro & Teberovsky, 1982).

In almost all homes, children are involved with literacy events from very early on in life. Not only the number of language experiences but the quality of that event will directly affect the literacy development of that child.

### Developing a Love for Reading from Joyful Interaction with Books

Children's first experiences with books should be positive, supported by joyful interactions. The affective behaviors associated with literacy development are often the result of the kinds of interactions that parents and children have during literacy event. "The warm, human sharing which occurs when books, parents, and children come together becomes permanently associated with reading and creates an inner drive for gaining personal control over this experience" (Doake, 1986, p. 4).

A parent's positive attitude exhibited during reading to his child helps to build an inner drive about wanting to learn to read. This is where it all starts! In Doake's (1986) report on one observational study of parent and infant during reading, after only 2 months and 3 weeks of warm and happy interactions during lap reading, the infant began to show animation when a familiar book was read to him.

### Developing Literacy Behaviors Through Extensive and Early Reading

Since all forms of language support each other, the role that reading to children plays is critical in developing writing as well as reading and other forms of language. Studies of young children indicate that literacy development occurs early when children have come from print-rich environments and had been extensively read to at an early age (Clark, 1976; Durkin, 1966).

While children are listening to stories being read to them, they are learning many concepts about print needed to write. Among others they see how spoken words look on a page; they learn that print reads in a linear direction, from left to right; they begin to see boundaries between words. Reading to children from books with illustrations helps children develop the notions that pictures and text together convey meaning. They not only learn where the print ends on one page and where it begins on the next page, but they know how to turn the page to get there. These are necessary book behaviors and print concepts children need to know when writing as well as reading.

### Learning to Write Stories from Listening to and Reading Stories

In an environment where familiar stories are read to children over and over again, they learn the language of stories, and they develop a sense of story that enables them to retell the story and to construct their own stories.

Listening to stories that are well structured helps children develop a concept for story. This concept for story aids them in story recall: It facilitates their memory for the major story elements, for specific details, and it enables them to make predictions about "What will happen next?" In asking one class of first graders to retell a simple fable, *The Lion and the Mouse*, in writing, I have found that the children who come from homes that are print-rich and who are read to extensively produced the best story recalls in writing. These children are also the ones who are engaged in self-initiated literacy events, including reading at a higher frequency.

Figure 5.1 is a sample of one story retelling. In Brian's written retelling of the story, notice his use of story language. A further analysis of his retelling determining his recall for story elements, using the procedure suggested in Chapter 2, "A Portfolio Approach for Documenting Literacy Development" shows that Brian recalled all of the story elements along with some specific details. Thus reading stories to children does help them to recall orally (Morrow, 1982) and in writing as well.

### Learning About the Functions of Language

Children learn about the functions of printed language by demonstration of family members within their home and community, and in a similar way they learn about the value of their language (Wells, 1986). Children are surrounded by print and they see its use for a variety of purposes. In

**Figure 5.1.   Brian's story retell of "The Lion and the Mouse."**

The Lion and the Mouse

Wans       a       Lion     was     sleping  and  a  mouse
was         on       his     back    and    when  he   wacke up
he          was     going    to      eat   him up   but   the
mouse      mode     a      promis that he   will  help  him
one         day.      but    not    Log    afta
The Lion   wos       thrapt.  The Mouse  monch and mon
in,tel.     he       was     out.    littl  anomls  can
do  defret  thegs.

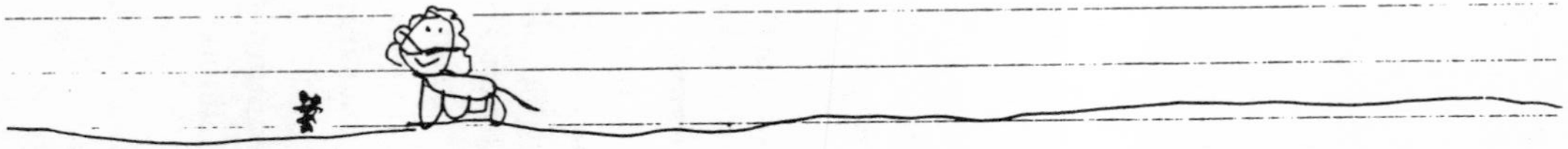

THE LION AND THE MOUSE

*Once a lion was sleeping. And a mouse was on his back, and when he woke up he was going to eat him (the mouse) up. But the mouse made a promise that he will help him (the lion) one day. But not long after, the lion was trapped. The mouse munched and munched until he was out. Little animals can do different things.*

print-rich environments, they see adults writing for numerous reasons: creating a shopping list, writing a phone message, recording a recipe, writing a set of directions to get to a specific place. When children are involved in these literacy events, they begin to realize that we write for a variety of reasons.

When children are involved in literacy events that include magazines containing pictures and captions or longer text or advertisements in newspapers or fliers, they are introduced to how pictures or illustrations represent meaning (Wells, 1986). Drawing becomes an important part of their construction of meaning. Children's written productions begin to take on the use of other media. They integrate pictures, scribbles, words, letters, and drawings; they use a variety of materials that are pasted, stapled, and attached in creative ways. Through various engagements with print and the embedding of print in illustrations of all kinds, they are learning new ways to deliver meaning.

### Learning About the Tools for Writing

Children who are in homes where there are a variety of tools to write with and different kinds of paper and material to write on will come to school feeling comfortable in using different instruments. It is their open invitation to write, to explore, to express themselves. Young writers do not need direct instruction on how to use pencils, crayons, and markers to write; they do need demonstrations by other writers in the family. With the availability of writing tools along with sufficient interaction from adults, emergent writers become independent in the use of these instruments, creating their own written productions.

## CHARACTERISTICS OF EMERGENT WRITING

To facilitate our understanding of how emergent writing develops in literacy-rich homes, Sulzby, Teale, and Kamberelis (1989) have reduced the findings of numerous researchers to five important themes. These themes provide insight to teachers and parents on the descriptive nature of emergent writing. Therefore, the themes reported by Sulzby et al. (1989, pp. 65–69) are reported below.

### Transience

An interesting characteristic of emergent writing is transience. One researcher explains that a few lines of scribble by a child may be described by him once as a story but at another time as a letter to Grandma. Another explanation of transience in early writing is in the child's shift of interest. The young writer may be engaged in writing activities for very long periods of time during the day, and maybe over a few weeks. Suddenly, his interest shifts to a different activity, such as to a form of play. A third example of transience in early writing can be observed in the emergent writer's use of various forms of writing.

## Power

Writing empowers an author; after all, it is not only a form of expression, but it is a means to assign permanency to the writer's ideas. Writing is indeed an expression of oneself. Empowerment has been defined as "a positive force and literacy is the medium" (Fagan, 1989, p. 573). This empowerment through writing is first felt when a child becomes intrigued by his initial markings and realizes who is the agent of those markings.

Through a variety of diverse and natural ways emergent writers receive encouragement to write. Part of that encouragement is in the form of negotiation when parents provide limits or restrictions. They detail safety rules, insist on furniture and wall restrictions as well as make available materials (Temple, Nathan, & Burris, 1982) to their children. This concept of negotiated power continues as children develop with writers: Parents help children to form words, and sometimes they resist; teachers may give assistance in showing how to make words mean, and depending on the child's writing development the suggestion may be facilitative or frustrating to his written productions.

## The Forms of Writing

In literacy-rich homes, the five most common forms of writing used by emergent writers are scribble, drawing, nonphonetic strings, phonetic (or invented) spelling, and conventional orthography. Children may use one or more forms of writing in a single production. This, as mentioned above, is a mark of transience.

In discussing the forms of writing, it is important to show the relationship of the writer's purpose or function and the form(s) of writing that he chooses to use. Research does show that certain forms of writing do appear at home at approximate ages. At 2 years of age, scribble is used which develops into a differentiation of scribble for drawing and scribble for writing. At 3 years of age, letterlike features appear in scribble along with the beginnings of conventional letter forms. They combine scribble, drawing, letterlike features to produce messages and stories. At four, some attempt to use phonetic spelling, though this is more prevalent at 5 and 6 years of age.

While one might look at age relations, it is important to focus on language use of purpose. Transiency of writing forms is characteristic of early writing even in the first grade. This is especially true when the young writers are producing a complex story; they utilize scribble and drawing to get finished.

### Engrossing Construction

An engrossing or a multimedia construction is produced by young children who have the opportunity to convey their meaning not only through print but through the use and integration of a variety of materials and of different art forms. Children construct elaborate stories by pasting or taping decorations made from drawings, cutouts, pieces of wool, pictures from magazines. They may continue to add three-dimensional pieces made from a variety of materials, wood, paper popups, plastic tops, and toy figures who become the main character in their stories.

In sharing their creations, they may continue to add other art forms, such as music, puppetry, and dramatization. This movement across media enhances their development because such activities produce tensions within children's thinking about literacy.

### Aesthetic Creation

Emergent writing is filled with examples of aesthetic creations or the poetic voice. This occurs when children use language in unusual ways, which results from playing with language, making fun with language, and investigating different language expressions. Figure 5.2 is an interesting example of aesthetic use of language found in one first grader's writing.

**Figure 5.2. Denny's story, telling about how he felt.**
**Note his aesthetic creation in language.**

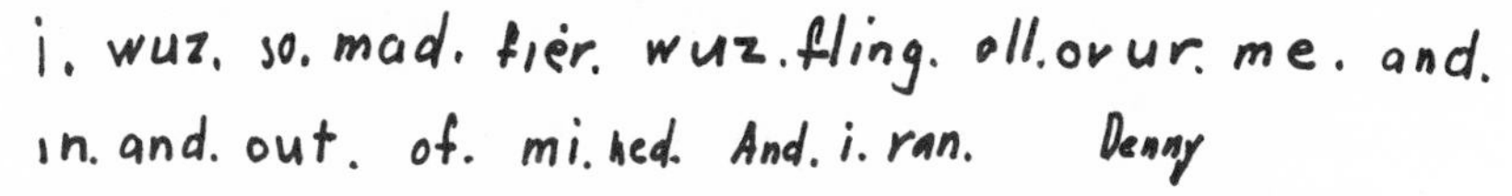

i. wuz. so. mad. fiér. wuz. fling. oll. ovur. me. and. in. and. out. of. mi. hed. And. i. ran.     Denny

*I was so mad. Fire was flying all over me. And in and out of my head. And I ran.*
*Denny*

## Classrooms That Develop Writing

The insights that we gain from research on children's writing development will enable us to create classrooms where writing is promoted.

We know that children understand that writing has many functions and that children write for many reasons.

We know that children use many forms of writing, from scribbling to drawing, and when they are busy writing they are constructing meaning or composing—not practicing letter forms.

We know that literacy development is marked by transiency, a shifting of interest in the language form in which they are engaged or in another interpretation of "what they mean to mean."

We know that children need encouragement, which means that we need to understand their point of literacy development to bring them to the next point. "Pushing" only leads to frustration.

We know that writing development is supported by all forms of language use, and all forms of language develop concurrently.

We know that children's writing is further developed by their use of multimedia constructions and aesthetic engagements while they are writing.

Using these basic understandings on writing development in young children, we can create classroom environments that foster writing. The conclusions of this chapter will describe natural approaches that can be used with the young child to promote writing development.

## The Classroom Environment that Promotes Writing

A classroom environment that promotes literacy development in the young child is one that is designed based upon the "portrait of the emergent reader and writer." What we know with regard to how language develops needs to be used in instructional planning, which includes the physical environment of the classroom.

We simply cannot tell the child that print is important. We need to show the child. Therefore, writing development is supported and nourished in a print-rich environment. The use of print for many purposes is part of this classroom environment. Labels, instructions, messages, directions, signs, and so on are examples of functional uses of print in the classroom.

Most classrooms for the young child are arranged with activity centers, each center designated for specific activities, such as science, art, math, social studies, play, creative dramatics, and literacy. The literacy center should be attractive and include a quiet library corner with open-faced shelves that are well stocked. An attractive area for free reading as well as a small place for shared reading are also part of the library corner. In addition, the literacy center needs a well-stocked writing area. The writing area should include appropriate tables and chairs for writing. A variety of types and sizes of lined and unlined paper should be stocked in a way that's easy to get to. All of the writer's tools should be available to the young writer—pencils, pens, colored felt-tipped marking pens, crayons, erasers, paste, scissors, and rulers. There should be a place in the writing center for keeping a Literary Folder for each child to store finished works and to keep works in progress.

## Literacy Across the Curriculum

Children learn language when it becomes purposeful, not when it becomes the object or the goal of learning itself. Therefore, when writing is used in each area of the curriculum, it becomes interesting to the child because he sees a function or a purpose for his writing.

Integrating writing in content areas provides opportunities for the young child to engage in expository writing or informational writing. Children have their own interests, and each child is an expert on a particular topic (Graves, 1983). Social studies and science are content areas that include numerous topics that are related to the child's world waiting to be explored, discussed, acted on, and written about. Keeping live animals can be made into a literacy event. Reading about the animals to give them proper care, writing logs about the animals' behaviors, writing animal stories, writing a book on animal care using the entries from the logs, writing poems are just some ways that writing can be integrated in the content areas.

In a first-grade class ducks were being hatched. The children were in charge. They kept individual logs, recording what they had observed. After being instructed on how to turn the duck eggs and how to keep the incubator, Amanda made the sign shown in Figure 5.3 to help her friends when it was their turn to turn the eggs. Additionally, Adam kept a schedule of children's names and times of those whose turn it was for egg turning. These are examples of how literacy is integrated throughout the curriculum; they are demonstrations of how writing can be used for specific functions.

## Promoting Story Writing Through Retellings

The teacher of the young child realizes that children engaged in story-writing before they entered school, and children do not need to know

**Figure 5.3.    Amanda's entry into her learning log after a discussion and demonstration on how to turn the duck eggs.**

Turning the duck eggs

1. Wosh your hands.
2. Opin the tgo Jetlee.
3. Trn the eggs.
4. Cows the top Saftlee.
5. Teck the tepacr for 100°F.

1. Wash your hands.
2. Open the top gently.
3. Turn the eggs.
4. Close the top softly.
5. Check the temperature for 100°F.

the 26 letters to start writing stories. Teachers know when children greet them in the morning, it is often with a story. The teacher of the young child needs to capitalize on the children's interest to tell their stories. What is one specific strategy that a teacher of emergent writers use to facilitate their written expressions of stories?

Retelling stories before writing is an effective strategy for the young writer. Britton (1970) studied the effects of retelling stories on writing and argues that through this activity children learn to dominate the conversation; they learn to stay on the topic without the feedback awarded them in a conversation. It is the story retell that provides the connection between speech and writing, with the oral language experience providing the ready-made content for writing.

Researchers (Mandler & Johnson, 1977; Rumelhart, 1975; Stein & Glenn, 1979) on the structure of stories have used the retelling of stories to provide the basis for analyzing stories and to show how stories are represented in memory. This research also supports the notion that story sense is acquired through hearing and reading stories as well as retelling them and further suggests the effects that a well-developed story concept has on creation of good stories.

In one study with first graders, the supportive link between the oral reproduction of stories and story writing was confirmed (King & Rental, 1983). Since literacy can be traced to the earlier developments of speech in the young child, it makes sense to employ a strategy for story writing that will incorporate the acquired linguistic competencies of the young child.

### Personal Communication in the Classroom

Birthdays are very important to young children. Almost every day there are at least two or three children announcing the birthday of a parent or sibling. This provides a wonderful opportunity to create a special-event message—the birthday card (Taylor, 1983). Instead of throwing away used commercially prepared birthday cards, as well as other greeting cards, collect and save them as a source for children to examine in their free time. This gives them some ideas of format and decoration; they will also try to read them. There are many occasions during the course of the school year that children can send greeting cards to members of their family as well as their classmates. A classroom mailbox is a good idea to encourage sending birthday cards to members of the class.

Personal communication comes in forms that are quite appropriate for the classroom. Children love to write notes and messages to each other. It might be a reminder to do something, a complaint, or just a simple "Hello." Such message writing should be encouraged, since it is a legitimate function of print that it often overlooked in traditional class-rooms. To encourage message writing, provide a message board to which the children have access. Demonstrate how to use the message board. To further strengthen the use of the message board, the teacher can engage in writing messages to the children. A teacher's written message may be for the purpose of reminding someone to do a job, or a personal invitation to engage in a special event, or a special note of thanks for the job that was well done. (The procedure for message boarding can be found on p. 96.)

### The Functional Use of Writing

Young children will participate in writing experiences that are meaningful to them. When literacy events are meaningful and purposeful to the child, he will develop functional principles for language in print. In emergent literacy classrooms, teachers find many ways to engage children in functional writing activities, so these children will develop functional principles. They will understand the myriad reasons for which print is used because they will be actively engaged in print use for varied functions. What will we see these children doing?

A classroom that has functional literacy environments requires children to make use of reading and writing for their direction and guidance during the course of the day. The following are some examples of functional writing that may be used with young children:

*Job lists.* Have children sign up for classroom chores.

*Daily weather board.* Have children listen to the news on the classroom radio and record the weather.

*Lunch counts and attendance.* Have children sign up for buying lunch. Have a child write down the names of children who are absent for the day.

*Passes to leave the classroom.* Have children sign out to leave the classroom.

*Signs for the classroom.* There are numerous signs that need to be made for the classroom. Children should be part of making these signs.

*Labels for displays.* Children's work needs to be displayed. This too is a form of publication; children get a sense of ownership. This is particularly true when the child can attach his own label to his display.

*Sign-on charts.* When children are invited to volunteer for a job, when they want to participate in a particular activity, when they need to register their choices, they can do it by signing on a specified chart.

*Name writing.* Cunningham (1988) suggests name writing to develop children's linguistic understandings and specific skills related to literacy. Young children are expected to write their names on all of their work. Even though the young child scribbles his name, it is important to let him write his own name: This is an act of declaring ownership. When children consistently engage in this practice, they learn to write their own name correctly and to recognize the names of others.

## CONCLUSION

There are a number of ways, in addition to those described above, that we can use to facilitate writing in an emergent literacy classroom. Lengthening the list above is simply a matter of being responsive to how the child learns language naturally. The kinds of literacy experiences that the teacher designs for the child will take into account his experiences, his interests, and his abilities. Sulzby (1988) suggested that the teacher accept whatever form of writing the children use, that the teacher make direct invitations to write, and that the teacher encourage the child to write at his development by reassuring, "You don't have to write like grown-ups!" and "Write your own way." To grasp support in the belief that natural approaches for developing strategies in the young child are effective, we need only reflect on how we as children learned language in natural settings.

## REFERENCES

Bissex, G. (1980). *GNYS AT WRK: A child learns to write and read.* Cambridge, MA: Harvard University Press.

Britton, J. (1970). *Language and learning.* London: Allen Lane, Penguin Press.

Clark, M.M. (1976). *Young fluent readers.* London: Heinemann.

Clay, M.M. (1975). *What did I write? Beginning writing behavior.* Portsmouth, NH: Heinemann.

Cunningham, P. (1988). Names: A natural for early reading and writing. *Reading Horizons, 28,* 114–122.

Doake, D.B. (1986). Learning to read: It starts at home. In D.R. Tovey & J.E. Kerber (Eds.), *Roles in literacy learning: A new perspective.* Newark, DE: International Reading Association.

Durkin, D. (1966). *Children who read early.* New York: Teachers College Press.

Fagan, W.T. (1989). Empowered students; empowered teachers. *The Reading Teacher, 42,* 572–578.

Ferreiro, E. (1984). The underlying logic of literacy development. In H. Goelman, A. Obert, & F. Smith (Eds.), *Awakening to literacy.* Exeter, NH: Heinemann Educational.

Ferreiro, E., & Teberosky, A. (1982). *Literacy before schooling.* Exeter, NH: Heinemann Educational.

Graves, D.M. (1983). *Writing: Teachers and children at work.* Portsmouth, NH: Heinemann.

King, M., & Rental, V. (1983). Present at the beginning. In P. Mosenthal, L. Tamor, & S. Walmsley (Eds.), *Research on writing: Principles and method.* New York: Longman.

Mandler, J.M., & Johnson, N.S. (1977). Remembrance of things passed: Story structure and recall. *Cognitive Psychology, 9,* 111–151.

Morrow, L.M. (1982). Relationships between literature programs, library corner designs, and children's use of literature. *Journal of Educational Research, 75,* 339–344.

Rumelhart, D. (1975). Notes on a schema for stories. In D. Bobrow & A. Colins (Eds.), *Representation and understanding: Studies in cognitive science.* New York: Academic Press.

Stein, N.L., & Glenn, C.G. (1979). An analysis of story comprehension in elementary school children. In R.O. Freedle (Ed.), *New directions in discourse processing: Advances in discourse processing.* Norwood, NJ: Ablex.

Sulzby, E. (1988). *Emergent literacy: Kindergartners write and read, including Sulzby coding system.* Ann Arbor, MI: University of Michigan and North Central Regional Educational Laboratory.

Sulzby, E., Teale, W.H., & Kamberelis, G. (1989). Emergent writing in the classroom: Home and school connections. In D.S. Strickland & L.M. Morrow (Eds.), *Emerging literacy: Young children learn to read and write.* Newark, DE: International Reading Association.

Taylor, D. (1983). *Family literacy: Young children learning to read and write.* Exeter, NH: Heinemann.

Temple, C.A., Nathan, R.G., & Burris, N.A. (1982). *The beginnings of writing.* Boston: Allyn & Bacon, Inc.

Wells, G. (1986). *The meaning makers: Children learning language and using language to learn.* Portsmouth, NH: Heinemann.

# Chapter 6

# Strategies for Young Authors: Making Writing Work in the Primary Grades

## Patricia A. Antonacci

All children enter first grade with print concepts, and most educators are aware of this. Teachers now know that children have been read to and that parent–child book-reading interactions play a critical role in their literacy development. Such awareness has changed the reading programs in the primary grades.

However, writing in the primary school has not been given the same consideration. Teale (1986) calls for a greater emphasis on writing experiences in the early school years. His suggestion is supported by his research that demonstrated preschool children who were engaged in literacy experiences spent half of the time writing. Thus learning to write, like reading, begins early at home in a natural setting. Children do not first learn how to write when they are engaged in formal language instruction. Rather learning about writing begins when children learn about the language system acquired through use in natural contexts, not through practice exercises on how to use language (Harste & Woodward, 1989; Harste, Woodward, & Burke, 1984).

There are two major purposes of this chapter: The first is to create a place in the primary grade curriculum for writing; the second is to explore how teachers can set up classrooms that offer natural contexts and functional uses for writing with young children. To implement these objectives, the first part of this chapter surveys a rationale for extending students' writing using natural contexts; the second part describes a writing program that employs a process approach to the teaching of writing, followed by writing activities that extend and support a literate environment for young writers.

## THE DEVELOPMENT OF WRITING

If writing has always been in the classroom, why has it been the subject of considerable focus over the past 10 years? Increased interest in writing was generated as a result of researchers studying children's use of written language. Britton et al.'s (1975) studies revealed that the function of classroom assignments is to transmit information to the teacher; thus the teacher is the primary audience. Clearly, his studies raise the question about the limited writing contexts that such classrooms provide and their effects on students' writing development. In other words, how do children develop a sense of audience when they write for one audience, their teacher? The concept of audience is critical to the development of a writer (Graves, 1983). To develop a sense of audience, young writers need a community of authors who will listen, react, and discuss their writings. They must "feel" their audience; they must know who is listening to their writing. So there must be a change from the traditional classroom where the teacher is *the* audience.

When children are immersed in natural language contexts, we seem them experimenting with the print in their environment. Dyson (1984) explains that while children are constructing meaning, they are also learning about the language: Their learning is centered about the visual features of the printed code, the purposes of language, the processes and strategies that others utilize to read and write. As children are engaged in meaningful print uses, they gain control over it (Taylor, 1983) and their concepts about purposes for print use become varied. In their multifunctional use of print, children integrate literacy with other areas of learning and problem solving. Classrooms cannot simulate the rich informal language contexts found in some home environments. However, meaningful and natural instructional contexts can be created in classrooms that employ the functional use of print to strengthen students' grip on literacy concepts they have already acquired and to develop new ones.

Authorship is critical to literacy development and needs to be nurtured in the writing classroom. When considered apart from the act of writing, the concept of authorship may be impaired. Many young children do not regard a book as the creation of an individual person who is a writer, an author. Children who are given the opportunity to make the connection link a book to a person's work; they view the writing of stories as a distinctly human activity (Hall, 1987) within their own capabilities. Writing stories that lead to publishing along with reading their stories to a variety of audiences help to develop this critical concept of authorship in young children (Calkins, 1986). Among the many benefits attributed authorship—children's writing and telling of stories—is the development of oral language. Children learn language within natural social contexts, and when writing a story to be told to other children and adults, they "actually construct (or reconstruct) language" (Strickland & Morrow, 1990, p. 260) to communicate what they mean. Children not only learn about their language system during this process of writing; they are also learning how to think as well as how to "mean."

We certainly want young writers to evolve into authors. Providing them with a map of the writing journey will help students take their good writing and make it their best. The map is of the writing process, from rehearsal of an idea to it publication; the creation of a writing-process classroom is how children learn to use the map. One benefit of process writing is that it leads to critical thinking. When young children use this approach to writing, they do more than just copy words on paper. Emig (1971), who observed students write, found that the writing process provides opportunities for decision making. Her writers decided to select components of texts; they corrected, revised, drafted, and they redrafted and they rewrote, during which time they stopped to think. Graves's (1984) study of young writers led him to conclude that during the writing process, children learn to mean: Their intricate interplay among talking, reading, drawing, and writing helped them to construct meaning while they wrote. Children write about what they know and what they feel is important, not about a topic selected by the teacher. They become part of the community of authors, where writing is respected and celebrated. Children change: They begin to see themselves as we and others see them. They realize our expectations for their ability to communicate through writing and they are affected by teacher and peer expectations. So if we view our students as authors, writers, meaning makers with useful ideas to share among a community of authors, then our students will develop similar self-perceptions. If we provide children with classrooms that promote natural language contexts for writing within risk-free environments, students' literacy will flourish.

The following sections will focus on using what we know from current research on language learning to create classrooms that support optimum literacy development through a meaningful writing program.

## A WRITING-PROCESS CLASSROOM

The importance of "process" in instruction cannot be discounted. Process approaches are concerned with how students "get at" learning a concept or skill. In most traditional classrooms, the focus is on the finished product, not on the steps that were taken by the writer to complete his text. Among the negative effects resulting from this approach is the failure by young writers to realize the importance of revision so that few students will revise on their own (Fitzgerald, 1988). In a process class-room, students look critically not only at the product of their efforts but on what steps they took to get there.

According to Murray (1980), writing is a process of continuous think-ing, experimenting, and reviewing. The process of writing develops in the following three stages: rehearsing, drafting, and revising. It should be emphasized that there are times when these stages occur sequentially; more often, they do not. Two stages may be operating at the same times, such as drafting and rehearsing, or revising may direct the writer back to rehearsal. In any case, all professional writers realize the importance of each stage. They don't deny any part of the process because they know it is the natural approach to the end product.

## The Stages of the Writing Process

*Rehearsing* is the first stage of the writing process which begins when the writer gathers ideas and thoughts about a topic. It is thinking a written piece through; it is the sifting and the sorting through our past experience to determine what needs to be written about. When we teach children to rehearse, we get them to talk it out, to practice it outwardly; the assump-tion is that they will learn to perform it inwardly and privately (Vygotsky, 1978). So rehearsing takes time; time to think and to reflect, time to talk out and practice with others. When children encounter "road-blocks," we may ask children questions to help them focus on the topic, elaborate, and make connections from their own bank of experiences with the topic. *Our writing classrooms must allow them the leisure of this time.*

*Drafting,* the second stage of the process, implies that our piece is undergoing change. Students in writing-process classrooms know that nothing is written in stone; drafts change. While drafting, writers are taught that it's okay to be messy, to scribble out their ideas, to move ideas around (cut and paste), to "try new words on old ideas." Calkins (1986) encourages students to be messy: "Make it messy to make it clear."

*Revision* is the central component of the writing process: Its significance is founded in research that demonstrates that revision is responsible for the development of thought and knowledge and that revision is a prob-lem-solving process (Scardamalia & Bereiter, 1983, 1986).

Revision means making changes at any point in the process. Even before the writer makes a mark on paper, the writer may designate changes. These would occur when planning text is off the paper. In some cases revision takes place after the final editing, when the writer's story is ready for publication. As writers grow in competence, the kinds of revision change: Younger, inexperienced writers view revision as editing, making only surface changes, such as spelling and punctuation, while older, more competent writers revise for meaning (Lehrer & Comeaux, 1987). In any case, research reveals that young writers need considerable external support from their peers and teachers to ameliorate the problems associated with revision.

*Editing and publishing* are at the final stage in the writing process. With the publication of a piece of work, the impact on young writers is momentous: The act of publication brings the students to a new passage, taking them from writers to authors. Now the young authors read with a critic's eye: ''Who would ever write this?'' They begin to view books as products of human beings, who must write for the same reasons they write. Making passage through the writing process has given them stronger connections to the community of writers; they now belong.

Not every piece from the student's folder will be published. Like professional writers who choose to publish only those drafts they consider worthwhile, the student will select one for publication from among a number of pieces. It is this piece that must go through the rigorous procedure of proofing and editing. The young writer is now aware that his work must stand on its own; when the writer is not present, someone may read it and meaning must be delivered through the words of the story. Together in conference, the teacher and student writer or the student writer along with peer writers proof the draft for spelling, punctuation, language use, and other writing conventions. Like at any other step of the writing process, revision may take place here as well.

## Launching a Writing-Process Program

Beginning a writing-process program in a self-contained elementary classroom of 25 students with one teacher may seem to be the ultimate challenge. However, using a systematic approach and starting ''small'' will make this goal attainable. The following is a summary of suggestions from Parry and Hornsby (1985) on how to initiate a writing-process program in an elementary classroom:

*Know the Process.* If you plan on implementing a process approach in teaching writing, it is important that you are aware of the stages in the process. The best way of learning the stages is to be a writer yourself. Take each step from topic selection, through the painful decision of revision, to publication and sharing your work with your students.

*Know ''Whys'' of Change.* Read the rationale for using a writing-process program in your classroom. This involves understanding the current literature on language learning and knowing the language development of children in your classroom.

*Obtain the Support of Administrators and Parents.* Inform your administrator of your intent by describing the writing process to her and discuss your plan of implementation. Support from administration will facilitate the process. Discussion on the writing process with parents will also win the necessary assistance in making your program a success.

*Start with a Small Motivated Group.* Don't try to involve the entire class at once. Select independent workers who show a need to write. Teach the process to them. Give them a set of well-defined routines and model the process from rehearsal to publication. Motivate the rest of the class by moving the members of the small group to publish their first draft. This event serves as a tangible incentive for others to become members of the writing group. With this small motivated group, work out the procedural difficulties.

*Progress to Include Another Group.* After the first group is established, with major difficulties worked out, organize the next group until the entire class is included in the writing program.

*Secure the Assistance of Parents.* Further support for the newly founded writing program may be acquired when parents become involved. Parents can be especially helpful in book production: They may type drafts that have been edited, procure and prepare materials for book-binding, and help children with their illustrations.

*Celebrate Authors.* Publishing assures writers that they have arrived. However, their attempts must be celebrated and shared with other members of the community of writers. Start the author celebration with simple activities, such as displaying young authors' books next to outstanding works of E.B. White and Tommie de Paola, having the young author sit in the special "Author's Chair" to share his published book, displaying books with similar themes. A more elaborate author celebration may be to conclude the school year with an "Author's Luncheon" where parents are in attendance while the celebrated authors have the unique opportunity of discussing their books before the community of writers.

### The Classroom Environment

The physical appearance of the classroom should support the writing as a process approach. The organization and the management of a classroom are directly related to the teachers' instructional beliefs that govern the teaching strategies they employ.

In a writing-process classroom, there is a writing center that contains a variety of writing supplies to which children have free access. A small out-of-the-way comfortable corner for conferencing is part of the physical arrangement. In another area that is quiet there are tables for writing. Next to the art center, the publisher's table is set. A computer, typewriter, materials for bookbinding, and free access to the art supplies for final illustrations are available at this center.

In a prominent place in the classroom is the "Author's Chair," which is appropriately decorated and used specifically for sharing a work by a young writer. Bulletin boards, in and out of the classroom, are attractively decorated for displaying the writers' works.

### The Teacher's Role

The role of the teacher is one of facilitator who provides the support from behind rather than engaging in direct instruction and telling what is right or wrong. As participant-observer, "kidwatcher," the teacher knows the literacy development of each child and makes critical decisions of nudging the child, not pushing, by providing him with opportunities for more and appropriate literacy events to further his growth. The teacher becomes an honest collaborator with the students, helping them find their own stories to write and to share with the community of writers.

### Writing Folders

The writer's folder is an important tool of organization for both the student and the teacher. The primary function of the folder is to hold the writer's story that is in progress. Additionally, the folder serves as a record-keeping service as well as a writer's notebook. Graves (1983) suggests making use of four sides of the folder by recording books written and published on the front cover, new ideas to write about on the inside front cover, skills the writer needs to learn on the inside back cover, and topics that the writer knows much about on the back cover. Because there is so much writing in a process-approach classroom, the writing folder helps to keep the student from losing important drafts. A simple procedure to follow is to distribute the folders, which are kept in a central area, at the beginning of the writing period and to collect them when the period is over.

In the primary grades, children's stories are shorter and they will produce more than older students. It is a good idea to maintain another folder of finished stories that have not been published. On parents' day, these folders may be displayed, and at the end of the year children may take them home.

## Publishing

Publishing students' stories is an important part of the writing process; it is the reason for writing. Publishing is a form of literary recognition that empowers writers, providing them with a greater self-esteem and motivation to keep them writing. It gives the young writer a reason for polishing up, revising, and focusing on the conventions of print.

Sitting in the "Author's Chair" and reading his story in print to the community of writers expands the writer's sense of audience. When the student's published story is placed on the bookshelf next to E.B. White's *Charlotte's Web* and read by his peers or chosen by the teacher for a read-aloud book, the writer's concept of authorship is even further developed. These young writers now know that books are creations of real people, and they, too, have a worthwhile story that will be read by others. They are authors!

## The Conference

Calkins (1986) calls the conference the "heart" of the writing process. A good conference keeps the writer on track, helps the writer to focus, puts the responsibility on the writer to think for himself.

Because writers in a process-approach classroom are at different stages in their stories, there will be different types of conferences conducted within a day, each based on the individual needs of the writers.

*The Individual Conference.* During the revision stage, the writer may need a question to help him regain focus on his topic. In a short discussion, maybe two minues, the teacher asks an open-ended question about content, the meaning that the author wants to deliver. Several students may need an individual conference within the writing period.

*The Group Conference.* This conference consists of the writers' peers and the teacher as facilitator. Its purpose is to discuss the completed drafts which may lead to the final revision. Within a low-risk environment, five or six writers hear their peer's draft to help him decide on the strong points of the draft and ways to reconstruct its weak parts.

Each writer is using her critic's eye in responding with positive feedback, while the author listens and reacts, gaining a further sense of audience. The teacher guides this critical analysis through well-formulated questions. Graves (1983) suggests three types: (a) *Opening questions* will get the discussion going; (b) *following questions* nudge the student-writer to delve into his topic relating more of what he knows; and finally, (c) *process questions* direct the writer to rethink the writing strategies that he employed and target those that he needs to develop the piece.

*The Workshop Conference.* The process approach to teaching writing emphasizes the mastery of skills, however, within the writer's context based upon need and use. That is, at the time of publication, the conventions of language—spelling, punctuation, capital letters, word usage, grammar, and handwriting—become a critical vehicle to convey meaning to the writer's audience. The workshop conference is the place where the writer learns these language conventions; he is there for that purpose, knowing these conventions have significance.

Using each writer's draft, the teacher calls together a group of students who need a minilesson on a particular skill. Then application is made to each student's work.

*The Publishing Conference.* The purpose of this conference is to bring a story from draft to publication. Not every story that a child writes will be published. In the lower grades, the number of stories may reach high numbers, averaging five per week for some writers. The number of publications will be dependent on the publishing resources of the writing classroom. Parry and Hornsby (1985) suggest that joint decisions are made based on the suitability for book form, the originality of the piece, and the writer's individual effort. These criteria generally follow those that guide a professional publisher's selectivity of drafts.

## Final Comments on the Writing-Process Approach

Writing is a celebration of what one knows and needs to communicate in print. Setting up a writing-process classroom may be tedious, but the results are joyous. In natural settings, children grow and develop, unrestricted by barren contexts that bring no meaning to these young writers and block learning.

At first, the process approach may seem overwhelming; at second, it is probably a challenge; and finally, when routines are firmly established and the process is clear in our own heads, we will modify and expand knowing that there will be no other way.

## NATURAL CONTEXTS FOR WRITING

Creating natural contexts for students to grow and develop literacy skills rests on a strong foundation of research on language learning. Writers learn to write best when they write about things that interest them; when their own experiences are the basis of their writing, they will write effort-lessly and share with others freely and conversantly.

Unlike the restrictive work sheets that solicit one-word answers and exact copying ideas, providing natural writing experiences fosters critical thinking and creative problem solving. The writers are chal-lenged to extend what they know, using their favorite experiences on an audience that they believe and love. They are challenged to retell, to create, or to invent new stories. Their writing abilities will develop and progress as we give them time to write, expose them to natural and functional writing activities, and respect and celebrate their attempt at literacy. The following are some suggestions for providing natural writ-ing experiences for children in primary grades.

### Message Boards

One of the easiest ways of getting started is through message boarding. When I first read about it (Newman, 1985), I tried it with first graders. Sending messages across the classroom is one of the most natural ways of communicating, so why not facilitate it through establishing a sys-tem? It caught on almost immediately with no direct teaching, and even after the first month, it needed no external motivators to keep it going. Simply put, the students send messages to one another by tacking them up on a message board. The procedure follows:

1. Choose a large, easy-to-get-at bulletin board. Decorate it attractively using an appropriate caption.
2. On small white 2 x 2 cards print the names of everyone in class along with your own and other staff with whom children interact. Staple the names onto the bulletin board, leaving enough room around the name to tack notes.
3. Under each name pin a push-pin to be used in tacking up messages and notes.
4. Write a set of rules for using the message board and secure it to the bulletin. Such rules might include the following: "Always sign every message." "If you receive a note, answer it." "Use language you won't be ashamed of later on."
5. Discuss the use of the message board, and model the process by sending a message to each student.

Message boarding may be used pragmatically, sending such notes as reminders to students to carry out classroom chores. This strengthens the functional nature of writing for young authors. Another way a teacher may take advantage of message boarding is scaffolding the lan-

**Figure 6.1.**

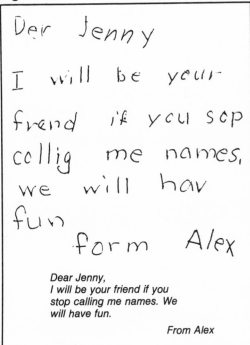

Der Jenny

I will be your

frend if you sop

collig me names,

we will hav

fun

form Alex

*Dear Jenny,*
*I will be your friend if you*
*stop calling me names. We*
*will have fun.*

*From Alex*

guage of children. When children write messages to the teacher and these contain errors, such as in spelling, her reply message can work as a scaffold. Simply, the teacher's answers to these children will contain the misspelled words spelled correctly.

The message board demonstrates the communicative nature of language; the writers may use it to work out problems that demand decision making. Such was the message in Figure 6.1 of one first grader to a girl who kept calling him names.

In these language exchanges, the emphasis is on meaning. Demonstration with their newly found activity has led to writing, reading, more writing and reading. The result of this natural language activity is growth in literacy.

## Journals

Journals provide another natural context for writing that is nonevaluative and nonjudgmental. That is, the student is free to write without being corrected for content or for any language convention. This aspect of journal writing makes it a vehicle that can be used to help students gain confidence as fluent writers who so often feel restricted by what they view as the insurmountable conventions of print.

Over the years, a number of different types of journals were developed for classroom use. Each has a different purpose and at least one can be selected to fit the students' needs.

*Diaries.* One of the easiest ways to begin writing with young children is providing them with small notebooks to be used consistently for writing down their thoughts and ideas. Before I distributed their diaries, a discussion ensued on funny things that happen to us, everyday occurrences that make us annoyed and upset, people we love to talk to, and so on. Children were then given a little notebook (receiving it with great joy and delight) and told they could write whatever they felt—what we were talking about.

I, too, have a diary and immediately began to write with the children. We decided as a group that we would keep a privacy code: We would only share the contents if we felt we wanted to. No one should feel free to read another's diary without permission. There are a number of ways to deal with the privacy of content and the sharing of a journal.

*Dialogue Journals.* Dialogue journals are usually kept between two writers, defined as a "written conversation between two persons on a functional, continued basis, about topics of interest" (Staton, 1988, p. 312). Here again emphasis is placed on the communicative nature of language.

Bode (1989) underscores the importance of using dialogue journal writing as a means of personalizing education as well as empowering students through literacy. When teacher and student speak through print, the teacher is meeting each child at his own developmental and interest level. This is indeed important in the primary grades when children are beginning to read and write, each with varying levels of competency.

Bode (1989) also noted that many students chose to write about complaints when dialoguing with their teacher. Certainly, this is not the case of a traditional classroom that emphasizes the rule of silence. To speak out and define one's complaint, to ask and to challenge, are ways of gaining control. In essence dialogue journal writing leads to student empowerment through literacy development.

*Group Journals.* Children in the younger grades will especially enjoy and benefit from the group journal. This type of journal capitalizes on experiences that are thought about and talked about, and then these same experiences are represented in writing and drawings.

In a group discussion, the children talk about their ideas and feelings. The teacher works as a scribe, recording the ideas of the students and modeling the process of writing at the same time. The group read these meaningful entries after the teacher. They may go back time and again to reread various entries made by the group. Strickland and Morrow (1990) suggest ways of sharing group journals through chart displays, creations of Big Books, and bulletin board displays.

*Journals Across the Curriculum.* Content areas provide a natural context for using journal writing. Response journals are used for responding to literature that students have read or heard. Used in the early part of the first grade, children's responses will be through drawing, which will progress to a few sentences about how the story was received. In upper primary grades, the children's focus may be directed to different elements of the story.

The log is used in science, and it, too, is a variation of journal writing. The purpose of the log is to note observations made on a particular scientific phenomenon being studied. For example, daily observations of weather may be recorded or the behavior of classroom animals. Keeping logs may be individual or in lower primary grades, the log may be a group activity.

These are only a few of the natural approaches that may be used to extend writing. During the course of a busy day, the teacher and children are presented with numerous opportunities to write. The teacher can take advantage of these opportunities to extend the literacy development by encouraging children to engage in these natural writing activities.

## REFERENCES

Bode, B. (1989). Dialogue journal writing. *The Reading Teacher, 42,* 568–571.

Britton, J., Burgess, T., Martin, M., McLeod, A., & Rosen, H. (1975). *The development of writing abilities* (pp. 11–18). Urbana, IL: NCTE.

Calkins, L. (1986). *The art of teaching writing.* Portsmouth, NH: Heinemann.

Dyson, A.H. (1984). "N" spell my grandmama: Fostering early thinking about print. *The Reading Teacher, 38,* 262–271.

Emig, J. (1971). *The composing process of twelfth graders.* Urbana, IL: NCTE.

Fitzgerald, J. (1988). Helping young readers to revise: A brief review for teachers. *The Reading Teacher, 42,* 124–129.

Graves, D. (1983). *Writing: Teachers and children at work.* Portsmouth, NH: Heinemann.

Graves, D. (1984). *A researcher learns to write.* Portsmouth, NH: Heinemann.

Hall, N. (1987). *The emergence of literacy.* Portsmouth, NH: Heinemann.

Harste, J., & Woodward, V. (1989). Fostering needed change in early literacy programs. In D.S. Strickland & L.M. Morrow (Eds.), *Emerging literacy: Young children learn to read and write.* Newark, DE: International Reading Association.

Harste, J., Woodward, V., & Burke, C. (1984). *Language stories and literacy lessons.* Portsmouth, NH: Heinemann.

Lehrer, R., & Comeaux, M. (1987, April). *A developmental study of the effects of goal restraints on composition.* Paper presented at the American Educational Research Association, annual meeting, Washington, DC.

Murray, D.M. (1980). How writing finds its own meaning. In T.R. Donovan & B.W. McClelland (Eds.), *Eight approaches to teaching composition.* Urbana, IL: NCTE.

Newman, J.M. (Ed.). (1985). *Whole language: Theory in use.* Portsmouth, NH: Heinemann.

Parry, J., & Hornsby, D. (1985). *Write on: A conference approach to writing.* Portsmouth, NH: Heinemann.

Scardamalia, M., & Bereiter, C. (1983). The development of evaluative, diagnostic and remedial capabilities in children's composing. In M. Martlew (Ed.), *The psychology of written language: A developmental approach.* London: John Wiley & Sons.

Scardamalia, M., & Bereiter, C. (1986). Research on written composition. In M.C. Wittrock (Ed.), *Handbook of research on teaching.* New York: Macmillan.

Staton, J. (1988). An introduction to dialogue journal communication. In M. Farr (Ed.), *Interactive writing in dialogue journals: Practitioner, linguistic, social, and cognitive views.* Norwood, NJ: Ablex.

Strickland, D.S., & Morrow, L.M. (1990). The daily journal: Using language experience strategies in an emergent literacy curriculum. *The Reading Teacher, 43,* 422–423.

Taylor, D. (1983). *Young children learning to read and write.* Portsmouth, NH: Heinemann.

Teale, W.H. (1986). Home background and young children's literacy development. In W.H. Teale & E. Sulzby (Eds.), *Emergent literacy: Writing and reading.* Norwood, NJ: Ablex.

Vygotsky, L.S. (1978). *Mind in society: The development of higher psychological processes.* Cambridge, MA: Harvard University Press.

Wells, G. (1986). *The meaning makers: Children learning language and using language to learn.* Portsmouth, NH: Heinemann.

**Chapter 7**

# I Can Read!
# Empowering Young Readers
# for Success

## Christine Bluestein

Four-year-old Natasia is so small that the big book on her lap nearly covers her feet as she sits on the rug, singing the song text of the book as she remembers it.

Several children are turning the pages of the big book *Chicken Soup with Rice* (Sendak, 1962). Each page is headed by the name of a month. The children argue about the word, trying to decode it with initial consonants. Sometimes they ask the teacher for help.

Suddenly Eliot runs in from the hall where he was reading with the educational assistant. "I can read! I just read this to Mrs. Teruel!" He is holding *Brown Bear, Brown Bear, What Do You See?* (Martin, 1967). Wanting to read by himself and feeling unable has been frustrating him.

At the group meeting, the children read a favorite big book in unison with the teacher as she tracks the print with a pointer. Next they will be shown phrase cards of the text to read and sequence as the first step in making their own version of the big book.

In this whole-language kindergarten, children in various stages of reading development are having a variety of reading experiences, some independent, some mediated by the teacher, some teacher-directed. Judged by the traditional definition of reading as independent decoding of unfamiliar material, none of them can read. Yet they feel and act like readers: confidently in control of the text, involved in the story, motivated and happy as they learn.

An increasing number of educators, informed by current theory and research, are creating classroom environments that encourage the development of literacy in all forms, including reading, in ways that are developmentally appropriate for young children. This new approach is based on:

- The commitment that all children can learn to read without stress and can enjoy reading, if materials and instruction are matched to their learning needs, styles, and interests.
- Recognition that motivation is a key factor in learning, and it depends on success and confidence.
- Knowledge gained from observing young children as they interact naturally with books: that reading is a developmental process, like learning to talk, and it proceeds along a continuum of stages. Learning needs and capacities differ from one stage to the next. The term "emergent reader" describes this view of the learner.
- The understanding that reading is an active process of meaning making in which children use many strategies to make sense of texts. Because of this emphasis on meaning, whole, meaningful stories ("whole language"), rather than isolated phonics skill-and-drill exercises, form the basis of the curriculum. Skill teaching is integrated into meaningful texts.
- Recognition that children have achieved competence in many areas of language development before they even enter school, and that instruction should build on this competence.
- Emphasis on total literacy development, not just reading skill; understanding that experiences in each of the language arts—reading, writing, speaking, and listening—have beneficial effects in the other areas. The term "whole language" refers also to this integration of the language arts.

Certainly all parents and teachers want to see their youngsters succeed in learning to read. In a larger sense, our national concern over widespread school failure and illiteracy has united us in a common goal of universal literacy. But the philosophy, content, methods, and timing of beginning reading instruction are very much disputed. The peaceful classroom scene described above is surrounded by controversy. Some journalists even call it a "war" ("Phonics vs. Whole Language," 1990; "The Reading Wars," 1990), portraying proponents of traditional phonics and basal programs and proponents of meaning-based whole language programs as doing battle with each other over the correct emphasis for reading instruction.

Another battle in the war is being fought over the age at which reading instruction should begin. Whether alarmed by statistics about reading failure in documents like *A Nation at Risk* (National Commission on Excellence in Education, 1983), anxious for improved standardized test scores, nostalgic for a "return to basics," or pressured by ambitious parents, many school districts are replacing the active, interactive traditional early childhood programs with formal phonics drill and basal reading programs in kindergarten or earlier. Some have even instituted a "pacing" system to achieve accountability in teaching with the result that children who have not mastered a certain skill by a target date can get an "F" in kindergarten!

But all is not well with an "earlier is better" policy. Articles appear in the popular press about "flunking kindergaren" ("Can Kids Flunk Kindergarten?," 1988) and "tense tots" ("Tense Tots," 1988). Anxious parents consider "red-shirting" their children: keeping them at home for a "catch-up" year so they will be mature enough to withstand the rigors of kindergarten ("The Redshirt Solution," 1989).

The casualties of this mismatch between the child and the curricululm speak eloquently for a reexamination of "pushing down" formal skill-based programs. Recently a child came back for a visit who had moved to a suburb in midyear. His mother complained that, although the family had chosen the new community because of the reputation of the schools, Chris hates school now because all they do in kindergarten is phonics and handwriting drill! A colleague in a nearby city told me that her students who had phonics instruction in prekindergarten initially resist coming to "reading time" because they think it means doing more phonics drill instead of enjoying stories!

So many early childhood classrooms are structured around narrowly defined academic skills like rote learning of letter names and sounds that some early childhood education authorities have issued strong policy statements defining and advocating appropriate practice for young children (Early Childhood and Literacy Development Committee of the International Reading Association, 1985; National Association for the Education of Young Children (NAEYC), 1988).

Below is an excerpt from the NAEYC (1988) Position Statement:

*Appropriate Practice*
The goals of the language and literacy program are for children to expand their ability to communicate orally and through reading and writing, and to enjoy these activities. Technical skills or subskills are taught as needed to accomplish the larger goals, not as the goal itself. (p. 70)

*Inappropriate Practice*
Instructional strategies revolve around teacher-directed reading groups that take up most of every morning, . . . and paper-and-pencil practice exercises or worksheets to be completed silently by children working individually at desks. . . . Reading is taught as the acquisition of skills and subskills. (p. 72)

Despite these guidelines, isolated skill instruction dominates the early school experience of more and more young children.

Obviously children's motivation suffers when they are asked to do things that do not make sense to them and that they do not enjoy. The NAEYC Position Statement also states:

> Longitudinal research indicates that curriculum and teaching methods should be designed so that children not only acquire knowledge and skills, but they also acquire the disposition or inclination to use them. Compelling evidence exists asserting that overemphasis on mastery of narrowly defined reading and arithmetic skills and excessive drill and practice...threaten children's dispositions to use the skills they have acquired....It is as important for children to acquire the desire to read...as it is for them to acquire the mechanics of reading. (p. 68)

It seems that in the rush to achievement many policymakers and parents have strayed far from what we know about children's needs and have forgotten their stated goals that every child should learn to read and to love reading. It does not make much sense to persist in a reading curriculum that spends most of its time in isolated skill work instead of reading books, and that has not been successful with large numbers of children. Given our dismal national statistics, should we push these same methods down to younger and younger children?

Instead of defending their territory, the opponents should lay down their weapons and examine both traditional and whole-language reading instruction. They might be surprised to find out that the war between phonics and meaning is fallacious. They are not mutually exclusive; rather, both are essential strategies in the reading process.

M. Adams, in a newly released comprehensive review of reading studies entitled *Beginning to Read,* summarized by Stahl, Osborn, and Lehr (1990), cites research indicating that children build letter sound knowledge on a foundation of letter name knowledge. While advocating explicit instruction for young children in both these areas, she acknowledges that "such instruction must take place in an environment where they [children] are surrounded by print" (p. 48).

> The goal is not to transport the first-grade curriculum down to the kindergarten or the preschool. It is to encourage teachers to select and structure preschool and kindergarten games, songs and storybook sessions with their students' linguistic growth in mind. It is to acknowledge that there is much that must be learned before a student can make sense of formal instruction. (p. 58)

> So why the dispute...All of its [the reading process] component knowledge and skills must work together within a single integrated and interdependent system. (p. 122)

This chapter will examine the interconnected processes of children learning to read and suggest some ways teachers can balance skill instruction and focus on meaning.

## RESEARCH IN LEARNING AND READING

Whether individual teachers or high-level policymakers make the decisions about reading, the best knowledge about learning to read, from research and observation of children, has to inform their choices.

### Cognitive Model of Learning

The work of Piaget is a good starting point in understanding why instruction should focus on integrating meaning with skills. Two of his key concepts, cognitive stages and constructivism, revolutionized the way we think about learning and teaching, changing the emphasis from acquiring facts to the problem-solving processes of the learner.

Each stage of cognitive development permits mental operations characteristic of that stage, and children are limited by their present level of development. Young children, up to the age of about seven, are in the preoperational stage and cannot yet mentally manipulate abstract symbols. They need active learning and the opportunity to experience new information within a meaningful context. Efforts to push children too far beyond their cognitive abilities will fail or cause stress in children as they learn without understanding.

As children encounter unfamiliar events, they construct new knowledge as they struggle to relate new to existing knowledge in a process of meaning making. Learners do not passively absorb knowledge transmitted by the teacher; they have to create it in their own minds (Ginzburg & Opper, 1988).

Recent theory and research from cognitive psychology suggest that the mind of the learner is like a construction of tinkertoys. Learning is the making of connections between new information and the learner's existing network of knowledge. In a network theory of cognition and learning, lower order skills do not necessarily precede higher order problem-solving activities. Skills and concepts are learned together in the process of problem solving, and instruction should facilitate the making of connections (Peterson, Fennema, & Carpenter, 1988).

This research explains why a narrow-focus, abstract reading curriculum based on letter sounds and word identification is so difficult for so many children and why they need so much review: The learning often does not transfer to the reading process because it does not have enough points of connection. Viewed from this perspective, the sequential skill model, based on building concepts by mastering small bits of knowledge, does not make sense. It is also clear that the better the fit between the instructional task and the cognitive network of the learner, the easier it will be for the learner to make sense of the new information.

### Implications for Instruction of Current Research

Understanding the learning process presents far-reaching implications for the structure of our educational programs: We have to alter the traditional view that children learn only because we teach them. They come to us curious and motivated, already equipped with their own strategies for problem solving. We have to look much harder at their natural learning processes so we can facilitate their attempts to learn. We have to help provide ways for children to expand their network of knowledge through appropriate experiences, so they will have a good foundation upon which to construct new knowledge. Since each child's network is unique, we cannot know exactly what a child can learn, so we have to provide learning experiences that are open-ended and broad-based enough so that each child can get what he needs out of it. Our role as teachers has to change: No longer only imparting information, we need to focus on modeling and facilitating learning strategies, questioning, and eliciting thinking.

Kamii (1989), a leading Piagetian educator, stated:

> Procedures children invent are rooted in the depth of their intuition and their natural ways of thinking. If we encourage them to develop their own ways of thinking rather than requiring them to memorize rules that do not make sense to them, children develop a better cognitive foundation as well as confidence. Children who are confident learn more in the long run than those who have been taught in ways that make them distrust their own thinking. (p. 14)

### Research into the Reading Process

How does a constructivist view of learning apply to reading? Psycholinguistic research originally conducted by K. Goodman (1976, 1987, 1989) confirms that the process of reading, though it includes decoding by phonic analysis, is far more concerned with meaning. "Attention is on meaning, and anything else such as letters, words, or grammar only gets full attention when the reader has trouble getting to the meaning" (K. Goodman, 1987, p. 207).

Effective independent readers make use of four language cueing systems as they try to decipher a text:

- Semantic: meaning, derived from context and personal knowledge.
- Syntactic: intuitive knowledge of parts of speech and word order.
- Grapho-phonic: letter-sound correspondence, spelling patterns, punctuation, word length and shape.
- Pragmatic: knowledge of the type of text, e.g., folk tale, newspaper, and what kind of language would be in it.

Successful readers use context to create meaning from a text: The immediate context surrounding the unknown word, the wider context of the passage, and their own knowledge about the subject and about print.

As proficient readers read, they mobilize a wealth of strategies. First they skim the text, using all the cueing systems to predict what is coming next. Readers use graphophonic cues minimally: Initial and final consonant, and perhaps word length are usually all a reader needs to predict a word. When they have a tentative interpretation of the text, they use the context following the passage to confirm or correct this guess. If their hypothesis was incorrect, they either go back to try again, rethink without referring to the text, or read on for more information. When good readers make miscues, they still preserve the sense of the text: For example, the reader may read, "He went to the corner," where the text is "He walked to the corner." The reading strategies just described interact continually with the four language cueing systems. Goodman, Watson, and Burke (1987) stated:

> Each follows the others but at the same time precedes them, always moving toward constructing a text and making meaning. Each cycle is tentative and partial, melting into the next. Inference and prediction make it possible to leap toward meaning without fully completing the cycles. (p. 33)

The flowchart in Figure 7.1 illustrates this cyclical process.

Young readers or readers in trouble have not successfully coordinated this complex interaction of cueing systems and reading strategies. Troubled readers have often been taught to "sound out" words as their only strategy, and many do not know that reading is supposed to make sense. Of course this misplaced emphasis obstructs the reading process, since the reader's attention is fixed on the parts instead of the whole. As Frank Smith (1975) puts it, "Reading depends more on what is behind the eyes—on nonvisual information—than on the visual information in front of them" (p. 35).

Recently I observed a second grader get struck sounding "liss-ten" (pronouncing the "t"), although semantic cues like "What do you hear?" were in the text. She wasy applying correct principles of phonic analysis, but without checking to see if it made sense in the context, she could not turn these sounds into a word! It is no surprise that children

**Figure 7.1. Interactive strategies in the reading process**

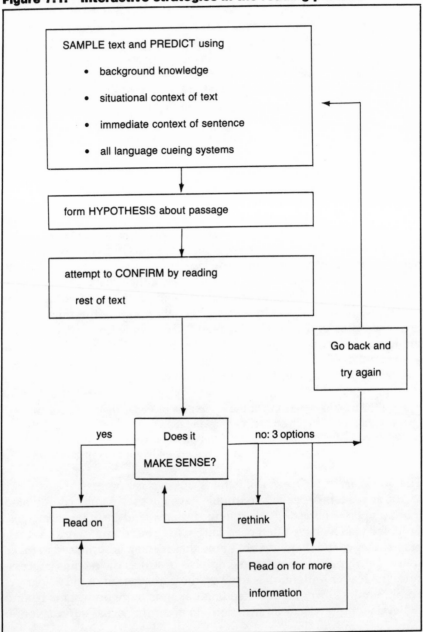

who find reading such an unproductive struggle feel frustrated and unsuccessful.

Clearly letter-sound knowledge is an essential element in the reading process, but we need to send a message to children that it is not an end in inself, only a means to unlock the meaning of a text. By integrating phonics into meaningful reading experiences and by modeling the functional use of letter-sound knowledge, early childhood educators can help children become aware of how the cueing system interrelate and lay a foundation for future success.

Writing furnishes a real reason to know letter sounds. Teachers can model the composing process informally; for example, by writing the daily news with the children's help. Composing stories or captions for pictures motivates children to apply what they know.

I will never forget the look on Lindsay's face she first understood the purpose of letter sounds. She entered kindergarten already knowing the letter sounds. One day early in the year, she asked me to write a caption on her picture of a boat. When I demonstrated how to stretch the word out so she could hear the sounds in the word "boat," she immediately identified the b, o, and t. Her eyes opened wide in amazement; from that time on she has spontaneously used her phonics knowledge for writing.

### Stages of Reading Development

Even the youngest children are primarily concerned with making meaning as they interact with books, though they also show interest in the features of letters and words. Long before they achieve the stage of independent reading with coordinated cueing systems, children who have access to books spontaneously pass through many other stages of reading development. As crawling is to walking, as babbling and baby talk are to speaking, as scribbling is to writing, these early reading behaviors are also necessary steps along a continuum culminating in independent reading. Studying children's natural reading behavior before they have had formal instruction gives us a direction for developmentally appropriate instruction.

Many investigators have described the stages of reading, among them Holdaway (1979), Chall (1983), Cochrane, Cochrane, Scalena, and Buchanan (1984), and Ferreiro and Teberosky (1982), whose categories are condensed in this summary:

- Stage 1: Emergent Reading (Schema Emphasis, Pre-Independent Stage): The child turns pages of books, engaging in reading-like behaviors like reciting memorized stories. He self-corrects for sense, but does not match his words to the written text. Natasia is in this stage.

- Stage 2: Advanced Emergent Reading (Semantic-Syntactic Emphasis, Bridging Stage): The child begins to match the oral and printed text, can pick out individual words and letters. He relies heavily on familiar context and may not recognize words out of context. He may use semantic cues but not correlate them with grapho-phonic cues (reading "leg" for "knee").
- Stage 3: Early Reading (Grapho-Phonic Emphasis): The child concentrates on sounding out words and is not satisfied with substitutions. Most children are using context cues but are also struggling to identify words. Eliot and the *Chicken Soup* group are beginning to move into this stage.
- Stage 4: Independent Stage (Simultaneous Use): The child is able to coordinate all three cueing systems and read independently in meaning clusters.

### Implications for Reading Instruction of Stages of Reading

From these descriptions three points are clear which have important implications for reading instruction:

- That children are engaged in active attempts to process written language and make meaning with it, using self-formulated strategies, long before they receive formal instruction.
- That children proceed from whole (meaning) to part (words, letters, and sounds) and not the other way around. Decoding is the end point of this progression, although many children who lack experience with books are asked to begin with decoding in school.
- That children progress through these stages gradually, making many approximations and partial successes before they achieve solidity in the next stage.

## CREATING LITERACY CLASSROOMS

### Integration of Literacy Experiences

The word "literacy" implies so much more than reading and writing skill:

Using reading, writing, thinking, and speaking daily in the real world, with options, appreciation, and meaningful purposes in various settings and with other people. An actively literate person is constantly thinking, learning and reflecting, and is assuming the responsibility for continued growth in personal literacy. (Routman, 1988, p. 15)

So an environment that fosters emergent literacy must integrate all the language arts in meaningful ways.

The focus of this chapter requires a false separation of reading from the other literacy experiences addressed in other chapters. But it is understood that reading should take place in an environment furnished with accessible materials for reading and writing, filled with environmental print. A balanced reading program includes reading *with* children, as in shared reading, reading *to* children good literature, and reading *by* children independently from self-selected books. Such an environment offers many "teachable moments."

Writing focuses children on letter sounds and the way print functions on a page. Children can read what they have written or dictated more easily than unfamiliar texts. Oral language—play, expressing ideas, listening to, retelling and acting out stories—all contribute to the background knowledge, story patterns, vocabulary, and interest which will foster success in reading. Each experience in any aspect of language development enhances all other aspects.

An example of the interactive nature of literacy activities comes from my kindergarten on a recent February morning during self-chosen activity time. To see so much spontaneous literacy activity by this diverse group of children was deeply satisfying to me: It felt as though all the year's literacy activities were coming together for the children as they made reading and writing their own:

Michael was writing a joke book in invented spelling. He later "read" it at group meeting, which started a rash of similar books. Lindsay was making a birthday card for her mother and trying to write the greeting. Shevonne and Maritza were acting out "the Frog Prince" with puppets and a prop box, referring to the text now and then and trying to read it. Serena, one of my least mature language students, was having a breakthrough: She wanted to write "ice skating" on her picture and was able to hear some of the sounds for the first time! At Steven's request I wrote "See you later, alligator; after while, crocodile!" on oaktag, which he illustrated and read to children around the room. Other children were playing "teacher," sitting in my meeting chair and reading big books to each other and to our educational assistant and student teacher. It was a delightful hour!

## Classroom Conditions That Facilitate Reading

In an attempt to define some of the qualities present in a program that supports children's literacy development, Cambourne (1987) and Cutting (1989) identified several key factors which facilitate oral language learning. Since oral language development closely parallels reading development, these conditions, when adapted to the reading process, will facilitate reading in the classroom.

- Immersion: Surround children with language and print experiences used in meaningful, purposeful ways. Give them many opportunities to hear good literature and to read alone and with other children from a wide variety of materials.
- Modeling: Demonstrate constantly the joys of reading, the sound of fluent reading, the purposes of reading, interest in the forms, and meanings of print. Shared reading with big books is an important modeling technique in the classroom.
- Acceptance of Approximations/Feedback: Just as parents do not expect their child to master the process of learning to talk immediately, so we need to accept children's efforts as they progress through the stages of reading development. We need to see their errors as strategic attempts to make patterns in this universe of print. But because children must learn that the words of the text are fixed, we need to call their attention to the actual text, not in a spirit of correction, but as something interesting to notice. Judicious, nonjudgmental feedback can help a child move to the next stage.
- Practice: As children learn language by using it, they learn to read by reading, not by doing exercises about reading. But studies have demonstrated that in the typical basal reading classroom, a child is actually reading only about seven minutes of each "reading" hour! As children practice reading, they work out strategies for making sense of stories. Even emergent readers, when given the opportunity, develop strategies for making sense of books.
- Choices/Responsibility: Because we can never know exactly what each child is ready to learn, children must have some chance to select the materials and means of their learning. We must nurture their self-responsibility, not take it away from them. Children need many opportunities to read self-selected books using their own reading strategies.
- Success/Motivation: Success is crucial for learning to read. When children are successful, they want to read more. The more they read, the better they will get. When children are unsuccessful, they become anxious and want to avoid reading. It seems so obvious, but so many educators seem to have forgotten the importance of these

two key factors when they insist that children engage in reading tasks that are cognitively and developmentally inappropriate.

Viewed in a literacy context, direct reading instruction and developmental appropriateness may initially seem like "strange bedfellows"; but a study by Slaughter (1988) demonstrates that both direct and indirect instruction can occur in a whole-language classroom. It is the nature of the event, not the style of instruction, which determines its appropriateness.

If children are invited, not forced, to read, if the teacher appreciates approximations and encourages children to take risks without anxiety, if the materials and procedures support children in many stages of reading development, reading instruction will be appropriate.

## SHARED READING

Shared reading, reading *with* children, is a major instructional technique for emergent readers. Observing the "lap method" of bedtime story reading, which had produced so many children who learned to read at home, Holdaway (1979) adapted it for classrooms with many children and one lap. Enlarging the book text ensures that all the children can see it as the adult reads. By tracking the print as she reads, the teacher can help emergent readers establish the vital one-to-one correspondence between oral and printed text. So much learning can happen with shared reading that children at many different stages of reading can benefit, all at the same time! In addition, shared reading gives children who have not had much experience with books a chance to acquire the background of familiarity with print and stories that is essential for success in reading as sense-making.

### Choosing Materials for Shared Reading

Not all enlarged format books called big books have the necessary characteristics to support emergent readers. What are these characteristics? A look at the language experiences children choose for themselves furnishes some answers.

### Characteristics of Texts for Shared Reading

*Brown, Bear, Brown Bear, What Do You See?* (Martin, 1967) was my introduction to whole-language learning. After I had read it for the first time, to my surprise the children clamored to hear it again, and before the end of the book, they were joining in. I began to hear it chanted in the classroom and in line (but I have never heard phonics exercises in their spontaneous language!). I wondered what magic this book held, and began to research whole-language reading.

As I listened to children on the playground I heard the same elements of rhyme, rhythm, and repetition that made *Brown Bear* so beloved:

> Mama, Mama, I feel sick,
> Call the doctor, quick, quick, quick!

> Jingle Bells, Batman smells,
> Robin laid an egg,
> Batmobile lost a wheel,
> And the Joker ran away!

I still remember a patterned-language book from my own childhood:

> I see a kitty, Away goes the kitty.
> I see a puppy. Away goes the puppy...
> Where is the kitty? Where is the puppy?...
> Here is the kitty! Here is the puppy!

All these patterns: of *text structure, of rhyme, rhythm, and repetition* of lines, have natural auditory appeal to children, as they show us by their spontaneous language behavior from crib to playground. But patterns also serve to increase *predictability*, making it easier for children to grasp the meaning of the text, anticipate what is coming next, and learn the words. Once children have internalized the text, it will be easier for them to focus on the salient features of print and the introduction of new words within this familiar context. Motivation remains high, because the children are having fun and mastering the text!

Educators sometimes object that a basal-style controlled vocabulary is necessary for children to build the automatic sight vocabulary required for independent reading. But it has been shown that the unnatural, decontextualized language of the preprimers actually makes reading harder for beginners, because it does not make sense and confuses children. Children who use predictable materials, whether trade books or language experience charts, learn not only "target" words better than those who use basal readers, but they learn nontarget words as well! (Bridge, Winograd, & Haley, 1983). The text of many big books designed for shared reading is above the instructional level of emergent readers so the book will be interesting and meaningful. The pattern and repetition control the variables while allowing for varied, natural language.

Clear pictures that directly illustrate the text help the reading effort as well. In one study, preschool children who associated words with pictures learned more words than did children who were taught to pay attention to the first letter (Mason, 1980). Using pictures is a reading strategy directed at creating meaning from a story, while phonic analysis is not. Eventually this reliance on pictures disappears as children achieve independence in reading.

### Commercial Big Books

During the last decade several publishers have been manufacturing big books which meet the requirements for shared reading with emergent readers, because their authors or consultants helped to develop whole-language reading (see list in bibliography). Others sell large format books which may or may not be predictable; teachers should try to preview the books, since they are expensive!

### Trade Books

There are many wonderful patterned-language trade books, and more are coming onto the market all the time. Classic folk tales often have text patterns and memorable refrains: "Run, run, as fast as you can, / You can't catch me, I'm the gingerbread man!" Once the text is familiar and the children can say it in unison with you, it can be copied onto large sheets of oaktag or double-folded brown paper and illustrated by the children. Now they have a big book for shared reading that they have created.

### Familiar Songs, Rhymes, Chants, and Poems

Any oral language activity that you and the children enjoy daily will make an ideal emergent reading activity, since the children already know it. Print the text on chart paper with an illustration by a child. After using it as a shared reading activity, mount it at the children's eye level. Or print it on oaktag cards covered with clear plastic. These can go in a box to be used as an independent center activity.

Some examples from my classroom:

- A "hello" song we sing at morning meeting:

    When ducks get up in the morning,
    They always say "Good-day." (repeat)
    "Quack-quack, quack-quack,"
    That is what they say, they say. (repeat)

I printed the text on sentence strips, leaving out "ducks" and "Quack-quack." I printed these and other animal names and noises on cards. Children can choose an animal for us to sing about, find its name and noise cards, and insert them in the sentence. Thus an ordinary kindergarten event becomes a shared reading activity.

- Chants like "Five little monkeys jumping on the bed" and favorite fingerplays become shared reading activities with the addition of the text in large print tracked with a pointer as we chant.

One of the comments that educators from New Zealand, where whole-langauge reading was born, make about American schools is that our classrooms are print-poor. Part of creating an environment for literacy involves making many forms of print available to children. What could be more fun than papering the walls with their favorite songs, jingles, and poems!

## Language Experience Materials

The Language Experience approach (Allen, 1976; Hall, 1976) has been used by early childhood teachers who recognized that children could learn to read with familiar, meaningful print. The children's own experiences and words form the basis of a text, which the teacher writes on large chart paper as the children watch. Language experience is meaning-based, it demonstrates how print is used, and it motivates because children want to read their own words. Teachers can create patterned text for shared reading by structuring the discussion to elicit a pattern of responses:

> **Teacher:** Tell us something you noticed about the chicks.
> **Chart of responses:**
> The chicks are fluffy.
> The chicks are yellow and brown.
> The chicks are dry.
> The chicks are cute.

After shared reading, leave the chart where the children can return to it on their own.

## Shared Reading Procedure with Big Books

Shared reading has many steps: You may work with a single book for a week or two, or even longer if your class makes a variation of it or dramatizes it. Repeated readings help children internalize the text, and an enjoyable book will be a pleasure to reread. You can work with the whole class, but smaller groups allow more children to participate. Following is a suggested sequence of activities. If you vary it, be sure not to overload the children, and save the introduction of language instruction activities until the children are familiar with the text.

The following sequence and activities are similar to those suggested by the Wright Group in their training sessions.

### Day 1: Introduction.

- Show the cover. Ask for predictions of what the story is about (a very important literacy activity).
- Read the title. Ask children to confirm or change their predictions.
- If the pictures are attractive and correspond closely to the text, you might want occasionally to begin by asking the children to infer the story by "reading the pictures."
- If you want to begin with the text, place the book on an easel and read it through, stopping at a few appropriate places to elicit predictions (not too many, or the thread of the story will be lost).
- Offer to read the book a second time. This time, while still reading fluently and with expression, touch under each word discretely with a pointer or your finger as you say it. This takes practice!

  Tracking the print is very important, since it helps establish one-to-one correspondence between oral and printed text, and it models the conventions of print: where to begin and end on a page, left-to-right and top-to-bottom progression, how punctuation influences oral reading. Some people are concerned that by pointing we are modeling word-by-word reading, but when we read flowingly and expressively, our oral fluency is a very poweful model in contrast to the usual negative model of halting word-calling children hear from other children in round-robin reading. If children persist in word-pointing after they read independently, they can be asked to stop tracking.
- After the reading children may like the opportunity to respond to the story by discussing it or drawing a picture about it.

### Day 2: Choral Reading, Participation.

- Read the book, again pointing to the words. Invite the children to join in the reading. A book with predictable text will enable children to memorize very quickly. They will already begin to feel they can read the book and will join in with enthusiasm. Unison reading particularly benefits young or hesitant readers: They can participate without risking failure, and they can model their reading after the fluency of the stronger readers. Later you may want to do choral readings where the children take parts, if the story lends itself to dramatizing.

- If the story is full of action, you and the children may want to choose gestures to go with the choral reading. They enjoy acting out the story, and it involves more sense modes, increasing the avenues for learning.

*Day 3 and Beyond: Language Instruction Activities.* Language instruction activities will be covered in detail below.

*Day 4 and Beyond: Reproductions and Variations.* Reproductions include any representation of the story where the text is used as it exists in the book. They can include:

- Masks, character cutouts, stuffed forms for dramatization.
- Wall stories or bulletin board stories: The pages of a big book your class has made can be sequenced by the children, then mounted unbound on the wall for a time before being stapled into a book. Or the text can be in a nonlinear form: The text of *Smarty Pants* (Wright Group, 1980) can be on a mural, with the "See me fly" text and illustration above, "See me swim" below.
- Child-made big books: Using large print, copy the lines as they appear in the commercial book onto cards. The children read and sequence the text cards before they are mounted on pages and illustrated. Children love to make a book their own by recreating it. Laminating or clear adhesive plastic make the book withstand its popularity.
- Small books: Individual books with the text reproduced on them provide another opportunity for ready children to recognize familiar text without the support of the pictures. Children can illustrate the pages after they are sure of the text on each page.

Variations on the text of a familiar book provide children with an opportunity to analyze and play with a book's patterns of story structure and language. The structure of the text is retained, but elements change to create a new story. Writing a variation can be a complex problem-solving experience lasting many days.

First, you and the children will decide whether the new story will be similar or opposite to the original in setting and characters. "In a Dark, Dark Wood" may become "On a Bright, Bright Street." Then, using structures that parallel the original, you will model how to make substitutions by placing the original text in a pocket chart, then covering words with new words as you and the children invent them (post-its are good for this). For example: "and on that bright, bright street there was a red, red building. And in that red, red building there was a fast, fast elevator."

Last year my kindergarten made a variation on *Mrs. Wishy-Washy* (Wright Group, 1980). In a flip moment a child suggested "Mr. Rock-and-Roll." The idea stuck, and to replace the washerwoman who scolds the dirty animals, they invented a grouchy teacher who confiscates the kids' tape player. Our authors had some sticky structural problems, especially an ending to parallel the newly washed animals jumping into the mud again. Eventually the characters got their tape player back and started singing and dancing again.

In addition to the problem solving during composing, the children had to figure out how to make the characters consistent in different children's illustrations so readers would recognize them. So we decided on costume and hair color for each. Looking at the book from the reader's point of view was a "decentering" experience for kindergarten children. This description illustrates how inextricably linked are the processes of composing and reading.

## LANGUAGE INSTRUCTION ACTIVITIES
## FOR SHARED READING WITH BIG BOOKS

Although the controversy surrounding skill instruction in whole language classrooms is far from settled—see, for example, Heymfeld (1989), "Filling the Hole in Whole Language," and Goodman's (1989) rebuttal, "Whole Language *Is* Whole"—many educators are convinced that skill instruction is necessary and desirable as long as it meets certain conditions. As Holdaway (1979) put it:

> Our teaching objectives are concerned with developing sound central strategies for reading and writing, and...the traditional "skills" are given meaning when they are seen to be abilities that may be called upon in applying strategies. (p. 136)

Skill instruction should be:

- Integrated into meaningful reading experiences.
- Introduced in connection with a book only after the child has internalized the text.
- Enjoyable and varied rather than drudgery.
- Secondary to the pleasure and mastery of reading itself, and should take much less of the allotted reading time than reading books. One teaching point each day should be the limit with young children.

- Only a means to the end of reading books not an end in itself. Children should receive only the minimum necessary to enable them to use strategies for reading.

Language instruction activities as a part of shared reading of big books begin only at the third reading or later to ensure that the text is familiar. As in all aspects of developmentally appropriate instruction, no child should ever be put on the spot with a right-answer question he has not volunteered to answer.

## CONVENTIONS OF PRINT

Clay (1985) identified concepts about books and print that proficient readers bring to the reading experience. Among these are:

- Format: front and back covers, title, how to turn pages.
- Directionality: moving left to right, top to bottom, where to begin on a page, where to go at the end of a line, page sequence.
- Visual discrimination: what a word is, spaces between words, what a letter is, reading words versus reading picture, punctuation marks.
- Auditory discrimination: one-to-one correspondence between spoken and printed text, letter-sound relationships, how punctuation affects oral reading of text.

Teachers often wrongly assume that children have these concepts. To increase children's familiarity with them, the teacher needs to demonstrate them by tracking during shared reading, and also by explicitly calling children's attention to them during language instruction activities. If children can articulate their knowledge about the conventions and forms of print, they can incorporate this knowledge into their repertoire of reading strategies. Aside from the common characteristics of all written texts, different books will lend themselves to emphasis on various conventions: For example, some will have quotation marks, some question marks.

## READING ACTIVITIES

Holdaway (1979), Johnson and Louis (1987), and McCracken and McCracken (1986) describe a wide variety of language instruction activities to use with familiar printed texts. Following are some of these procedures Johnson and Louis suggest to initiate the transition from reliance on memory to the use of all the cueing systems for independent reading.

## Recognizing Familiar Text

Demonstrate by framing a particular line with your hands and saying the line aloud:

> This line says "Ding dong bell."
> This line says "Who'll pull her out?"
>
> What does this line say? (Frame "Ding dong bell.)
> What does this line say? (Frame "Who'll pull her out?")

After a volunteer correctly identifies the line, ask the class to read it aloud. After a few times, call on the more advanced children to do the framing, since they will model it for the others.

After this procedure is familiar, you can repeat it using phrases, then words. Depending on their readiness to focus on small segments of text, children can work in small ability groups.

## Identifying Familiar Text

Demonstrate the procedure by framing the appropriate line with cupped hands.

> Here it says "Ding dong bell."
> Here it says "Who put her in?"
> Here it says "Who'll pull her out."
>
> Where does it say "Who put her in?"
> Where does it say "Who'll pull her out?"

Framing is recommended because it makes clear the line, phrase, or word boundaries. Recognition tasks are easier than identification tasks and should come first.

## Matching

Make a second copy of the text and cut into lines. Cut two other copies into phrases and words for later use. Display the line cards in random order in a pocket chart near the complete text. Ask the class to read the first line of the text in unison. Then invite someone to find the matching card. Incorrect responses can be teaching opportunities. Hold the incorrect card below the text and ask the children to compare. The cards can be used independently later as a center activity. You can use the same routine with the phrase and word cards with children who are ready.

## Cloze Activities

A cloze exercise, in which words are selectively omitted from text, is a technique to get the reader to mobilize meaning-making strategies in order to fill in the blanks. These are several kinds of cloze activities for emergent readers:

- Cloze with unfamiliar texts: As the text is read to the class, the child must use semantic cues from the surrounding text, the wider context of the story, or his general storehouse of knowledge to make sense. He also uses syntactic cues to determine what parts of speech the missing words are. Knowledge of story and language patterns can help a listener or a reader identify the missing words in predictable texts. McCracken and McCracken (1986, p. 22) demonstrate prediction as a sense-making strategy using a patterned story containing 36 words and 28 blanks, part of which is as follows:

> The skunk sat under the porch.
> The farmer sat on the porch.
> The skunk smelled the farmer.
>
> ____ ____ ____ ____ ____.
> The skunk saw ____ ____.
>
> ____ ____ ____ ____ ____.
> The skunk got on the porch.
>
> ____ ____ ____ ____ ____ ____.

As we supply the missing words, we call upon our knowledge of word order, our expectation of the story pattern, and our knowledge of the behavior of people when a skunk is near!

- Oral cloze with familiar text: Once the children are familiar with a book, you can pause in your oral reading to invite the children to supply the missing word or words. If the children have memorized the text, they will supply the words from memory. You can ask them to show you where the missing words are on the page, thus calling their attention to the one-to-one correspondence between your words and the text. They may count words from the beginning of the line, which forces them to attend to the correspondence. Children who are beginning to pay more attention to the features of words may rely more on decoding strategies and less on memory. With these children you can begin cloze activities before they have fully memorized the text.
- Cloze with post-its or masking device: Cover chosen words with post-it notes or a cardboard masking device. Ask the children to read

the line and guess what the hidden word is. An incorrect guess is a teaching opportunity: Repeat the line as the child said it, and ask, "Does that make sense? What else could it be?" Accept efforts to use semantic and syntactic cues, even if they are not correct. Then unmask the word or words and read the line with the children.

- Phonics cloze: Once the children have made a guess, as above, move to the post-it to reveal the initial consonant, and ask the children to confirm or adjust their original idea.

  Cloze with its post-its is a good example of an activity which invites participation and interest. When I use it with small groups of children who are interested in graphophonic cues, they are as excited and focused as any contestant on "Wheel of Fortune"! Removing the post-it to confirm their hypothesis about the word, they grin and exclaim victoriously. What a contrast to isolated, dry phonics drill!

- Progressive cloze: The complete text of a rhyme or several lines of a book are displayed with each word on a separate card. Read the rhyme aloud in unison. Then begin to remove individual words one or two at a time. As you reread the rhyme, ask the children to identify the missing words, and as they identify them, return the cards to their place. Repeat this procedure, removing progressively more words. If you leave structure or service words in the context, you will increase the children's exposure to them.

A variation of progressive cloze is to give the word cards to individual children and ask them to read and replace them as needed.

As educators increasingly realize the importance of comprehension in reading, cloze exercises are becoming a standard part of many traditional reading programs.

## Substitutions

In substitution activities, such as these suggested by Johnson and Louis, deliberate "errors" appear in the text, which the children find and correct. This kind of word play seems to tickle the emergent reader. Since this procedure involves detection of changes, the original text must be familiar. Print the sentence on cards or on the chalkboard.

> Word substitutions: Baa, baa black dog.
> Letter substitutions: There was a farmer had a fog (Bingo).

Letter substitutions provide a motivating opportunity for phonics learning with phonograms. One morning my class was intrigued and delighted to see that a mischievious imp had come during the night and changed the text cards of our current big book from "Sing, sing, sing a song" (Wright Group, 1980) to "Sing, ring, bing a long." Correcting involves noting which letters have caused the change: "This is an r, so it reads 'ring.' We need an s to make it say 'sing.'"

Sponerisms: Mazy Lary, will you get up?

Modeling the correction process is particularly important with this more complex activity. You could say, "The m and the l got switched. It says 'Mazy Lary.' To make it say 'Lazy Mary' we take the m off 'mazy' and the l off 'Lary' and put them back where they belong." Eventually, as children begin to understand the process, the correction should be turned over to them.

As this sampling of language instruction activities demonstrates, if we see reading skills as strategies children can use to further their understanding of texts, skill development does not have to be sterile or removed from meaning-making. As long as these activities are fun, short, and secondary to the real purpose of reading, they contribute to children's eventual mastery of independent reading while maintaining their interest.

## BEYOND SHARED READING

Kindergarten reading has been the focus of this chapter, but since children develop along a continuum, as they enter first grade there is no abrupt change into readiness for traditional formal instruction. It is heartbreaking to see a child who had a productive, positive kindergarten year begin to fail, show anxiety, or even develop school phobia because the nature of the reading task has suddenly changed before he was ready. Informed by knowledge about optimal conditions for beginning reading, we can continue to offer developmentally appropriate instruction beyond kindergarten. To replace the traditional reading groups, which allow little reading and require too much pencil-and-paper seatwork, small-group instruction can focus on a technique that guides children to use strategies as they move into independent reading.

Since some kindergarten and first-grade children will be moving from the emergent stages to the grapho-phonic stage, they should have the opportunity to decode new words without the support of familiarity. For this purpose some publishers have created graded series of small individual books carefully designed to gradually remove the support of language patterns and pictures. Although they consist of meaningful text like the big books, these books are easier to read without memorizing because they have less text on a page. As children become more able to read independently, the teacher can do less introductory reading to the children before beginning cloze activities or asking the children to read the book alone or in pairs (never ask a child to read aloud in a group without a rehearsal; we want children to feel comfortable, not on the spot!). This procedure, called "guided reading," is used as an adjunct to shared reading. The teacher models strategies which the children use more and more independently as they move toward fluency and a focus on literature.

## EVALUATION

Whole-language reading is holistic and not linear, so it is difficult to quantify for evaluation in the early stages. Because current standardized reading tests do not measure what children in whole language classrooms are learning, school districts which emphasize test results may have difficulty adopting this approach. However, a national consensus that we need to teach students to think is spurring research attempts to create reading tests which focus more on meaning than current standardized tests do. In the meantime teachers can use their own observations of their students' learning processes as a guide for planning instruction and can incorporate as much whole language practice as possible into the mandated curriculum. Teachers need to network for support and to take responsibility for educating administrators about more progressive ways to approach reading.

## CONCLUSION

Educators worried about pressuring young children with premature reading tasks are asking: "Should we be teaching reading to young children?" This question assumes that reading instruction means the sight-word and letter-sound skill model. A more complete question would be: "What reading experiences are young children ready for, and how can we best facilitate their learning?" A careful look at the research and at young children reveals how they learn what they teach themselves about language and reading. Using this knowledge, we can create an environment that will support the development or literacy. Whole language reading provides a developmentally appropriate, successful experience in reading when it is integrated without literacy activities.

Rightly or wrongly, the responsibility for reading failure is often placed squarely on the school system. We must do all we can to nurture new generations of children who know how to read well, who enjoy reding and who choose to read. We have an obligation to structure early reading instruction so that no child will fail, and to help each one begin the journey through reading education saying, as Eliot has, "I can read!"

## REFERENCES

Adams, M.J. (1990). *Beginning to read: Thinking and learning about print* (summary prepared by S.A. Stahl, J. Osborn, & F. Lehr). Urbana-Champaign, IL: Center for the Study of Reading.

Allen, R. (1976). *Language experience in communication*. Boston: Houghton Mifflin.

Bridge, C., Winograd, P., & Haley, D. (1983). Using predictable materials vs. preprimers to teach beginning sight words. *The Reading Teacher, 36,* 884–891.

Cambourne, B. (1987). Language, learning and literacy. In A. Butler & J. Turbill (Eds.), *Towards a reading-writing classroom.* Portsmouth, NH: Heinemann.

Can kids flunk kindergarten? (1988, April 25). *Time,* p. 86.

Chall, J. (1983). *Stages of reading development.* New York: McGraw-Hill.

Clay, M. (1985). *The early detection of reading difficulties* (3rd ed.). Portsmouth, NH: Heinemann.

Cochrane, O., Cochrane, D., Scalena, S., & Buchanan, E. (1984). *Reading, writing and caring.* Winnipeg, Canada: Whole Language Consultants, Ltd.

Cutting, R. (1989). *Getting started in whole language.* San Diego, CA: Wright Group.

Early Childhood and Literacy Development Committee of the International Reading Association. (1985). Literacy and pre-first grade. *Childhood Education, 63,* 110–111.

Ferreiro, E., & Teberosky, A. (1982). *Literacy before schooling.* Portsmouth, NH: Heinemann.

Ginzburg, H., & Opper, S. (1988). *Piaget's theory of intellectual development* (3rd ed.). Englewood Cliffs, NJ: Prentice-Hall.

Goodman, K. (1976). What we know abour reading. In P. Allen & D. Watson (Eds.), *Findings of research in miscue analysis: Classroom implications* (pp. 57–70). Urbana, IL: ERIC Clearinghouse on Reading and Communication Skills and the National Council of Teachers of English.

Goodman, K. (1987). *Language and thinking in school: A whole-language curriculum* (3rd ed.). New York: Richard C. Owen.

Goodman, K. (1989). Whole language IS whole. *Educational Leadership, 46*(6), 69–70.

Goodman, Y., Watson, D., & Burke, C. (1987). *Reading miscue inventory: Alternative procedures.* New York: Richard C. Owen.

Hall, M. (1976). *Teaching reading as a language experience.* Columbus, OH: Charles E. Merrill.

Heymsfeld, C. (1989). Filling the hole in whole language. *Educational Leadership, 46*(6), 65–68.

Holdaway, D. (1979). *The foundations of literacy.* Portsmouth, NH: Heinemann.

Johnson, T., & Louis, D. (1987). *Literacy through literature.* Portsmouth, NH: Heinemann.

Kamii, C. (1989). *Young children continue to invent arithmetic.* New York: Teachers College Press.

Martin, B. (1967). *Brown bear, brown bear, what do you see?* New York: Henry Holt & Company.

Mason, J. (1980). When do children begin to read? *Reading Research Quarterly, 15,* 203–227.

McCracken, R., & McCracken, M. (1986). *Stories, songs and poetry to teach reading and writing.* Chicago: American Library Association.

*Mrs. Wishy-Washy.* (1980). San Diego, CA: Wright Group.

National Association for the Education of Young Children. (1988). NAEYC position statement on developmentally appropriate practice in the primary grades serving 5- through 8-year-olds. *Young Children, 43*(2), 64–84.

National Commission on Excellence in Education. (1983). *A nation at risk: The imperative for educational reform.* Washington, DC: U.S. Department of Education.

Peterson, P., Fennema, E., & Carpenter, T. (1988). Using knowledge of how students think about mathematics. *Educational Leadership, 46,* 42–46.

Phonics vs. whole language: Can there by peace? (1990). *American Teacher, 74*(7), 2.

Routman, R. (1988). *Transitions: From literature to literacy.* Portsmouth, NH: Heinemann.

Sendak, M. (1962). *Chicken soup with rice.* New York: Harper & Row.

*Sing a song.* (1980). San Diego, CA: Wright Group.

Slaughter, H. (1988). Indirect and direct teaching in a whole language program. *Reading Teacher, 42,* 30–34.

*Smarty pants.* (1980). San Diego, CA: Wright Group.

Smith, F. (1975). *Reading without nonsense.* New York: Teachers College Press.

Tense tots: Some schools press so hard kids become stressed and fearful. (1988, July 6). *Wall Street Journal.*

The reading wars. (1990, Fall/Winter Special Issue). *Newsweek,* pp. 8–14.

The redshirt solution. (1989, November 13). *Time.*

## Publishers of Predictable Big Books

DLM (Bill Martin Books), PO Box 4000, One DLM Park, Allen, TX 75002.
Richard C. Owen Publishers, 135 Katonah Avenue, Katonah, NY 10536.
Rigby, PO Box 797, Crystal Lake, IL 60014.
Scholastic Inc., PO Box 7501, 2931 E. McCarty Street, Jefferson City, MO 65102.
Wright Group, 10949 Technology Place, San Diego, CA 92127.

## Chapter 8

# Tried and True:
# Books That Fit the Interests
# and Needs of Young Children

## Sally R. Costa

Children's literature is a topic that often arises when educators of young children get together. Questions are posed about how to find the best children's books and how to integrate these books into the classroom curriculum. Parents also are looking for guidance in the same areas. This chapter examines these two questions. It also raises some ideas, some cautions, and some recommendations. The books mentioned can be used in both the classroom and in the home.

Research shows that children who have been exposed to books and reading, who are "print literate," learn to read more readily than young-sters who have not had this exposure. Weir (1989) reviewed the research done in this area. She points out that studies indicate that young children can understand the purpose of print. At the preschool level the ability to associate separate sounds with separate letters is not expected (Lomax & McGree, 1987); neither is there an understanding of terms: letter, word, and sentence (Morgan, 1987, in Weir). However, parents and preschool teachers have an important role to play in teaching the purposes of read-ing (Wahl, 1988). Because of this, intelligent teachers and parents want to find the best books for their younsters. They are aware that reading aloud to children increases the likelihood that they will learn to read. Being interested in books and enjoying stories has helped many a child acquire reading ability.

Parents are sometimes hesitant to select books beyond Big Bird and Golden Books. These are readily available in the supermarket and parents know that they are safe choices. However, when these same parents enter the children's section of a bookstore or the public library where higher quality books are available, the choices can become overwhelming. Big expensive books may or may not be enjoyed by the child and parents are reluctant to invest in unknown books. At the other end of the ecomonic scale, there are so many paperback books that the adult has difficulty evaluating the choices. There is not enough time in the parent's busy schedule to stand and read these books before choosing one from the cluttered shelves.

Teachers, with experience in selecting children's books, have a clear advantage in evaluating stories. Therefore, they can be a big help to parents. Quality children's literature can be identified more easily in a group setting. Although some stories have a direct appeal to individual children (boys' and girls' tastes do differ) the children's response to particular stories seems to be fairly universal. Seldom does a book become a great hit with one group of younsters and not with another. When evaluating new books, no book critic can outdo the accuracy of the classroom. A teacher will receive a candid critique of the author's ability and success.

In selecting the right book for the individual child, parents have other guidelines to follow. They judge if their child is interested in a story about bugs or only wants information about dinosaurs. No book is right for every child. *Peter Rabbit* by Beatrix Potter, known and loved by so many, is not loved at all. Children who are concerned with right and wrong may see this tale as a frightening example of what happens to naughty children who do not obey their mother, rather than seeing it as a rollicking adventure story. Adults have to remain flexible in their judgment, listening to the child's comment and watching his or her reactions is what is needed.

## GUIDELINES

The following section of this chapter outlines some valid signposts for identifying superior picture books for children. One must remember that there are exceptions to each rule. However, before going into various exceptions, let's look at the "rules." Examining some of the characteristics of young children will help identify what is needed to interest and catch the imagination and intelligence of children.

### Attention Span

The young child has a short attention span. Books must be short enough to be read in one sitting. The length of the sitting depends on the age and disposition of the children. The story must move along so that each new page is interesting in either storyline, illustration, or both. *Drummer Hoff* by Emberley, like other repetitive and predictable stories, adds one new picture detail, one new name, and one new text component on each page. The illustrations and rhyme carry the story along to its surprise "KABOOM" ending. The story can be read in less than five minutes. Some children's attention may be focused on the rhyming text while others have a growing conviction that a cannon is being assembled. This story is often enjoyed much more on subsequent readings after the ending is known. The child's anticipation becomes the prime motivator. Being "in on the secret" is another reason youngsters enjoy this classic. Interest is high and the children's attention is riveted on each page. In this situation young children can extend their attention span without strain. As with many books, its quality is reflected in the children's focusing on the story.

### Self-Centeredness

Self-centeredness is the norm for this age range. From the young child's point of view, the closer one can be to the reader and to the book, the better. If the story is a good one and there is no major distraction going on close by, even active boys clamber for the seat next to the reader. With only one lap the teacher has a problem. This is one reason why the "big book" format works so well classroom setting. Even in a circle of children each child can easily see the pictures and print. Although the child cannot snuggle up to the reader, eye contact is easily established and no sharing or waiting for a turn to see the page is necessary. These oversized books are designed for group activities and are wonderful for classroom use.

### Language Learning

Developing an understanding of storyline and increasing vocabulary knowledge are two of the benefits of sharing a story. Books that allow time for talking and expressing ideas are especially important (Yaden, Smolkin, & Conlon, 1989). Although any book can be discussed and predictions solicited, the wordless picture books seem designed to accomplish these goals. "Oh look!" and "What happened here?" come naturally in this situation. These questions are the building blocks on which story structure and new words are learned. When in *Good Dog Carl* by Alexandra Day, the gifted dog, Carl, is left to mind the baby there are pages and pages of funny things to talk about. Tommie dePaola's *Sing Pierrot, Sing* gives the child much to reflect on. People's feelings are shown and can be talked about. In both books the construction of plot is clear but the selection of the words is left to the "reader." When the child says, "Here, I'll read it to you now" or more simply, "My turn," you have a child showing his or her understanding of language and story.

### Recognition and Understanding of Feeling

There are some fine books that address feelings of self-worth and of doubt, of acceptance and rejection. Young children need to know about these feelings; they need to talk about them and they need to know that others have these feelings too. Even at an early age, books can help children with their problems. Parents and educators may wish to help draw the parallels between characters in fiction and the child's own situation. "Remember when the little boy in *Will I have a Friend?* (Cohen) went to school the first day? He wondered if he would find someone to play with. Are you wondering about the same thing?"

Buckley's *Grandfather and I* centers around personal development and relationships with others. *Play with Me* by Marie Hall Ets tells of a child's attempt to make friends with shy animals. The lesson taught through this book can easily be applied to making friends with people. The question of "best friends" is in many books for older children but *Best Friends* by Miriam Cohen handles this problem in the kindergarten setting.

Some books reflect a special quality of personal identification. Ezra Jack Keats strikes this chord in several of his stories, perhaps the most outstanding one being *The Snowy Day*. This book reflects the essence of being little in a big world, of knowing less than is needed and yet having a safe home in which to grow and to learn. This insight can help children who find themselves in the same position.

### Rapid Growth of Knowledge

Young children are impatient to learn. Then they want to show off what they know. When asked if they know numbers or letters the answer is always along the line of "Lots!" If asked, "How high can you jump?" the answer is, "To the moon!" Books that foster school knowledge and learning are particularly tempting to parents. Numerous books expose youngsters to letters and numbers. Parents and teachers must remember that only one skill should be presented at a time. In looking for books that teach, simplicity is the key. Number and alphabet books should be fun. Books that have one picture per page are just fine. Keep borrowing library books at this stage. One or two will turn into favorites and should be bought but sampling different books should be done first.

Children of this age are learning a complex set of new concepts; the lines on the page have a particular shape; that particular shape has a special meaning and a special relationship with the word or the picture on the page. That is a lot to sort out and the process should not be hurried. The alphabet books with lots of pictures on the page are great for later on when the letter sound will act as a clue to remembering new words. But don't start here. Later on alphabet books that feature unusual representations of the letters such as "virtuous valentines" and "advancing aardvarks" can be lots of fun. When old enough to appreciate the jokes, *Hillary Knight's A B C* is a prime example of this type of language enjoyment.

Counting books have the same rules. To start, keep it simple. The wonderful illustrations by Steven Kellogg in the book written by David M. Schwartz, *How Much Is a Million?*, shouldn't be missed but this book will keep for a few years. The young children need to know what patterns and sequences are before they can or need to conceptualize millions and billions.

### Time and Place

Finding tiny pictures can be lots of fun to do for older children. No matter how wonderfully detailed the drawings, they are too complex for young children. Even older children may overlook the sophistication of the pictures in their search for the key figures on each page. There is nothing wrong in these activities but some adults think that by searching the detailed pictures their children will assimilate knowledge. They are mistaken.

The concept of time is a hard one to grasp. Stories that do not respect time concepts are not appropriate for little ones who are just now learning the meanings of the words *yesterday, today, now, in a little while,* and *tomorrow.* After these have been firmly established they can be "played" with. James Stevenson's wonderful stories about Grandfather, such as *No Friends,* flip back and forth in time so wait a bit before enjoying them with your younsters.

*Miss Rumphius* by Barbara Cooney tells a story in the sequence from being a little girl to growing old. The wonderful life of Miss Rumphius is told simply and beautifully. This book can be read again and again; it can be enjoyed at many ages.

Time and sequence play an important part in several children's stories. *Blueberries for Sal* (McCloskey) employs a strict sequence of events. As

Sal and her mother become separated, Little Bear and his mother do the same. In a step-by-step progression the tension of the story mounts. When the two mothers realize their respective losses, sort out their babies and then head home, the listener has enjoyed the humor of the sequence of events. The panoramic pictures in the book show the location and the action of the story.

Harold and his purple crayon (Johnson) progress in a linear fashion, each episode depends on what went before and anticipates what will come next. *Bubble Bubble* (Mayer) has the same plot structure. It is interesting to note that both of these books demonstrate this concept without the use of words.

"*Charlie Needs a Cloak*" (DePaola) also tells its tale in a structured sequence. The story unfolds as Charlie, a resourceful shepherd, goes through the process of making himself a new cloak. He is undaunted by the efforts of a sheep, who is not cooperative about his part of the cloak-making process, and an acquisitive mouse. Sequence and humor are the keys to enjoying this story. Again, children see the process, with each picture presenting a separate activity. Each one is dependent on what went before and leads to what will come next.

### Emotional and Social Skills

An important facet of uniting teaching and children's books is done by moving from the academic skills to the emotional and social skills. Children learn the values expressed by the author. *Little Toot* by Gramatky, *The Little Engine That Could* by Piper, and *Mike Mulligan and His Steam Shovel* by Burton all reflect the same values; hard work and perseverance will be rewarded in the end. Reading these books and talking about their meaning in an accepting environment leads to learning social values.

In order to promote the use of language it is important to design open-ended questions. "How do you think Little Toot learned to be a good tug boat?," "Why didn't the Little Engine give up when she heard the other engines say that she would not be able to get over the mountain?," and "How hard did Mike and Mary Anne work? Did you ever work that hard?" are all examples of this type of questioning.

### Humor

A developing sense of humor is part of growing up. Understanding what is funny and what isn't is part of parcel of the socialization process. Much of what is written for children is seen through the adult's eyes and often what we understand as irony is not appropriate for young children.

Slapstick humor, however, is understood and enjoyed. This is the level on which *Amelia Bedelia* (Parish) is so popular with first graders. Much of the play on language is far beyond most children's grasp but the sight of Amelia "dressing" the turkey in clothes before putting it into the oven or "changing" the towels by cutting them has obvious appeal. Seeing those naughty monkeys stealing the peddler's caps in *Caps for Sale* (Slobodkina) is another example of a story with age-appropriate humor. The visual humor and the strong action line make this story clearly understandable. The humor comes through loud and clear.

### Self-Esteem and Self-Concept

Accepting oneself is an important component of early childhood education. *Leo the Late Bloomer* by Kraus is perhaps the best known and best loved book of this genera. This story, however, is not the only one that recommends taking the longer view on life and its problems. Young children are often fearful of not meeting others' expectations and of not being able to deal with problems. Rosemary Wells presents children with two underdogs that make good: Morris, whose Christmas is almost ruined because he is the "baby" in the family, and Benjamin, who has a bully named Tulip for a neighbor, both have unusual adventures establishing their own identities. Judith Viorst's *Alexander and the Terrible, Horrible, No Good, Very Bad Day* is another winning book. Coping skills are an essential part of growing up and Alexander "hangs in there" even though his day is a horror by anyone's standard.

### A Few Surprises

With all our understanding of children, their likes and dislikes, and their characteristic growth and development, the magic of childhood sometimes proves us wrong. Therefore it is important in selecting books to keep an open mind. The classic example of this phenomenon is *Where the Wild Things Are* by Maurice Sendak. Who would have thought that little children would respond positively to monsters and to the threat to Max's life and limb? Today those very monsters are classic characters and even appear as stuffed animals.

Mike Mulligan and Mary Anne (Burton) lose none of their appeal because today we do not have shovels run by steam. Children have a code that lets the settings and the characters vary; however, the hero or heroine must be strong and/or worthy of the listener's consideration. In the book of this name, Bemelmans' *Madeline*, who lives in Paris in a convent boarding school with eleven other little girls and Miss Clavel, appeals to children even though both the location and the life are entirely foreign to their own existence.

What makes these books classics is the appeal of the characters. They convey a special response in children. Mike and Mary Anne are the underdogs. They are hardworking and fair in a land that doesn't need them anymore. Madeline is fearless even though she is the littlest. Max is a fighter who is not afraid even when he is punished. Children who are brave and strong are popular with the young child.

Mice are little in a big world and some attribute their popularity with children to this obvious parallel. However, Babar the elephant by de Brunoff is certainly not little and he is very popular. He is also upstanding and above reproach. He has his problems, but he is able to rise above them.

In identifying children's classic literature the test of time is the only one that holds true in all cases. If the book is good it will transcend the changes in the society and be as fresh to the new group of children as it was to the very first group of young readers and listeners.


## TRIED AND TRUE

With the above guidelines in place and the exceptions noted, what are some of the "tired and true" books that have earned the title of classic books for young children? How can they be incorporated into school activities and into the lives of the children we work with?

The early childhood teacher has many themes from which to choose. Since they are starting out with a "clean slate" the possibilities seem unlimited. So many things are brand new to the children and at these ages almost all the world is interesting. The children have not found out that it is fashionable to label anything the teacher presents as "boring." For example, there are so many books about animals that constructing a teaching unit seems easy. Stories about kittens, puppies, and bears abound. One could easily spend the whole year reading books about any of these three popular animals. However, teachers are entrusted to select the best quality ideas and concepts for their younsters.

A good teacher is able to avoid "cute syndrome" and make curriculum decisions about quality learning. Children do not need to learn that a duckling looks "cute" sitting in a tea cup. Children do demonstrate an affinity toward "baby" animals. Learning their names, where they live, and what they eat makes a fine teaching unit. The concept of nurturing and home can be added to the lessons.

Animal picture books can be selected and placed about the classroom. There are many books designed for young children but the teacher should not overlook books where writing is at an adult level. The quality of the pictures is the important factor here; if the pictures provide information they can become a key part of the lesson. The teacher provides the information at the appropriate level for the children.

Vocabulary instruction in this type of unit is carried out in the same way it is done in the home. The new word is pronounced and a few ideas are presented to tie the unknown to what is already known. "It's a tiger. Can you say *tiger*? See his stripes? He is like a very big cat. He lives in the jungle in India, a land far away from here. We would see a tiger at the zoo."

## Sometimes More Is Better

There are several characters in children's literature that have such wonderfully distinct personalities that one book is just not enough (Fisher, 1975). This is true in picture books as well as in longer books. Angus (Flack), the Scottie who is only a shade less curious than Curious George (Rey) rates several volumes; his adventures go on as he grows and his world becomes larger. Speaking of the most inquisitive monkey in the world, George has shown that variations on a good format can be repeated without becoming stale. Richek and McTague (1988) use these books in the classroom with much success. *Harry the Dirty Dog* (Zion) and *Frog and Toad Are Friends* (Lobel) also are greeted as old friends in their later exploits. The gentle and vulnerable Celestine (Vincent) has many adventures as Ernest tries to raise her with love and affection. The series deals with problems that speak to the needs of children.

Today we have several books that were written and conceived as a series, not simply as sequels. These books each tell a complete story but they are designed to continue the storyline over a longer period of time. They are very much like chapters in longer stories. The Polk Street School series (Giff), a series written about a year in the life of a second grade classroom, has been followed by the *Little Polk Street* books designed for the younger child. Miriam Cohen's stories about first grade are favorites with both teachers and children. The children sometimes require an explanation of the humor but they appreciate these books written about the things first graders experience and feel. Wanting to learn to read while being impatient about having to wait, not getting as many valentines as someone else, and taking tests are all topics that six-year-olds are interested in.

There are other series books like this on the market today. Although many may never become classics, they clearly have a place in the early childhood years. Judging from the number of books seen on the market today, they are popular. If they are well done they can provide the children with the idea that some stories can and do continue. When later books in the series are introduced to the children, they already have background knowledge about the characters and they will understand that they are about to find out more about their old friends. Like adults, children enjoy discovering what interesting characters like Little Bear (Minarik) do next.

### Pop-Up Books

Pop-up books have been around for a long time; they are often seen in displays of antique toys and playthings. Although the ones constructed with levers and strips to pull are not sturdy enough for very small hands, by the time the child reaches six the fine motor coordination and patience to move gently have usually developed. Today there is a renaissance of pop-up books. They cover a wide range of subjects (Bohning & Radencich, 1989). Locations as diverse as Pooh Corner and Buckingham Palace can be found. There are pop-up versions of *Winnie-the-Pooh* and *The House at Pooh Corner* (Milne), along with *The Royal Family Pop-Up* (Hodge) and *Pop-Up London* (Wild).

If travel and motors are a prevailing interest, there are many titles to choose from. *Sailing Ships* (van der Meer), *The Car* (Marshall), *The Train* (Marshall), and *Flight* (Moseley), along with many others, are all there for opening up and playing with. These books are meant for careful handling but their cleverness at adding a "new dimension" to the enjoyment of books is clear.

### ACTIVITIES

### Puppets

Puppets have always been a mainstay in the creative classroom. They offer the child the opportunity to reenact and create stories. Hand and finger puppets must be sturdy and safe to play with. There are very few commercially available puppets that match story characters. In order to have them the teacher must make them. Puppets made from felt are sensible for the early primary classroom. Stick puppets can be a problem. A simple cardboard cut out of the character sewn or glued on to a felt mitten shape with an extra long wrist is all that is needed. Because puppets receive hard wear and tear, they will not last very long. Angus (Flack) chasing the ducks will be chased back again; as the ducks will lose their tail feathers, so Angus will lose his tail. Even with these factors in mind, having puppets in the classroom is excellent for teaching and learning about language.

### Cooking and Eating

Although children tend to be no more flexible than Frances (Hoban) in their eating habits, cooking the food themselves sometimes carries the day. This is a theme in children's literature that easily leads to either actual cooking or play cooking. *The Little Red Hen* (Galdone), who works so hard to make bread, is an example. *The Gingerbread Boy* (Galdone) can be made from gingerbread or, second best, from brown paper. Tommie DePaola tells about Big Anthony's experiment with Strega Nona's magic pasta pot. This makes us all hungry for spaghetti, and his *Pancakes for Breakfast* is a natural mouth "waterer." *Bread and Jam for Frances* (Hoban) is easy to recreate in the classroom. However, most teachers draw the line at *Green Eggs and Ham* (Dr. Seuss) even though all it takes is green food coloring and courage.

### Acting

*Caps for Sale* (Slobodkina) and *The Three Billy Goats Gruff* (Galdone) lend themselves to play format because of their clear story progression. One of the interesting things to note about children's classics is that the traditional stories with clearly defined major characters, such as Little Red Riding Hood and Cinderella, are easy to act out. The simple story progression and the clear-cut winners and losers make these old favorites easy to perform and enjoy.

Props should be very simple; a basket and cape or a set of caps are all that are needed. The magic of acting brings along its own "magic wand." The child provides the script and often carries the story on beyond the book's ending. If you listen carefully you may find out how many children Cinderella and the Prince had and if they indeed lived happily ever after.

## CONCLUSION

We have looked at several facets of children's literature. In early childhood it is vitally important to expose younsters to good literature. The preschool child learns story structure, how to make predictions and inferences, new vocabulary, new concepts, socialization skills, and ideals. Our classrooms and homes have a golden opportunity to provide guid-

ance and care through the selection and use of quality children's literature. Reading early and often to children is a wonderful way to nurture
the young child both at home and at school (Rudman & Pearce, 1988).
Classrooms that have only one story time a day are not taking advantage
of the wealth of literature that is available.

In helping parents see the importance of reading in the home teachers
perform a great service. Parents want guidance and encouraging them
to read to their youngsters is a concrete activity that they can do. An
understanding of the interrelationships of reading, writing, listening,
and speaking is the key to such cooperation. The quality time between
parent and child reading and listening together can be the cornerstone
of the child's education.

## CHILDREN'S BOOK LIST

Bemelmans, Ludwig. (1977). *Madeline*. New York: Penguin.
Buckley, Helen E. (1959). *Grandfather and I*. New York: Lothrop, Lee & Shepard.
Burton, Virginia Lee. (1977). *Mike Mulligan and his steam shovel*. Boston: Houghton
 Mifflin.
Cohen, Miriam. (1967). *Will I have a friend?* New York: Macmillan.
Cohen, Miriam. (1971). *Best friends*. New York: Macmillan.
Cooney, Barbara. (1982). *Miss Rumphius*. New York: Viking.
Day, Alexandra. (1985). *Good dog Carl*. Hong Kong: Green Tiger Press.
deBrunhoff, Jean. (1967). *The story of Babar the little elephant*. New York: Random
 House.
dePaola, Tommie. (1974). *"Charlie needs a cloak."* San Diego: Harcourt.
dePaola, Tommie. (1975). *Strega Nona*. Englewood Cliffs, NJ: Prentice-Hall.
dePaola, Tommie. (1978). *Pancakes for breakfast*. San Diego: Harcourt.
dePaola, Tommie. (1983). *Sing Pierrot sing*. San Diego: Harcourt.
Dr. Seuss. (1960). *Green eggs and ham*. New York: Random House.
Emberley, Barbara. (1967). *Drummer Hoff*. New York: Prentice-Hall.
Ets, Marie Hall. (1955). *Play with me*. New York: Viking.
Flack, Marjorie. (1971). *Angus and the ducks*. New York: Doubleday.
Galdone, Paul. (1973a). *Little red hen*. Boston: Houghton Mifflin.
Galdone, Paul. (1973b). *The three Billy Goats Gruff*. Boston: Houghton Mifflin.
Galdone, Paul. (1983). *The gingerbread boy*. Boston: Houghton Mifflin.
Giff, Patricia R. (1984). *The beast in Ms. Rooney's room*. New York: Delacorte.
Gramatky, Hardie. (1939). *Little Toot*. New York: Putnam's Sons.
Hoban, Russell. (1964). *Bread and jam for Frances*. New York: Harper & Row.
Hodge, Lete. (1984). *The Royal Family Pop-Up*. New York: Outlet Book.
Johnson, Crockett. (1981). *Harold and the purple crayon*. New York: Harper & Row.
Keats, Ezra Jack. (1962). *The snowy day*. New York: Viking.
Knight, Hilary. (1962). *Hilary Knight's ABC*. New York: Golden Press.
Kraus, Robert. (1971). *Leo the late bloomer*. New York: Prentice-Hall.
Lobel, Arnold. (1970). *Frog and Toad are friends*. New York: Harper & Row.
Marshall, Ray. (1984). *The car*. New York: Viking.

Marshall, Ray. (1986). *The train.* New York: Viking.

Mayer, Mercer. (1980). *Bubble bubble.* New York: Macmillan.

McCloskey, Robert. (1948). *Blueberries for Sal.* New York: Viking Press.

Milne, A.A. (1984). *Winnie-the-Pooh: A pop-up book.* New York: Dutton.

Milne, A.A. (1986). *The house at Pooh Corner: A pop-up book.* New York: Dutton.

Minarik, Elsi H. (1957). *Little Bear.* New York: Harper & Row.

Moseley, Keith. (1985). *Flight.* New York: Viking.

Parish, Peggy. (1983). *Amelia Bedelia.* New York: Harper & Row.

Piper, Watty. (1979). *The little engine that could.* New York: Scholastic.

Potter, Beatrix. (1903). *The tale of Peter Rabbit.* London: Frederick Warne.

Ray, H.A. (1941). *Curious George.* New York: Scholastic.

Schwartz, David M. (1985). *How much is a million?* New York: Scholastic.

Sendak, Maurice. (1963). *Where the wild things are.* New York: Harper & Row.

Slobodkina, Esphyr. (1947). *Caps for sale.* New York: Harper & Row.

Stevenson, James. (1986). *No friends.* New York: Greenwillow Books.

van der Meer, Ron. (1984). *Sailing ships.* New York: Viking.

Vincent, Gabrille. (1981). *Ernest & Celestine.* New York: Greenwillow Press.

Viorst, Judith. (1972). *Alexander and the terrible, horrible, no good, very bad gay.* New York: Atheneum.

Wells, Rosemarie. (1973). *Benjamin and Tulip.* New York: Doubleday.

Wells, Rosemarie. (1978). *Morris's disappearing bag: A Christmas story.* New York: Dial.

Wild, Anne. (1983). *Pop-up London.* New York: Parkwest.

Zion, Gene. (1956). *Harry the dirty dog.* New York: Harper & Row.

## REFERENCES

Bohning, G., & Radencich, M. (1989). Travel the world with pop-up books. *The Reading Teacher, 42,* 444–445.

Fisher, M. (1975). *Who's who in children's books: A treasury of the familiar characters of childhood.* New York: Holt, Rinehart & Winston.

Lomax, R.G., & McGee, L.M. (1987). Young children's concepts about print and reading. *Reading Research Quarterly, 22,* 237–256.

Morgan, A.L. (1987). The development of written language awareness in black preschool children. *Journal of Reading Behavior, 19,* 49–66.

Richek, M.A., & McTague, B.K. (1988). The "Curious George" strategy for students with reading problems. *The Reading Teacher, 42,* 220–226.

Rudman, M.K., Pearce, M.A., & Editors of Consumer Reports Books. (1988). *For love of reading: A parent's guide to encouraging young readers from infancy through age five.* Mount Vernon, NY: Consumers Union.

Wahl, A. (1988). Ready...set...role: Parents' role in early reading. *The Reading Teacher, 42,* 228–231.

Weir, B. (1989). A research base for prekindergarten literacy programs. *The Reading Teacher, 42,* 456–460.

Yaden, D.B., Jr., Smolkin, L.B., & Conlon, A. (1989). Preschoolers' questions about pictures, print convention, and story text during reading aloud at home. *Reading Research Quarterly, 24,* 188–214.

# Chapter 9

# He's Not Looking at the Book!
# Metacognition and the Young Child

## Patricia Chiarelli Elfant

The bear, who was in search of a robber, picked up a tennis racket but James said it was a baseball bat. "Why did you say baseball bat?" I asked. He looked at the videotape of a recent shared book experience, saw the position of his eyes, and replied, "I wasn't looking at the book." Moments later, as I read the last page of *Hairy Bear*, James remarked, as six-year-olds have been known to do, "You did an accident; it doesn't say, 'Hello Mom—Hello dad'; it says, 'Hello Dad,' and look, you weren't looking at the book." James' observations were correct; the book was under my chin as I showed it to the children—*I* wasn't looking at the book!

Obviously James had formulated an important rule that children learn as they begin to read—that is, you look at the book, at the pictures, and at the print in order to understand what's happening in the story. However, we know that formulating a rule is not enough; a child becomes a strategic reader when he is able to apply the rule or transfer it to a new situation. Weeks later, as James was listening to another student read, he remarked, "Look, Jason did an accident; he read the wrong word and I know why. I watched his eyes and they weren't looking at the book!"

James learned an important rule about reading, not by filling in any worksheet, not even by teacher-directed instruction; he learned because he was motivated to make meaning—the intention is paramount. He learned also because of the structure of the teacher-student interaction in a shared book experience.

## THE SHARED BOOK EXPERIENCE

What attracts children to make meaning from what is read is the story, the possibility of penetrating new worlds (Bruner, 1984). The shared book experience, in which adult and child engage in an interactive negotiation of meaning (Cochran-Smith, 1984), is how children first learn about books and the power of the written word to expand their knowledge of the world  (Wells, 1986), to expand their vocabulary and learn concepts about print (Clay, 1982; Holdaway, 1979), and to develop a positive and aesthetic attitude toward reading books (Teale, 1984). Important elements of the shared book experience that combine to create an effective teaching-learning situation include rereadings, the nature of materials being read, meaningful tasks, and the collaboration of teacher and student in a negotiation of meaning.

In the shared book experience, the initial reading of a story by the teacher is usually followed by rereadings in which the children are encouraged to participate. Predictable books containing simple narratives are frequently used in shared book experiences with emergent readers because they contain a support system that enables beginning readers to read fluently despite their inability to decode the words. This support system includes repetition of phrases, rhythm, rhyme, simple plots, and close picture to print relationship (Holdaway, 1979).

## THE TASK OF PREDICTING OUTCOMES

In the initial reading of *Hairy Bear,* James and his peers were asked to make predictions about what would happen next. Research (Anderson, Shirey, & Mason, 1981; Au & Mason, 1981–1982; Hansen, 1981) provides evidence that the prereading strategy of asking students to predict is an effective instructional method that facilitates access to prior knowledge and the use of that knowledge in a strategy that constructs the meaning of the text. James understood the character's intention to protect himself or to attack the robber by readying himself with a weapon.

During subsequent discussion, he explained that he used his prior knowledge of robberies, robbers, and how to cope with them. James' verbalizations about strategy use was facilitated by focusing on a task that was specific and easily understood by an emergent reader, that of predicting outcomes. Pressley (1983) believes that tasks that are more concrete and explicit are more likely to trigger the retrieval and use of a child's experience.

## THE TEACHER'S ROLE

The role of the adult has been described as one that provides scaffolding upon which the child learns how to understand (Bruner, 1984; Heath & Thomas, 1984; Ninio & Bruner, 1978). The adult builds one comment or question on another, each time relinguishing more control to the child as the child internalizes the processes first modeled and guided by the adult until finally the child can perform the strategies independently.

Harste, Woodward, and Burke (1984) reject the notion of scaffolding and emphasize the child as having a more dominant role in formulating and using strategies. It is through the open-inquiry method in a shared book experience, such as those used in James' literacy event, that the *child* becomes the curriculum informer; the adult then makes informed choices about what kinds of learning activities to provide in order to help the child make his own discoveries. Wells (1986) views the child as an active maker of meaning and the adult as the one who triggers the mechanism and influences the rate to help children reinvent language for themselves.

## THE POWER OF VERBALIZATION

In James' literacy event, the shared book experience had an added element that was included to instigate the development of strategies; James had an opportunity to further discuss his thinking processes individually with the teacher while they viewed a videotape of the shared book experience.

James was asked to predict in the initial reading of the story and asked the reason for his prediction in the subsequent individual interview. The question was in the form of a nondirective probe: "How did you know that?" Ericsson and Simon (1980) believe that verbalization would accelerate the learning process or the development of cognitive strategies if subjects are asked to provide reasons for actions or a statement of a rule.

For young children learning to use language, especially in speech, invitations to verbalize their knowledge about language occur naturally in the course of interaction. However, as Wells (1986) concluded from his comparison of home and school language, children are not frequently given the opportunity to verbalize their knowledge about language processing during school instruction. Studies by Harste et al. (1984) and Langer (1986) examined children's strategies in the natural setting of reading and writing activities in the classroom. Both indicated the importance of allowing children to discuss and reflect on strategy use.

Successful intervention studies which emphasize the role of verbalization in strategic reading development (Brown & Palinscar, 1982; Miller, 1985; Paris, Lipson, & Wixson, 1983) involve the students in a discussion *during* the act of getting meaning from text. Brown (1987) does not advise the use of verbal reports during reading for young children because they do not seem able to cope with the split focus necessary to perform a strategy and verbalize about it at the same time. She believes the use of retrospective reports, in which the student verbalizes about strategy use *after* performance, is more appropriate but only if the strategy is made available in a concrete way, hence the use of the videotape to stimulate recall.

Peterson, Swing, Braverman, and Buss (1982) used a stimulated recall method to study the cognitive processes of fifth- and sixth-grade students involved in the study of probability. Following the lessons, each student viewed the videotape and reported individually to an interviewer what she/he was doing at the time. Results show that the students who were able to provide detailed explanations about their use of specific cognitive strategies did better on the achievement test than those that did not.

In summary, the structure of James' literacy event which facilitated the formulation of the strategy of "looking at the book" has been described as containing the following elements:

1. The use of the familiar simple narrative in the form of predictable books.
2. The adult support system inherent in the shared book experience.
3. The use of specific probing in the familiar task of predicting outcomes.
4. The use of a videotape of the shared book experience as concrete evidence of performance to stimulate recall and assist retrospection.

## THE SAILOR WHO BUILDS A SHIP WHILE AT SEA

Harste et al. (1984) liken the teacher to a sailor who must build a ship while at sea. *During* the subsequent individual interview in which James was asked for the reasons for his predictions, the teacher made an *informed choice* in guiding the dialogue that produced a teaching-learning situation. It did not happen serendipitously. Certain things were known about James:

1. He was motivated to make meaning in a shared book experience; he had experience in that context.
2. He had not yet mastered spoken to written word correspondence.

3.  He was more of a gist reader, readily filling in gaps of information created by his lack of fluency with print with his own prior knowledge; he used personal experiences or memory of the stories' language from initial readings.
4.  He was ready to perceive the difference in information gathered from the story text and that of his own head.

The teacher did not plan the error in order to provide James with the opportunity to formulate a strategy and advance his literacy development. The teacher used her knowledge of James' stage of development and the opportunity provided by his error to trigger a mechanism that would allow James to reinvent language for himself.

Vygotsky (1978, 1987) believed that we could only learn more about the learning process if we studied it as a living process, not as an object, if we examined the potential for learning, not just what has already been learned. In this way, learning is programmed to match the child's developmental level. Vygotsky (1978) terms that level the zone of proximal development, "the distance between actual development as determined by independent problem solving and the level of potential development as determined through problem solving under adult guidance" (p. 86).

## ARE THEIR REFLECTIONS ACCURATE?

In asking James to explain why he chose a baseball bat as the bear's weapon, he provided a report of his own cognitive or thinking processes; he stepped back and considered his own cognitive operations as objects of thought or reflected on his own thinking. One issue for gathering information from verbal reports is the distance between the thought and its expression: Can we trust that James' reflections will uncover the actual processes he used or will they be fabrications?

Rowe and Harste (1986) report from their extensive observations that young children naturally and spontaneously comment on the discoveries they are making as they solve literacy problems. Elements of the structure of James' literacy event increased the possibility that his reflections would match his performance: the familiar task of predicting outcomes, adult support, and the use of the videotape to provide concrete evidence of performance. If there were distortions between what James actually did and what he says he did, they are not as significant as the reasoning he reveals; we are still learning something about his cognitive operations that can be used to pinpoint his zone of proximal development, shape the literacy event, and advance his development as a strategic reader.

## METACOGNITIVE STRATEGIES

James was asked to explain what strategy he had used to make a prediction. Strategies are described by Paris (1990) as personal tactics for reading. They become metacognitive in nature when they reflect a conscious awareness of thinking as one plans, controls, or evaluates one's cognition (Brown, 1987). Paris (1990) defines metacognition as having "a mirror on one's knowledge and thinking" (p. 11) that can be generated by the individual and shared among people.

The ability to reflect on one's own activities when reading is necessary for effective comprehension (Brown & Palinscar, 1982; Flavell, 1981, 1987). Holdaway (1979) explains that self-regulation is crucial to the mastering of strategies: "There is no better system to control the complexities and intricacies of each person's learning than that person's own and self-determination within reach of humane and informed help" (p. 170).

## METACOGNITION AND THE YOUNG CHILD

Theorists and researchers generally agree that strategic behavior should begin in the initial stages of learning to read but some believe that young children tend not to employ strategies (Brown, 1987; Flavell, 1981; Paris et al., 1983). They are excluded from research because of their lack of fluency in reading (Forrest-Pressley & Waller, 1984). Yet the strategic behavior of young children has been described in studies of language development (Bissex, 1980; Harste et al., 1984; Wells, 1986) and of the development of phonemic awareness (Cunningham, 1986/1987). In studies of the shared book experiences, metacognitive constructs appeared in children as young as four (Mason, 1984; Sulzby, 1985).

It is not necessary to wait for children to become fluent readers before we can study the circumstances under which they become strategic readers. In a study by Elfant (1990), the cognitive and metacognitive strategies used by first graders in understanding a narrative during a shared book experience were identified and categorized. Twelve above-average first graders were chosen in order to ascertain what children are capable of knowing and doing under the best of circumstances. The children were randomly placed in three groups of four; each group met eight times, resulting in a total of 24 shared book experience sessions. Eight simple narratives were chosen from the Story Box collection of the Wright Group (San Diego, California) and the Ready to Read collection of the Richard Owen Publishing Company (Katonah, New York).

For each session, the teacher met individually with one of the children in the group after the shared book experience to discuss strategy use while viewing a videotape of the group session. Each child had the opportunity to be interviewed twice during the study. The interviews were audiotaped, transcribed into written dialogue together with the dialogue from the shared book experiences, and analyzed for strategy use.

The analysis generated seven broad categories of strategies:

1. *Predicting Outcomes* (O), used to generate ideas about what will happen next in the story: "I think the ghost will boo a cat or a dog next."
2. *Interpreting* (I), used to generate ideas about meaning: "The ghost was counting his scaring people."
3. *Questioning* (Q), used to state uncertainties or confusion: "Is there any such thing as a birdwoman?"
4. *Refining* (R), used to elaborate predictions/interpretations: "I changed my mind because the witch could throw a potion."
5. *Citing Evidence* (C), used to support predictions/interpretations: "I think it's a witch because of the crumbled-up face."
6. *Personalizing* (P), used to apply text to life situations: "If your hand could go through it (the ghost), I would kick it."
7. *Evaluating* (E), used to critique the text, to make judgments: "Her eyes is funny. One goes that way."

When the frequency of strategy use was analyzed, a pattern in use of the categories was found that was consistent across the 12 students, the eight stories, and the three groups, as exemplified in the percentage of the use of each category of strategy for the 12 students (Figure 9.1).

**Figure 9.1.    Pattern in strategy use for all 12 students.**

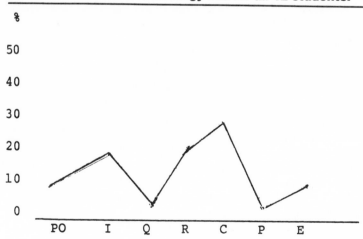

The analysis also revealed categories describing what point of information was being processed. For example, the students attended to the illustrations more than the written text as a source of information. When they elaborated on their initial predictions and interpretations, it was often in agreement or disagreement with their peers' ideas or reflected inferences they had made about the characters' motives or feelings. When they were asked to cite evidence for their interpretations, they used the text more often than their own experiences. Their evaluations were generally more concerned with their own performance than with those of their peers or the content of the text.

Individual differences in strategy use were most apparent in how the students supported their interpretations with prior knowledge in the category of citing evidence. Some students used a variety of informational sources while others concentrated on using one or two. Some were more general in citing the source of their understandings while others specified the text, another book, a movie, or a person. Some made generalizations and systematically searched the text and their own experiences to support them while others adhered to the script of planned predictions.

There were also differences among the students in the length of their elaborations (Refining). Some discussed their knowledge of literary genre and book-making conventions, made inferences about the authors' or the illustrators' purposes, and evaluated the content of the text to the point of making suggestions as to how it could be improved.

Analysis of their self-initiated questions revealed concerns about the picture-print relationship; they seemed to think that all the information in the written text should be depicted in the illustrations. There were also times in which their recent experiences created a misunderstanding of the main theme in a story; one student felt the robber was really after the dog and not the gold because she had just seen a movie about a dog-napping.

A second analysis of the students' responses during the shared book experiences and the subsequent interviews was made in order to ascertain which responses could be considered metacognitive in nature. A stricter definition of metacognition than that of Paris (1990) was used because there had been little research done in this area with emergent readers. Piaget's (1976) concept of reflected abstraction was applied so that only responses which concerned reflections that were abstracted from the context were considered metacognitive. For example, the response, "I know that because I read the title" would be considered merely cognitive; in order to be metacognitive, the response would be, "I know those things because I read titles."

As a result of using a strict criterion, very few responses were categorized as metacognitive, only 14 of the 1,974 responses analyzed.

Those responses included the students' discussing their knowledge of their own abilities; they know about illustrations because they can draw; they know about stories because they write them. They also talked about their strategies, how they use information from movies and other books in order to understand new stories. There were incidents in which the students were consciously aware that they were having difficulty understanding a concept: Chris could not predict the ghost would scare a milkman next because he had never learned what a milkman was; Frank reflected on the concept of a ghost who could not rest until someone knocked him down as being difficult for him to understand.

The inclusion of the individual interviews, as teacher and student watched the videotape, had a profound effect on the use of strategies. Initial predicting, interpreting, questioning, and refining occurred during the first reading of the story and the rereading. It was during the individual interviews that a large majority of the higher-level categories of citing evidence, personalizing, and evaluating were used, and metacognitive statements appeared.

Several attributes or characteristics of learners, some adapted from Flavell (1987), that would lead to the development of metacognition were proposed and supported with evidence from the analyses of the students' responses. The students' cognitive strategies surrounding the metacognitive statements were described as were the characteristics of the students as learners extracted from their performance in general. The attributes are the following:

1.  A developing sense of self: (a) an understanding of their own special talents; (b) courage to cope with cognitive confusion.
2.  An ability to evaluate their own cognition: (a) to evaluate others' interpretations including peers, authors, and illustrators; (b) to more deeply process the stories by personalizing.
3.  A sensitivity to imagery: (a) to imagine the thoughts of others, peers, characters, authors, illustrators; (b) to create a mental image of the events in the story, to relate the written text and the illustrations.
4.  An ability to interrelate information: (a) to cite evidence from many sources of information; (b) to use prior knowledge and information from peers to elaborate on understandings.

The findings of this study support the conclusion that strategy development, both cognitive and metacognitive, is *task*-dependent, *time*-dependent, and *knowledge*-dependent.

This study accomplished the development and implementation of appropriate tasks that provoked the use and development of young children's strategies. The first analysis of the students' responses revealed a pattern in the use of cognitive strategies that was consistent across all students, stories, and groups. It seems that the existence of this pattern, along with the increase in the use of more complicated strategies in the individual interviews, was dependent on the highly structured and appropriate procedures: The specific and understandable task of predicting outcomes, the concrete evidence of the videotape, and the opportunity to engage in a collaboration with the teacher who facilitated the verbalization of strategy use.

The procedures of this study provided time for the student to apply, formulate, and reflect on strategy use. The students had time in the first reading to get to know the events and characters, time in the rereadings to refine meanings, time to listen to peers, time to reflect while watching the videotape, and most important, time to be confused and attempt to resolve problems that were often self-initiated.

In this study, the use of the categories that described the sources of information being processed varied among the students. As the students cited evidence to support their predictions and interpretations, there seemed to be a progression from using a simple kind of knowledge about story characters and events to the use of more complex information about literary genre and book-making conventions. The students with more sophisticated knowledge were also those who were able to use the higher-level strategies of personalizing and evaluating.

This study offers important considerations for the formulation of instrucional practices that will help children develop cognitive and metacognitive strategies. It is important to give children the opportunity to tell what they know. That opportunity is provided through the teacher's questioning in a collaborative interaction with the students and through extended access to the stories that are presented to them.

In a collaborative interaction with students, the teacher strives to understand what a child already knows and needs to know. Langer (1986) states that it is a "sociocognitively sensitive" (p. 141) teacher that views the child from the child's point of view. The teacher can gather knowledge about students' comprehension by helping them verbalize about what they are doing to solve the problem of understanding stories. The procedure can be as simple as asking them, "How did you know that?"

The results of this study indicate that there are young children who are capable of verbalizations about their strategy use and metacognition emerges as early as they begin to learn to read. Teachers should be aware that there are children who are capable of reflecting consciously about their own cognition and raise their expectations about the development of metacognition to include the emergent reader.

It is important for teachers to understand when children would be able to reflectively access their strategies. The children need extended access to the stories. The findings of this study indicate that children first need time to get acquainted with the story's characters and events in the first reading. It is during the rereadings that they are given time to refine their interpretations through questioning, self-initiated concerns, and dialogue with peers that the teacher can begin to ask, "How did you know that?" The procedure in this study in which individual students viewed videotapes of the shared book experiences may be difficult to implement in a regular classroom setting. However, the opportunity to verbalize about strategy use can occur in the group setting of the shared book experience as children discuss their understandings.

The scope of this study does not support recommending that the descriptions of strategies serve as models for the formulation of instruction; the findings indicate that individuals differ in the amount and complexity of strategy use and knowledge. However, the strategies can serve as a guide to what children are capable of knowing and doing in understanding stories. This study indicates that first graders seem to be:

1. Ready to discuss their strategy use.
2. Ready to make their transition to using print.
3. Expecting a close relationship between the illustrations and the print.
4. Ready to interpret and evaluate their own cognitive talent and those of their peers.
5. Acquiring more sophisticated knowledge about stories, literary genre, book-making conventions, and the purposes of the author and illustrator.
6. Occasionally able to formulate generalizations about strategy use that are abstracted from the context of the stories.
7. Able to monitor their comprehension to alleviate cognitive confusion.

In the final analysis, what really determines the ability to understand anything is how much knowledge one has about the topic. Although James said "baseball bat" instead of the tennis racket in the picture, he was using his knowledge of how one copes with robbers. Pearson and Dole (1988) suggest that good readers may not need instruction in comprehension because they know more about everything they read and intuitively know how to get information from text.

The emphasis on knowledge as being the determinant of effective comprehension has implications for what we understand about the development of metacognition. If children are consistently given the opportunity to verbalize and reflect on their strategy use, they will begin to build a store of experiences that they can apply to future problems. They will generalize across experiences and create new rules for the use of strategies, develop a "mind set" for the kind of awareness, a self-reflection, that can travel with them throughout their school career.

The choice of task and materials also has an impact on the students' development of effective comprehension strategies. As sociocognitively sensitive teachers interact with students, they discover the level at which they are particularly sensitive to instruction, their zone of proximal development (Vygotsky, 1978). Teachers need to use this knowledge to choose materials and problem-solving tasks at the appropriate level of complexity. It seems that more complex tasks would provide a degree of instability which will provoke a "readiness for developmental change" (Kamberelis & Sulzby, 1988). The instability would cause the children to monitor their comprehension, and opportunity would be provided for a metacognitive experience.

This study suggests that metacognitive strategies develop along with literacy skills; these children were in the emergent stages of learning to read; hence their metacognitive strategies were in the emergent stage of development. It has provided some insight into those aspects of metacognition that are acquired early. Studies with a larger number of participants are needed to broaden that knowledge. Flavell (1987) believes that in the next few years more careful and critical examination of metacognition will occur and more theories will develop to more fully explain its development. Metacognition should be a priority in educational research because it is a necessary ingredient in effective comprehension.

## REFERENCES

Anderson, R.C., Shirey, L., & Mason, J.M. (1981). *An experimental analysis of round robin reading.* Paper presented at the annual meeting of the Psychonomic Society, Philadelphia, PA.

Au, K., & Mason, J. (1981–1982). Social organization factors in learning to read: The balance of the right hypothesis. *Reading Research Quarterly, 17,* 115–152.

Bissex, G. (1980). *Gyns at work: A child learns to read and write.* Cambridge, MA: Harvard University Press.

Brown, A.L. (1987). Metacognition, executive control, self-regulation, and other more mysterious mechanisms. In F.E. Weinert & R.H. Kluwe (Eds.), *Metacognition, motivation, and understanding* (pp. 65–116). Hillsdale, NJ: Lawrence Erlbaum Associates.

Brown, A.L., & Palinscar, A.S. (1989). Guided, cooperative learning and individual knowledge acquisition. In L.B. Resnick (Ed.), *Knowing, learning, and instruction: Essays in honor of Robert Glaser* (pp. 393–451). Hillsdale, NJ: Lawrence Erlbaum Associates.

Brown, A.L., & Palinscar, A.S. (1982). *Inducing strategic learning from texts by means of informed self-control training* (Tech Rep. No. 262). Urbana: University of Illinois, Center for the Study of Reading.

Bruner, J. (1984). Language, mind, and reading. In H. Goeman, A. Oberg, & F. Smith (Eds.), *Awakening to literacy* (pp. 193–200). Exeter, NH: Heinemann Educational Books.

Clay, M. (1982). *Observing young readers: Selected papers.* Portsmouth, NH: Heinemann.

Cochran-Smith, M. (1984). *The making of a reader.* Norwood, NJ: Ablex.

Cunningham, A.E. (1987). Phonemic awareness: The development of early reading competency (Doctoral dissertation, University of Michigan, 1986). *Dissertation Abstracts International, 48,* 282B.

Elfant, P.A. (1990). *The cognitive and metacognitive strategies of first graders during a shared book experience.* Unpublished doctoral dissertation, Fordham University, New York.

Ericsson, K.A., & Simon, H.A. (1980). Verbal reports as data. *Psychological Review, 87,* 215–251.

Flavell, J.H. (1981). Cognitive monitoring. In W.P. Dickson (Ed.), *Children's oral communication skills* (pp. 21–29). Hillsdale, NJ: Lawrence Erlbaum Associates.

Flavell, J.H. (1987). Speculations about the nature and development of metacognition. In F.E. Weinert & R.H. Kluwe (Eds.), *Metacognition, motivation, and understanding* (pp. 21–29). Hillsdale, NJ: Lawrence Erlbaum Associates.

Forest-Pressley, D.L., & Waller, T.G. (1984). *Cognition, metacognition, and reading.* New York: Springer-Verlag.

Hansen, J. (1981). The effects of inference training and practice on young children's reading comprehension. *Reading Research Quarterly, 3,* 391–403.

Harste, J.C., Woodward, V.A., & Burke, C.L. (1984). *Language stories and literacy lessons.* Portsmouth, NH: Heinemann.

Heath, S.B., & Thomas, C. (1984). The achievement of preschool literacy for mother and child. In H. Goelman, A.P. Oberg, & F. Smith (Eds.), *Awakening to literacy* (pp. 51–52). Norwood, NJ: Ablex.

Holdaway, D. (1979). *The foundations of literacy.* Portsmouth, NH: Heinemann.

Kamberelis, G., & Sulzby, E. (1988). Transitional knowledge in emerging literacy. In J.E. Readance & R.S. Baldwin (Eds.), *Dialogues in literacy research* (Thirty-seventh Yearbook of the National Reading Conference, pp. 95–106). Chicago: National Reading Conference.

Langer, J.A. (1986). *Children reading and writing: Structures and strategies.* Norwood, NJ: Ablex.

Mason, J.M. (1984). *Acquisition of knowledge about reading in the preschool period: An update and extension* (Tech. Rep. No. 318). Urbana: University of Illinois, Center for the Study of Reading.

Miller, G.E. (1985). The effects of general and specific self-instruction training on children's comprehension monitoring performances during reading. *Reading Research Quarterly, 20,* 616–628.

Ninio, A., & Bruner, J.S. (1978). The achievement and antecedent of labeling. *Journal of Child Language, 5,* 1–15.

Paris, S.G. (1990). How metacognition can promote academic learning and instruction. In B.J. Jones & L. Idol (Eds.), *Dimensions of thinking and cognitive instruction* (Vol. 1). Hillsdale, NJ: Lawrence Erlbaum Associates.

Paris, S.G., Lipson, M.Y., & Wixson, K.K. (1983). Becoming a strategic reader. *Contemporary Educational Psychology, 8,* 293–316.

Pearson, P.D., & Dole, J.A. (1988). *Explicit comprehension instruction: A review of research and a new conceptualization of instruction* (Tech. Rep. No. 427). Urbana: University of Illinois, Center for the Study of Reading.

Peterson, P.S., Swing, S.R., Braverman, M.T., & Buss, R. (1982). Students' aptitudes and their reports of cognitive processes during direct instruction. *Journal of Educational Psychology, 74,* 535–547.

Piaget, J. (1976). *The grasp of consciousness: Action and concept in the young child.* Cambridge, MA: Harvard University Press.

Pressley, M. (1983). Making meaningful materials easier to learn: Lessons from cognitive strategy research. In M. Pressley & J.R. Levin (Eds.), *Cognitive strategy research: Educational applications* (pp. 239–266). New York: Springer-Verlag.

Rowe, D.W., & Harste, J.C. (1986). Metalinguistic awareness in writing and reading: The young child as curricular informant. In D. Yaden & W.S. Templeton (Eds.), *Metalinguistic awareness and beginning literacy: Conceptualization what it means to read and write* (pp. 235–256). Portsmouth, NH: Heinemann.

Sulzby, E. (1985). Children's emergent reading of favorite storybooks: A developmental study. *Reading Research Quarterly, 20,* 458–481.

Teale, W.H. (1984). Reading to young children: Its significance for literacy development. In H. Goelman, A.P. Oberg, & F. Smith (Eds.), *Awakening to literacy* (pp. 110–121). Exeter, NH: Heinemann Educational Books.

Vygotsky, L.S. (1978). *Mind and society.* Cambridge, MA: MIT Press.

Vygotsky, L.S. (1987). *The collected works of L.S. Vygotsky* (R.W. Rieber & A.S. Caron, Eds.). New York: Plenum Press.

Wells, G. (1986). *The meaning makers.* Portsmouth, NH: Heinemann.

# Chapter 10

# Literature Webbing: Literacy Across the Curriculum

## Patricia Chaplin

A literature web is a framework that functions to integrate literacy across the curriculum. As a curriculum model, it can be used most effectively in preschool and primary-grade programs. A major purpose of the integrated model is to develop literacy skills in the context of a subject area. Such an approach is not only an efficient approach to managing the curriculum, but it is supported by current research findings on children's language learning (Strickland, 1989): Language is learned most effectively in meaningful contexts; the least effective way to teach language is through practice of isolated skills.

Literature webbing is referred to as thematic teaching, because a piece of children's literature becomes the theme or focus. From the central theme in the selected literature, natural experiences from content areas are related. Children's literature with similar themes are a major support of the literature web. Thematic teaching and learning is a way to bring together meaningful experiences that are otherwise separated into specific content areas and isolated concepts and skills. Literature is the major vehicle to achieve this goal. It is through whole texts, books, that a meaningful experience is introduced, and the story is further used to network this experience to others, resulting in the macroexperience or theme.

Thematic teaching has its foundations in recent findings on language learning and child development. Language is acquired and developed most effectively through meaningful contexts (Wells, 1986); they are the real experiences children use to learn language. Literature provides the basis to bring such natural experiences into the classroom because it is the human condition that is the core of each good story.

## LITERACY DEVELOPMENT OCCURS
## IN MEANINGFUL CONTEXTS

Learning takes place when the learner is involved in a thoughtful, goal-oriented task. When reading and writing evolve from real situations, literacy is used to accomplish goals (Teale & Sulzby, 1989). When reading and writing are embedded in activities directed toward some goal, other than literacy, children learn literacy (Taylor & Dorsey-Gaines, 1988).

Language becomes meaningless when it is an object of study; such teaching/learning is inefficient. Consider: why should young children want to spend 20 minutes on learning vowels? Another reason such an approach is ineffective for young children is that age and cognitive maturity have appeared as problematic in the acquisition of isolated literacy skills (Hiebert, 1980; Morgan, 1987). Teaching language skills devoid of context to young children does not promote the functional uses of language where it can be viewed by the student as a larger system to accomplish a real goal.

Clearly, concept and literacy development will occur when children are engaged in meaningful activities with objects and situations that are part of their environments (Strickland & Taylor, 1989). These experiences that we offer children will be beneficial to them only when they are part of the child's world. Using this same framework, language learning by the young child is nurtured when the adult offers a *meaningful content*, meaningful to the child not the adult. Such an environment can be shaped by the adult who knows the world of the child. Taylor (1987) has emphasized the need for adults to understand the worlds of childhood:

> Classrooms are part of the child's small world and we can fill them with an abundance of objects, images, and symbols that are meaningful to the young child. There is room for children to create their own magic when researchers and teachers recognize the authenticity of their experience, and see learning as a joint enterprise between adults and children, rather than imposing a system that encourages and often demands a one-way transfer of knowledge. We can begin ourselves by considering imaginatively what the smallness of our prepackaged world is likely to mean to the young children that we parent, study and teach. (p. 106)

## THE USE OF LITERATURE

In addition to engaging children in meaningful contexts to learn language, they also need to become involved in excellent forms of language. To foster their ability to use language, our young students need a language form that is more mature than their own. Children's literature is created for the world of the child without having an oversimplification of language forms.

Unlike workbook pages that distort language forms and preprimers and primers that rely heavily on word counts and sound/symbol regularities to teach language, literature attempts to present language in its best and most natural forms. Children's literature is drenched with words that paint pictures with rhythmic language and interesting vocabulary, unrestricted by formulas and word lists. Vocabulary development is the result of many book experiences (Chomsky, 1972; Fodor, 1966; Irwin, 1960; Ninio & Bruner, 1978).

Stories that we read in good children's literature are built on real situations that are part of the child's world. These natural experiences found in literature are constructed on the conceptual level of children and aimed at satisfying their insatiable curiosity. For example, Thalami Catterwell's *Aldita and the Forest* tells the story of a white butterfly who, because of her late hatch, was left alone by the other butterflies that migrated. Numerous concepts, central to the life-cycle of a butterfly, can be learned by young children because these are experiences that are real and natural. Beautiful illustrations are an additional source of information.

These are the stories that enable children to understand their world and to organize their minds. They allow the teacher to integrate content areas of literacy, science, math, social studies, and creative arts. They are the delights of childhood that bring the child to literacy growth and concept development using natural approaches.

## USING LITERATURE WEBBING
## TO TEACH LITERACY ACROSS THE CURRICULUM

Not only do most of the stories we read to our children contain events, themes, or characters that suggest activities and concepts from content areas, but they provide for skill and concept learning that are part of the suggested curriculum. Stories can introduce or reinforce ideas in science, social studies as well as literature. Mathematical concepts can be embedded in related experiences. Physical education and creative dramatics can be equally incorporated. Since these experiences are derived from the children's world, learning is meaningful and lasting.

Often many concepts and experiences will be an obvious outgrowth of the story. With thoughtful planning, the creative teacher will find even more ways to extend the story events across the curriculum to further affect the children's learning. While every story won't have experiences for every content area, the teacher can choose related stories which will provide the activities for other content areas. Children's literature may be related in several ways: Authorship, themes, character development may be used to develop the literature web across all areas of the curriculum.

## THE FORMAT OF A LITERATURE WEB

A literature web format is easy to develop and facilitates holistic teaching/ learning. A webbing format is a graphic that instantly clarifies what content areas the story overlays; it points to content areas that may need elaboration. As a visual, it displays the interrelatedness of the activities and the nature of their "fit" to the macroexperience.

Using the draft, or the first literature web, the teacher may make many determinations with respect to the individual needs of the students and group goals. Do these experiences fit the cognitive development of each student who will be a participant? Are additional experiences and activities needed to expand concept development? Is there a natural relationship among experiences? Are they part of the "Child's World"?

It is more likely that many of the activities and experiences will have overlap into two or more content areas. For example, puppetry is considered art as well as drama, when the puppets are used to dramatize the story or an event. Further, in an activity such as baking, several objectives from each of the major content areas are included: Measuring ingredients and keeping time can be considered math; observing changes in the dough before and after baking can be considered science; decorating the cookies or cakes can be an art experience; following directions is related to literacy development; and working as a group in baking demands cooperation, which may be categorized as social studies.

The more we explore and analyze literature webbing, the more proficient we become in recognizing the interrelatedness of activities and in finding experiences and activities in the story that are suitable for utilizing in the curriculum for the young child.

The following is a list of activities by content area that may have application in planning a literature web:

### Literacy Development

> Reading aloud
> Shared book experience
> Storytelling
> Independent reading
> Reading related literature: books with the same theme,
>     by the same author, having a similar main character, etc.

Creating big books and individual books with the same theme
Making shape books
Creating wall books
Creating comic strips
Keeping a literary journal
Writing in science and social studies logs
Making a literary poster
Writing a poem, a rhyme, a story
Writing directions for...
Discussing...
Writing a play
Telling adaptations of stories using the flannel
Playing book games (use pictures of the story to retell the story)
Writing newly discovered words in personal dictionaries

## Creative Arts: Music, Movement, Art, Drama

Dancing to depict some story element
Singing about a story element
Running, walking, jumping, stalking, etc., in response to or like
  story character
Using games, such as a tag game, to relate story event to
  movement
Engaging children in story related fingerplays
Singing
Rhyming activities
Choral speaking
Storytelling
Engaging students in plays and role playing
Making masks
Making puppets from paper bags, paper plate, socks,
  popsicle sticks
Sculpting figures with clay or flour-and-salt dough
Making murals
Illustrating books
Making props for plays
Leaf rubbings
Painting with vegetables and fruits

## Mathematics

Counting
Weighing

Measuring
Computing
Sorting
Matching
Graphing facts in a story or favorite choices
Making number problems about the story and solving them

## Science

Learning about story animals
Keeping a pet animal in the classroom
Visiting the zoo
Learning about plants and growing seeds in class
Observing
Keeping a science log (individual or group)
Baking
Making healthy snacks
Engaging in personal care and grooming
Learning about proper clothing for different weather types
Learning about the seasons

## Social Studies

Taking a trip to the post office, fire house, supermarket, police
station, library, etc.
Making maps depicting places in stories or showing where story
characters travel, for example, a map to show where the
Gingerbread Man went until he reached his encounter with
the Fox at the river
Board games using the story elements
Sharing and cooperating activities
Exploring careers through role playing
Acting out relationships between story characters
Discussing feelings demonstrated by characters

Presented above is a list of categorized activities that are generic in
nature. These can be used by applying them to different stories in specific
ways. Figures 10.1 through 10.4 show examples of literature webs using
some of these activities. These webs were developed by a group of teachers
and administrators who participated in an institute on natural approaches
to reading and writing for young children, sponsored by the New York
State Reading Association's Annual Conference in November 1989. The
show some of the ideas that can be developed with these principles. Let
them be the springboard for your own literature webbing and curriculum planning!

**Figure 10.1. A suggested literature web for the book *The Gingerbread Man*.**

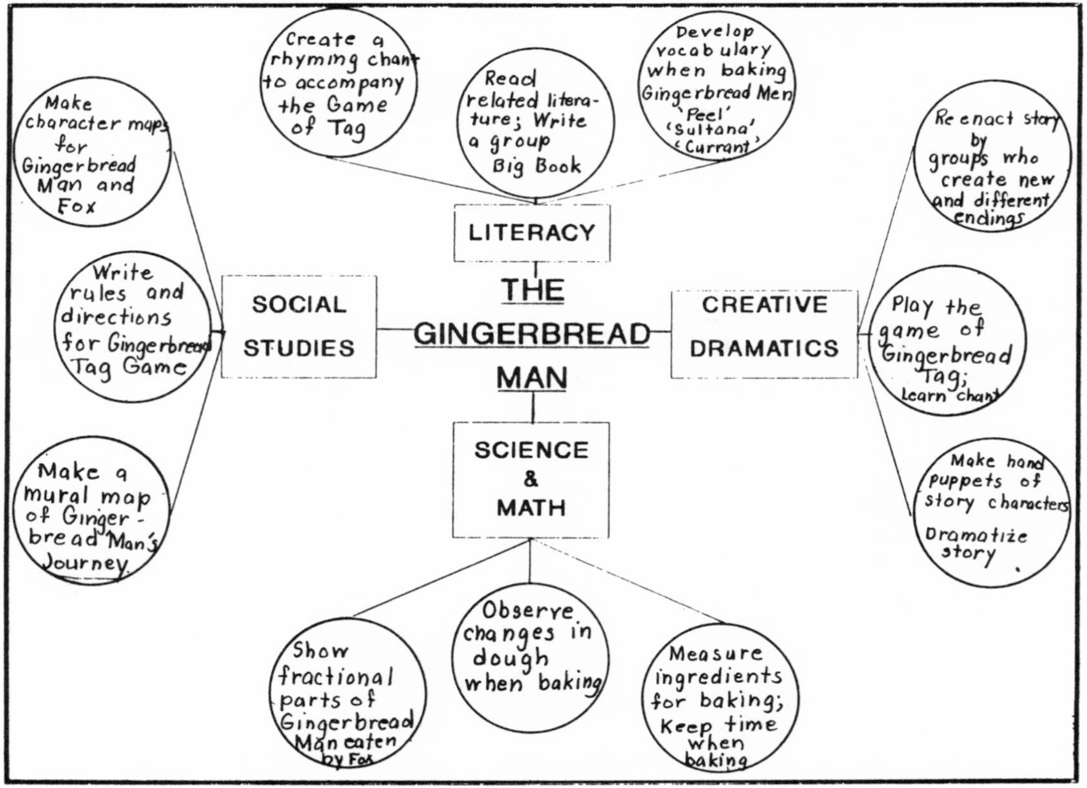

Reenact story by groups who create new and different endings

Play the game of Gingerbread Tag; learn chant

Make hand puppets of story characters; Dramatize story

Develop vocabulary when baking Gingerbread Men 'Peel' 'Sultana' 'Currant'

Read related literature; Write a group Big Book

Create a rhyming chant to accompany the Game of Tag

Measure ingredients for baking; Keep time when baking

Observe changes in dough when baking

Show fractional parts of Gingerbread Man eaten by Fox

Make character maps for Gingerbread Man and Fox

Write rules and directions for Gingerbread Tag Game

Make a mural map of Gingerbread Man's Journey

CREATIVE DRAMATICS

LITERACY

THE GINGERBREAD MAN

SCIENCE & MATH

SOCIAL STUDIES

**Figure 10.2. A suggested literature web for the book Stone Soup.**

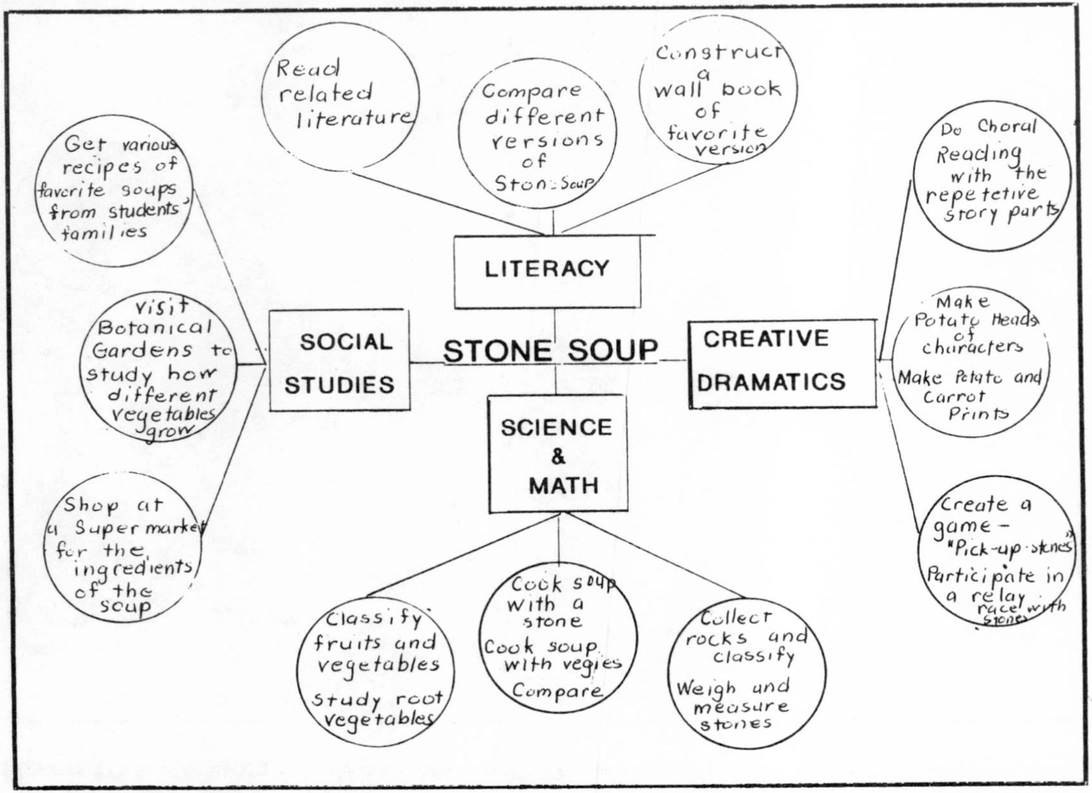

**Figure 10.3.  A suggested literature web for the book *Where the Wild Things Are*.**

Create Monster Runs Walks Dances Hops

Dramatize the story Choral read Mon

Make props for play! - Monster Masks - Paint a mural of a junk

Make a journal entry about "My Monster Manners"

Write Monster rhymes and riddles

Read related literature involving monster character(s)

CREATIVE DRAMATICS

LITERACY

**WHERE THE WILD THINGS ARE**

SCIENCE & MATH

SOCIAL STUDIES

Create a story map and study the time concepts and relationships of events

Find out whether there are "real" monsters

Make Healthy Monster Snacks

Classify behaviors as Polite or Monster Manners

Write sets of manners for different occasions

Discuss consequences of positive and negative behaviors

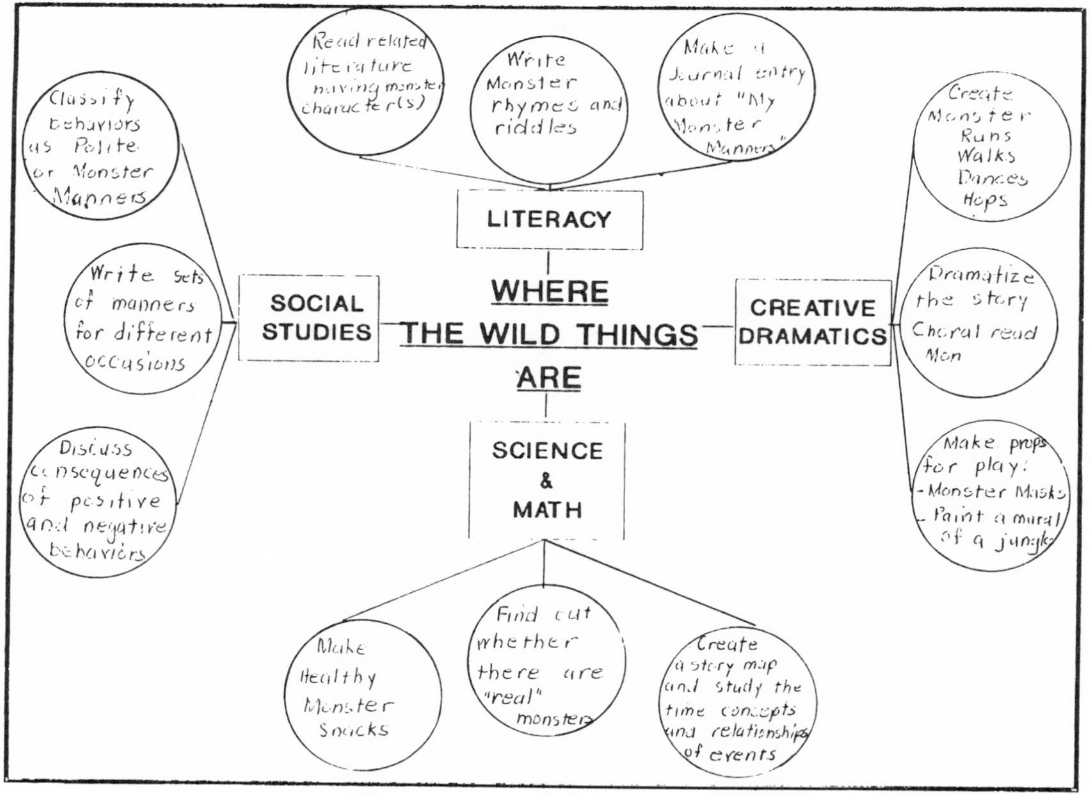

**Figure 10.4.   A suggested literature web for the book *If You Give a Mouse a Cookie*.**

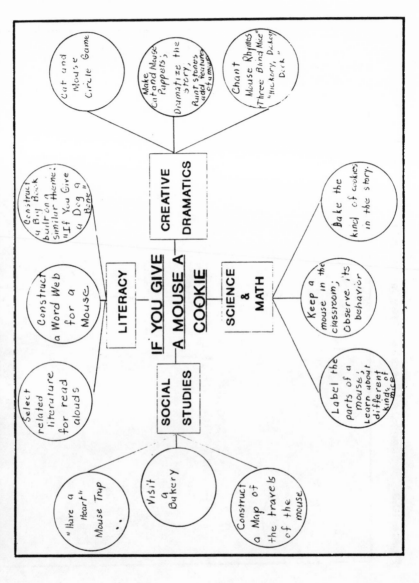

# REFERENCES

Chomsky, C. (1972). Stages in language development and reading exposure. *Harvard Educational Review, 42,* 1–33.

Fodor, M. (1966). *The effect of systematic reading of stories on the language development of culturally deprived children.* Unpublished doctoral dissertation, Cornell University, Ithaca, NY

Hiebert, E. (1980). The relationship of logical reasoning ability, oral language comprehension and home experiences to preschool children's print awareness. *Journal of Reading Behavior, 12,* 313–324.

Irwin, O. (1960). Infant speech: Effect of systematic reading of stories. *Journal of Speech and Hearing Research, 3,* 187–190.

Morgan, A.L. (1987). The development of written language awareness in black preschool children. *Journal of Reading Behavior, 19*(1), 49–66.

Ninio, A., & Bruner, J. (1978). The achievement and antecedent of labeling. *Journal of Child Language, 5,* 5–15.

Strickland, D.S. (1989). A model for change: Framework for an emergent literacy curriculum. In D.S. Strickland & L.M. Morrow (Eds.), *Emerging literacy: Young children learn to read and write.* Newark, DE: International Reading Association.

Strickland, D.S., & Taylor, D. (1989). Family storybook reading: Implications for children, families, and curriculum. In D.S. Strickland & L.M. Morrow (Eds.), *Emerging literacy: Young children learn to read and write.* Newark, DE: International Reading Association.

Taylor, D. (1987). The (con)textual worlds of childhood: An interpretive approach to alternate dimensions of experience. In B. Fillion, C. Hedley, & E. DiMartino (Eds.), *Home and school: Early Language and Reading.*

Taylor, D., & Dorsey-Gaines, C. (1988). *Growing up literate: Learning from inner city families.* Portsmouth, NH: Heinemann.

Teale, W.H., & Sulzby, E. (1989). Emergent literacy: New perspectives. In D.S. Strickland & L.M. Morrow (Eds.), *Emerging literacy: Young children learn to read and write.* Newark, DE: International Reading Association.

Wells, G. (1986). *The meaning makers: Children learning language and using language to learn.* Portsmouth, NH: Heinemann.

# Part III

# Supporting Literacy Development

# Chapter 11

# Creating Environments That Promote Literacy

## Florence D. Musiello

According to Fillion (1987), "Schools influence children's language, not only through the nature and content of instruction, but also through the linguistic environment they create" (p. 161). However as Halliday (1973), Fillion (1983, 1987), Mayher and Lester (1983), and others indicate, the range of language uses encouraged by schools is far more restricted than what children generally experience in natural environments such as the home.

Fillion (1983) argues that the most significant uses of language in many classrooms are by the teachers and textbook writers. Teachers set the tasks, select the topics, specify the procedures, explain the information, and ask the questions. Activities that require students to repeat almost verbatim material from the basal reader, workbook, blackboard, or other resources to answer comprehension, phonic, or other "test" questions teach children that their task is to acquire someone else's language, and that for every bit of knowledge there is a predetermined right answer.

If we accept that "language is the medium of interpersonal relationships, the medium of our mental life, the medium of learning" (Cazden, 1977, p. 42), then it appears that the creation and use of a natural language environment can be powerfully extended in the service of emergent literacy by giving students the opportunity and the means of using their language as a means of learning. However, the potential and actual connection of language and learning requires American educators to reconceptualize learning itself.

## PSYCHO-PHILOSOPHICAL PERSPECTIVES
## OF KNOWLEDGE AND CLASSROOM PRACTICE

Having examined some of the major themes in differing educational ideologies, Pope and Keen (1981; Pope, 1982) observed that the cultural transmission approach, which has dominated Western education, sees the primary task of the educator as the transmission of the information, rules, and values which form the "truths" of the cultural heritage. The teacher's philosophical view is that absolute truth can be accumulated bit by bit, subject by subject, since "true knowledge" corresponds to the world as it is, and is therefore independent of the subjective constructions of the learner. Traditional teaching methods are not only based upon the cultural transmission philosophy but are often derived from the behaviorist educational psychology, which suggests that learning and student achievement are primarily responses to particular educational stimuli (Fillion & Brause, 1987). According to Barnes and Shemilt (1974) and Pope (1982), these teaching methods emphasize the student's role as a passive receiver rather than as an active participant. Curriculum content and the manner in which it is taught place little emphasis on the students' individual conceptions and active participation.

However, for major 20th-century theorists such as Bruner, Dewey, Kelly, Piaget, and Polanyi, the mind is dynamic; "knowing" involves the construction of reality and is therefore a personal, active, creative, rational, and emotional experience. Knowledge is seen as being produced by the transactions of an active person reaching out to make sense of the objects and events of the environment by constructing and interpreting experience. The constructivist view of knowledge supports the teacher who is concerned with the investigation and use of students' views in a teaching/learning dialogue, and who encourages students to create, reflect upon, and make known their individual constructions of some aspect of reality (Pope, 1982).

Kelly (1970) viewed learning as a personal exploration; for him, the teacher's role is to help children design and implement the experiments that result in learning. In order to become a participant in each enterprise, the teacher must try to see through the child's eyes. For Kelly, successful communication depends upon the extent to which people construe each other's construct systems. For the teaching-learning dialogue to be effective, the teacher must attempt to understand the student's frameworks. What is relevant to the learner is central if education is to be a joint venture between teacher and learner.

Kelly's theory is a human construct, a hypothesis waiting to be put to the test. Therefore, Pope (1982) argues that the challenge for educators is to create ways to experiment with constructivist notions in order to enhance our knowledge of the teaching-learning process.

According to Fillion and Brause (1987), "virtually all children have a natural facility with language learning that we have failed to recognize or exploit in our schools and classrooms" (p. 216). The creation and use of natural language environments to promote literacy depend on theories about how language develops and is influenced.

## LANGUAGE AND THINKING, AND LEARNING

Although the relationship of thought and language continues to be a controversial issue, various schools of psychology have proposed an explanation. Both Piaget (1959) and Vygotsky (1962) believed that in order to understand the nature of the relationship between mature thought and language, it is necessary to study their growth in the period from infancy to adolescence. Since they hypothesized that children's thought differed from adults' not only in degree but also in kind, they studied children's use of language. Piaget and Vygotsky both observed that, in fact, language did serve different functions in childhood than in maturity, and that parents, peers, and others played a role in the growth of children's thought and language. Piaget proposed that egocentrism, the cognitive inability to differentiate one's own perspective from another's, is a stage in the growth of children's thought which is reflected in their use of language. Furthermore, he maintained that adults think socially even when alone, while children think individually even in the company of others.

Piaget speculated that social experiences that rely on language may facilitate the growth from egocentric to logical thought. He argued that in their interactions with each other, children often realize that they have failed to communicate. With this realization, attempts are made to consider, even anticipate, another's viewpoint and to speak accordingly. Therefore, Piaget proposed that open-ended exchange among peers is an important factor in the growth of thought and the use of language (DeLisi, 1981).

Although Vygotsky (1962) agreed with Piaget that there are differences between children's and adults' use of speech, he did not believe that egocentric speech disappeared in late childhood. Instead Vygotsky argued that the direction of intellectual growth was from social to individual. He believed that the early forms of thought and speech are at first performed in a social context but that once mastered, psychological functions are gradually transformed or internalized. Vygotsky explained that while speech and thought have independent origins, they merge during childhood.

Vygotsky (1962) argued that in the final stages in the merger of speech and thought, egocentric speech precedes action, and eventually "goes underground." It is no longer egocentric speech but has become inner speech. Vygotsky believed that egocentric speech is the first form of speech in the service of thought, and that when it becomes internalized as inner speech, the shift from the interpersonal to the intrapersonal is complete.

Furthermore, Vygotsky claimed that speech and thought are integrated into one psychological function as a consequence of social experience. He argued that early forms of speech are primarily communicative and that speech is the main mechanism by which adults assist and direct a child's problem-solving and goal-directed behaviors. Gradually children learn to use speech not only to communicate but also in the service of thought by using their own inner speech to monitor and guide thoughts and purposeful actions. The work of Vygotsky (1962) demonstrates that children's capacity for symbolic representation at first allows them to learn language and later to achieve powers of conceptualization in thought which exceed their powers of organization in speech.

According to DeLisi (1981), there is a similarity between Piaget and Vygotsky that may be more important than their points of contrast. Without denying that innate ability and learning are necessary components of the growth of thought and language, Piaget and Vygotsky both argued that they were not sufficient. Both focused on children's active involvement in the growth of their own intelligence, by pointing out that although the environment may attempt to provide answers and solutions, transmission of information or knowledge is rarely automatic when children are the pupils. Piaget and Vygotsky both proposed that the growth of thought and language separately and in the service of each other involves a process that is more than either maturation or rote learning. Instead, the child must order and regulate the contributions of his maturing natural abilities and the information from the environment through the process of development.

The Bullock (1975) report stresses that the teacher must create a classroom environment that encourages a wide range of language experiences in order for language to play its full role as a means of learning. Fillion (1985) maintains that "both in and out of school, learning often involves and occurs through language." Children describing their experiences to family and friends, and students discussing new ideas and concepts in classrooms, are both involved in shaping and extending their own understandings. Children are born learners; they not only learn language but they use that language as a means to learn (Britton, 1977).

It is Britton's (1970) contention that language is a major intellectual tool. Through language, experiences are interpreted and organized into generalized representations, which help us to formulate and reformulate what we know about the world. Through the processes of talking and writing and the internal language that accompanies listening and reading, knowledge is actively brought into being and at the same time the mental operations necessary for cognitive growth are developed (Fillion, 1985).

Fillion (1985) further maintains that children's language, especially their informal, personal, expressive language is important to the learning process in four critical ways: First, language is involved in developing interest in learning because it is through talking and writing about a given topic that children forge links between the information and personal experience. Second, language in the form of talk and print is part of the process of establishing relationships between prior knowledge and new information and concepts, since it helps children understand and appreciate it. Also in the process of solving problems through talking and writing, children will develop the mental operations that will help them with subsequent thinking and learning. Finally, since language is the "exposed edge of thought" (Britton, 1970), expressed language provides teachers and learners with the means to assess and develop the learner's cognitive processes (pp. 2880–2881).

The Bullock (1975) report indicates that language development is characterized as a facility in using language for an increasing range of purposes. The report further emphasizes that the real "basics" in language development are motivation, intention, and the opportunity to use language for one's own purposes including purposes generated by school learning.

In a natural language environment, emphasis must shift from language teaching to language learning, from skill building to intentional use, and from teacher as corrector to teacher as audience. Thus, the classroom becomes a language-learning environment and the search for ways to improve students' reading and writing is not restricted to a particular subject or time of the day but includes all areas of the curriculum and all areas of physical space. Arguing that language competence grows through the interaction of writing, talk, reading, and experience, the Bullock report advocates an educational approach patterned after natural language acquisition in the home environment in which the child encounters the need to use more elaborate forms to satisfy his own purposes, and is motivated to extend the complexity of his language. Therefore, the teacher's role in the language environment is of great significance.

## A DEVELOPMENTAL MODEL FOR TEACHING

A teaching model needs to be created by examining initial language learning; such a model is developmental rather than instructional. According to New Zealand educator, Don Holdaway (1979, pp. 22–23), developmental learning begins with immersion in an environment in which the skill to be learned is being used in purposeful ways. The adults create an environment that is emulative rather than instructional—that is, they set up a model of the skill in operation and induce activities that result in the child experimenting with successive approximations toward the use of the skill. Initially, the child attempts to do something like the skill he is trying to emulate; the activity is then refined by assistance from an adult with patience and tolerance for less than exact responses. Reinforcement, both intrinsic and extrinsic, is almost ideal since immediate rewards are available for almost every approximation regardless of the distance between the initial response and the "correct" response. The learner determines the aspects of the task that will be practiced as well as the length of the practice. Since the reinforcement is generally intrinsic, practice occurs whether or not the adult is attending. For example, the infant experimenting with oral language is rewarded by auditory sensations which he/she can compare with previous models and continues approximating mature speech even in the absence of a reinforcing adult. Therefore, practice tends to continue until critical aspects of the task are under comfortable, automatic control.

The developmental environment is secure and supportive; it provides help on call and freedom from any threat associated with learning a specific skill or accomplishing a particular task. It is understood that development proceeds continuously and in an orderly sequence but varies considerably among individuals.

Holdaway further theorized that the factors that influence natural literacy in the home could be applied to literacy instruction in the classroom. Researchers in different parts of the English-speaking world such as Marie Clay of New Zealand, Dolores Durkin of the United States, and Margaret Clark of Scotland had observed that the home environments of natural literacy learners (children who learned to read and write before coming to school) are similar in very specific ways. The factors researchers observed as common to those homes defined as positive literacy environments include:

1. Children are read to often, and frequently the same book is repeated a number of times.
2. Parents, siblings, and significant others serve as reading models since they are seen reading a variety of materials for pleasure as well as for purposes related to work and problem solving (cooking, assembling toys, etc.).
3. A wide variety of reading materials, including storybooks, newspapers, magazines, nonfiction, and work-related texts, is available throughout the home. Children are frequently taken to libraries and bookstores.
4. Children are involved with various forms of writing and writing materials including scribbling, copying, printing, and writing on

paper of different sizes, shapes, and colors with pencils, pens, magic markers, and crayons. Writing activities are generally functional and arise from such real-life situations as preparing shopping lists and following directions for activities worked on in cooperation with parents as well as writing and receiving personal notes and invitations.

5. The adults generally value reading and associate literacy with pleasure; therefore the children receive positive interactive responses to their questions and attempts at any activities related to literacy (Clark, 1976; Clay, 1967; Durkin, 1966; Morrow, 1983, 1989; Routman, 1988).

## NATURAL LANGUAGE ENVIRONMENTS AND SCHOOL-BASED LITERACY

The classroom that nourishes natural literacy requires the teacher to integrate a developmental model of teaching with a language-rich environment. Since there are so many attractive books written especially for children, literature provides a natural entrance into school-based literacy. By using memorable songs, poems, and stories in a shared-book experience, the teacher can recreate both the corporate spirit of the oral language tradition, exemplified in church services and playground games, and the visual intimacy with print characteristic of the bedtime story and lap reading (Holdaway, 1979).

Big Books and other stories from children's literature are selected for sharing because they are perennial favorites or have highly predictable texts. The book is placed on an easel or book stand so that all children can easily see and follow along while the teacher points distinctly to each word as she reads in a natural and lively manner. Children are encouraged to join in the reading whenever they are ready. They are invited to predict story events and vocabulary by using cues from illustrations and personal experience, and to listen to confirm or reconsider their predictions. With teacher guidance, the children naturally become aware of the correspondence between the spoken and written word, left to right, top to bottom progression, some sight vocabulary, the concept of a word and the spaces between words, as well as the conventions of print such as capital letters, punctuation, and indentation.

Each new book is introduced by developing the necessary background knowledge for understanding the story. Purposes for reading are set, and questions asked that focus on prediction and higher levels of thinking. Discussion includes reactions to the title and illustrations, information about the author, comparisons to personal experience and other stories, as well as responses to the behavior of the characters, the mood, and/or setting. Vocabulary is discussed in context while personal interpretation and reactions are encouraged. The experience is filled with energy as teacher and children mutually enjoy literature.

Rereadings, usually on request, increase unison participation by deepening understanding and enjoyable listening, especially for children who need more repetition in order to develop strong memory models. Independent experience and expression is encouraged by creative exploration that involves all the expressive arts. Children may engage in readinglike and reading behaviors using both the big and little book versions of the shared book texts. They may work alone or with peers to dramatize, create illustrations, build scenes with blocks, or role play "as teacher" using materials and experiences based on the shared books.

As with reading, the developmental model can be applied to writing. In traditional classrooms when teachers begin writing lessons, they instruct. They stand up and transmit information about letter-sound correspondences while children sit and listen. Although this may be the logical starting point from the perspective of adults who know the written system, Bissex (1987) argues that children are already keenly aware of the sound systems of language as revealed by the invented spellings they create. Since children come to school with knowledge that could make literacy learning more sensible and efficient for them, Bissex maintains that the environment must build on that knowledge by allowing children to show us what they already know.

The research of Emilia Ferreiro (1982, 1984) demonstrates that knowledge about literacy cannot simply be handed down to children, for when children learn to write, they reinvent the historic evolution of the writing system. They begin by drawing and representing ideas and objects with a single symbol or letterlike shape and continue to puzzle over the relationship between the printed marks and the meaning in speech until they discover the very nature of the system. They experiment by separating words with dots, writing from right to left, using one letter for each syllable, and inventing spellings. Each step in the process is fueled by the power of discovery as children come to understand that writing conveys meaning.

In a natural-language environment children learn how to write by writing. Developmental progression from symbol to scribble to standard orthography, from invented to standard spelling is tolerated, even encouraged. Children's writing is functional and arises from personal needs to communicate in real-life situations. They write and receive notes, letters, and invitations from each other, the teacher, and pen pals. They write in personal diaries and dialogue journals. The teacher responds to journal entries with sensitive feedback in the form of verbal or written comments that relate to the content rather than form. The children write books based on personal or shared-book experiences which they share with classmates and parents. The environment is alive with talk and information about print and language, and through the motivation to be understood skills develop.

## CREATING A PHYSICAL ENVIRONMENT
## TO SUPPORT NATURAL LANGUAGE LEARNING

Since the physical setting influences movement, behavior, and learning. Loughlin (1977) argues that the physical environment of the classroom is a powerful instrument that can become an extension of the teacher. Knowledge of the relationship between physical surroundings and behavior can help a teacher create an environment that is in harmony with the philosophical view of learning and the model for teaching.

The organization of space and materials influences children's cognitive and affective behaviors. For example, Loughlin points out that complex learning environments tend to promote sustained involvement, a long attention span, and independence from the teacher, while the side-by-side placement of materials often suggests to children useful ways to combine objects as well as links between ideas.

Therefore, it appears that in order to support the natural-language process and the development of emergent literacy, space, and literacy-oriented materials can be arranged to encourage group inquiry and foster interactive language between children, as well as between teacher and children. According to Morrow (1989), the physical environment for optimum literacy development must be designed around the concept that reading, writing, and oral language are interdisciplinary and should be integrated throughout the day, and in all areas of physical space.

In order to dramatize the importance of literacy behaviors, the Literacy Center, which includes the library, oral, and written language areas should become the focal point in the room (Morrow, 1989). Research (Morrow, 1987; Morrow & Weinstein, 1982) demonstrates that a well-designed library corner with a wide variety of easily accessible books and comfortable seating stimulates children to explore and enjoy books even during free-choice periods. Furthermore, while open shelves filled with display books and attractive posters capture children's attention and stimulate curiosity, well-stocked shelves organized with a system easily understood by young readers sustain interest. Huck (1976) recommends that a classroom library include at least 5 to 8 books per child while Morrow (1989) suggests that approximately 25 new books be introduced every two weeks to keep the collection stimulating. In addition to a wide variety of books representing many types of children's literature at a range of reading levels, the library corner should contain manipulatives such as stuffed animals and soft toys based on book characters, a feltboard with story props, puppets, and costumes to stimulate reading and readinglike behaviors, and oral language activities. Pillows, rugs, and rocking chairs can be used to create a cozy, homelike atmosphere that invites both interactive and independent experiences with books.

Since "writing floats on a sea of talk" (Britton, 1970), the writing area of the Literacy Center should support the cooperative spirit. A round table with chairs encourages small-group talk. For many children talk is a form of first draft; it allows students to share and test ideas. Observations by Dyson and Genishi (1982) demonstrate that the writing process is as much an oral as a written activity. They argue that the "muttering" of young children to themselves and their "chattering" with each other can be critical factors in the process of learning to write. As children interact in the writing area they serve as their own teacher-coaches. By questioning, modeling, and providing feedback, Dyson and Genishi observed that young writers developed the sense of audience and encouragement that enabled them to persevere.

The classroom environment must involve the children in an exploration of both oral and written language by providing a supportive social context. Therefore, the writing center should include materials such as puppets, flannel boards, tape recorders, and literature, as well as paper of various sizes and colors, magic markers, crayons, pencils, newspapers, and magazines to instigate talk, writing, and illustration. The teacher should create activities to demonstrate both the creative and functional uses of language. Children should be encouraged to write their own stories and poems as well as to write messages to each other, and to children and other personnel in the school, in addition to parents, relatives, and friends. Letters and cards may be written as holiday, birthday, or get-well greetings, as well as to say "thank you" for gifts, special assemblies, musical or dramatic performances.

Environmental print such as signs and labels can be used to help children recognize the functional nature of the printed word. Coat hooks, cubbies, and mailboxes can be labeled with children's names. Printed signs, such as "Don't feed the hamsters," or "Hang wet paintings here," help children cope with written directions and allow the teacher to work with individuals and groups without interruption. Classroom charts that list daily tasks, attendance, job responsibilities, work-center or independent assignments help the classroom function smoothly and efficiently while encouraging student independence. Similarly, bulletin boards and experience charts that include vocabulary lists as well as connected text from literature and content area instruction can be used to stimulate interest in a topic and word recognition practice.

Finally, in order for children to use their natural language abilities to support the growth of literacy and creative thinking, talk, reading, writing, and questioning must be integrated with all areas of the curriculum. The language arts must be seen as part of the environmental and curricular design of math, science, social studies, drama, music, and art rather than as a content area itself. Through the use of a linguistic, social, and physical environment that encourages natural language to evolve developmentally, the teacher can help children increase their conscious control of learning and develop a positive, successful attitude toward school-based literacy.

## REFERENCES

Barnes, D., & Shemilt, D. (1974). Transmission and interpretation. *Educational Review, 26,* 213–238.

Bissex, G.L. (1987). The beginnings of writing. In B. Fillion, C. Hedley, & E. DiMartino (Eds.), *Home and school: Early language and reading* (pp. 47–63). Norwood, NJ: Ablex.

Britton, J. (1970). *Language and learning.* Middlesex: Penguin.

Bullock, A.L.C. (1975). *A language for life.* London: Her Majesty's Stationery Office.

Cazden, C. (1977). Language, literacy and literature: Putting it all together. *National Elementary Principal, 57,* 40–42.

Clark, M.M. (1976). *Young fluent readers.* London: Heinemann Educational.

Clay, M. (1967). The reading behavior of five-year-old children: A research report. *New Zealand Journal of Educational Studies, 2,* 11–31.

DeLisi, R. (1981). Children's thought and language. *New York University Education Quarterly, 13,* 29–32.

Durkin, D. (1966). *Children who read early: Two longitudinal studies.* New York: Teachers College Press.

Dyson, A.H., & Genishi, C. (1982). Whatta ya tryin' to write? Writing as an interactive process. *Language Arts, 59,* 126–132.

Ferreiro, E. (1982). The relationship between oral and written language: The child's viewpoints. In Y. Goodman, M. Haussler, & D. Strickland (Eds.), *Oral and written language development research: Impact on the schools.* Urbana, IL: National Council of Teachers of English.

Ferreiro, E. (1984). The underlying logic of development. In H. Goelman, A. Oberg, & F. Smith (Eds.), *Awakening to literacy.* Exeter, NH: Heinemann.

Fillion, B. (1983). Let me see you learn. *Language Arts, 60,* 702–710.

Fillion, B. (1985). Language across the curriculum. In T. Husen & T.N. Postlewaite (Eds.), *The international encyclopedia of education research and studies* (Vol. 5, pp. 2878–2883). New York: Pergamon Press.

Fillion, B. (1987). School influences on the language of children. In B. Fillion, C. Hedley, & E. DiMartino (Eds.), *Home and school: Early language and reading* (pp. 155–168). Norwood, NJ: Ablex.

Fillion, B., & Brause, R.S. (1987). Research into classroom practices: What have we learned and where are we going? In J.R. Square (Ed.), *The dynamics of language learning: Research in reading and English.* Urbana, IL: National Conference on Research in English and ERIC RCS Center.

Halliday, M.A.K. (1973). *Explorations in the functions of language.* London: Arnold.

Holdaway, D. (1979). *The foundations of literacy.* New York: Ashton Scholastic.

Huck, C. (1976). *Children's literature in the elementary school* (3rd ed.). New York: Holt, Rinehart, & Winston.

Kelly, C.A. (1970). Behaviour is an experiment. In D. Bannister (Ed.), *Perspectives in personal construct theory* (pp. 255–269). London: Academic Press.

Loughlin, C.E. (1977). Understanding the learning environment. *Elementary School Journal, 78,* 125–131.

Mayher, J.S., & Lester, N.B. (1983). Putting learning first in writing to learn. *Language Arts, 60,* 717–722.

Morrow, L.M. (1983). Home and school correlates of early interest in literature. *Journal of Educational Research, 76,* 221–230.

Morrow, L.M. (1987). Promoting innercity children's recreational reading. *The Reading Teacher, 41,* 266–274.

Morrow, L.M. (1989). Designing the classroom to promote literacy development. In D.S. Strickland & L.M. Morrow (Eds.), *Emerging literacy: Young children learn to read and write.* Newark, DE: International Reading Association.

Morrow, L.M., & Weinstein, C.S. (1982). Increasing children's use of literature through programs and physical design changes. *Elementary School Journal, 83,* 131–137.

Piaget, J. (1959). *Language and thought of the child* (M. Gabain, Trans.). Paterson, NJ: Littlefield, Adams. (Original work published 1924)

Pope, M. (1982). Personal construction of formal knowledge. *Interchange, 13,* 3–14.

Pope, M.L., & Keen, T. (1981). *Personal construct psychology and education.* London: Academic Press.

Routman, R. (1988). *Transitions: From literature to literacy.* Portsmouth: NH: Heinemann.

Vygotsky, L.S. (1962). *Thought and language* (E. Haufmann & G. Vakar, Trans.). Cambridge, MA: The MIT Press. (Original work published 1934)

## Chapter 12

# New Directions in Literacy: The Empowerment Movement

**Regis G. Bernhardt**
**Anthony N. Baratta**

### INTRODUCTION

Previous chapters of this book focused on presentations of theoretical perspectives of language learning in young children and on descriptions of literacy programs that incorporate natural language approaches. The present chapter considers the dynamic interplay of the roles of school personnel in the implementation of literacy programs in school settings.

The thesis of the chapter combines two powerful dimensions of the school: (a) the critical impact of literacy and (b) the phenomenon of empowerment. The press for universal literacy in our society is a significant national goal, and the press for teacher empowerment is at the inchoate stage of development.

Our concept of literacy involves persons becoming educated, competent, and knowledgeable. Baratta (1990) stated that the goals of literacy will continue to be expanded in our country and in the world. There will be requirements for macroliteracy skills involving competency in multiple languages. The concept of tech-literacy will become increasingly important as advances take place in computer/technological dimensions.

Baratta also observed that degrees of competence in literacy differentiate between the haves and the have-nots in societies. The economic welfare of nations will be dependent upon advances made in expanding the definitions and goals of literacy and in increasing the literacy levels of citizens. The national and international emphases on literacy will continue to be stressed.

Empowerment is typically focused on teachers, but our concept of empowerment is not restricted to this level. Rather, it is focused on all of the persons who work directly with students in the achievement of the objectives of literacy efforts.

Environmental and cultural factors in society play heavy roles in the operation of the school as a social institution. No one actor, no constituency, no policymaker, nor any single citizen has exclusive dominance or control in the operation of the school. Thus the concepts of alliances, collaboratives, partnerships, and cooperatives become important in understanding the different nature of schools and the manner in which they respond to the press for universal literacy.

## THEORETICAL FRAMEWORK

The framework upon which the chapter is based was taken from the work of Duckworth (1981) who developed a paradigm for research on the contribution of school administration to student achievement. The administrator is characterized as the agent of educational policy. It is the task of the administrator to operationalize policy by influencing what takes place in classrooms. Duckworth's illustration of the paradigm is presented in Figure 12.1.

In the present context, the student achievement goal of the system is to produce a literate population. Definitions of what "a literate population" means vary among the members of the internal and exernal environments, as do ideas as to how a literate population can be achieved. In the present book, a variety of definitions have been presented, and a number of approaches and programs have been described.

Members of the environment press the educational policy-making bodies to decide upon and to implement policies which are intended to achieve the expressed goals. Political, economic, and social forces are brought to bear on the decision makers. They act in response to these influences, and they decide upon the operational goals and the overall framework to achieve the goals.

Our intent here is not to focus on the influence processes or the decision-making processes, but rather to accept as a given the fact that a definition of the desired outcomes and an overall strategy for its accomplishments are selected by the policymakers. Our focus is on the implementation of the overall strategies.

Our discussion concerns the work environments of students, teachers, administrators, and others within the school context. To successfully accomplish the goals of student literacy, new demands are placed upon all of the roles within the school. These demands require changes in the manner in which role incumbents function and in the responsibilities they are given.

**Figure 12.1. Research paradigm. Contribution of school administration to student achievement (Kenneth Duckworth, *Linking Educational Policy and Management with Student Achievement*, Center for Educational Policy and Management, University of Oregon, September, 1981).**

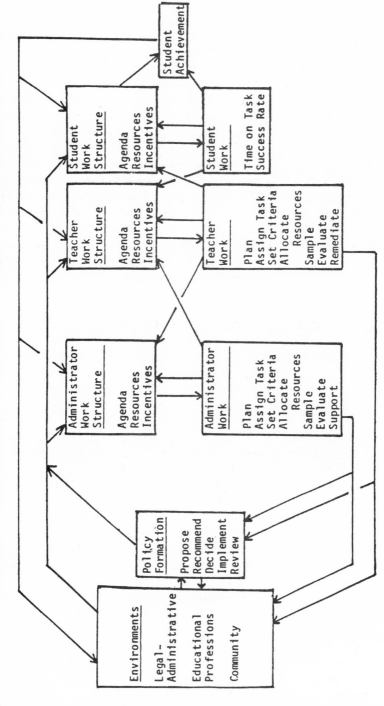

In the theoretical framework, the work structure of administrators focuses on their responsibilities to provide leadership in establishing goals and objectives, to assign tasks and responsibilities, to provide support, resources, and incentives, to evaluate processes and outcomes, and to make appropriate adjustments and changes in the school.

Teachers participate with administrators in establishing goals and objectives, and they define the work environment for students. Students, in turn, work within the environment provided for them by the teachers. The degree to which they achieve success, become literate, is dependent upon the structure and processes with which they are provided and the quality of the work that they perform. However, as illustrated in the theoretical framework, their work structure is determined through the complex interactions among the members of the environment in which schools exist, the policymakers of the system, and the educational personnel.

Given the complex nature of these interactions, it is essential that change take place in the basic structure of schools.

## RESTRUCTURING THE SCHOOL FOR LITERACY

The concept of restructuring the school for literacy may appear to some to be a simple process. Persons may have the mistaken view that officials possess the power to effect such changes through administrative decisions. Complex changes require the development of appropriate strategies and tactics well before the change process is even initiated. Changes required to implement programs intended to achieve even a universally supported concept, such as the development of a literate population, require more than a decision to act.

An example of the complexity of change in school settings is described in a recent volume of the National Society for the Study of Education in a chapter entitled, ''Textbooks, Textbook Publishers, and the Quality of Schooling'' (Westbury, 1990). Textbooks are defined as central books and central objects of attention in all modern forms of schooling. The roles played by persons, particularly the important roles of teachers, in decisions about textbooks are described.

Schools must be restructured in the immediate and long-term future for literacy programs to become effective. Such restructuring will have to occur in many areas. Physical plants will have to be restructured in order to respond to technological advancements. Governance systems will have to be restructured to more effectively respond to environmental demands. Formal recognition of the multiplicity of actors in the operation of schools will have to take place.

We expect that the hierarchical organizational chart of the governance structure of schools will become obsolete. We propose that it be replaced by a Concentric Model for School Restructure with students at the core and rings of actors surrounding the core (Figure 12.2). These rings include parents, teachers, support personnel, administrators and supervisors, government levels (local, state, federal), and the general environment.

In this model the hierarchical nature of the structure has been altered by expanding the influence and responsibilities of the persons having the most direct contact with the students. They will have greater control of the work environment of the students, and they will have greater responsibility for student performance. In turn, they will have greater support from school personnel and from governmental bodies.

## THE FOCUS ON STUDENTS

Literature concerning children is extensive and it comes from a vast array of unique and overlapping fields. Extensive research has been conducted in the disciplines of pedagogy, psychology, sociology, and so on. The dynamic and complex factors that influence children must be recognized, understood, and considered in deciding upon and implementing educational programs. The focus should not be on the environment, the policy makers, or the educational personnel.

Kirst and McLaughlin (1990) provide thoughtful analyses of the redefinitions of the contours of childhood. Among the problems facing children are: (a) poverty: nearly 20% of children in the United States live in poverty, up from 14% in 1969; (b) family structure: about one-half of all children and youth will live in a single-parent family for some period of their lives; (c) work: nearly 70% of mothers with children aged 6 to 17 were seeking work or worked in the formal labor market outside the home, and almost two-thirds of all 16- to 19-year-olds worked during some part of the year; and (d) health: health problems of the children of poverty have increased dramatically.

The implications of these facts require us to refocus our attention in policy-making and decision-making processes. Students must be directly involved in the interactive process. Kirst and McLaughlin (1990) talk about creating institutions and institutional tasks that actively engage children in identifying and solving their own problems and that involve them in tasks, group support systems, and long-term commitment.

## THE FOCUS ON PARENTS

In the Concentric Model for School Restructure, parents are in the ring surrounding the student. They are considered to be the student's first teachers.

**Figure 12.2. Baratta Concentric Model for School Restructure**

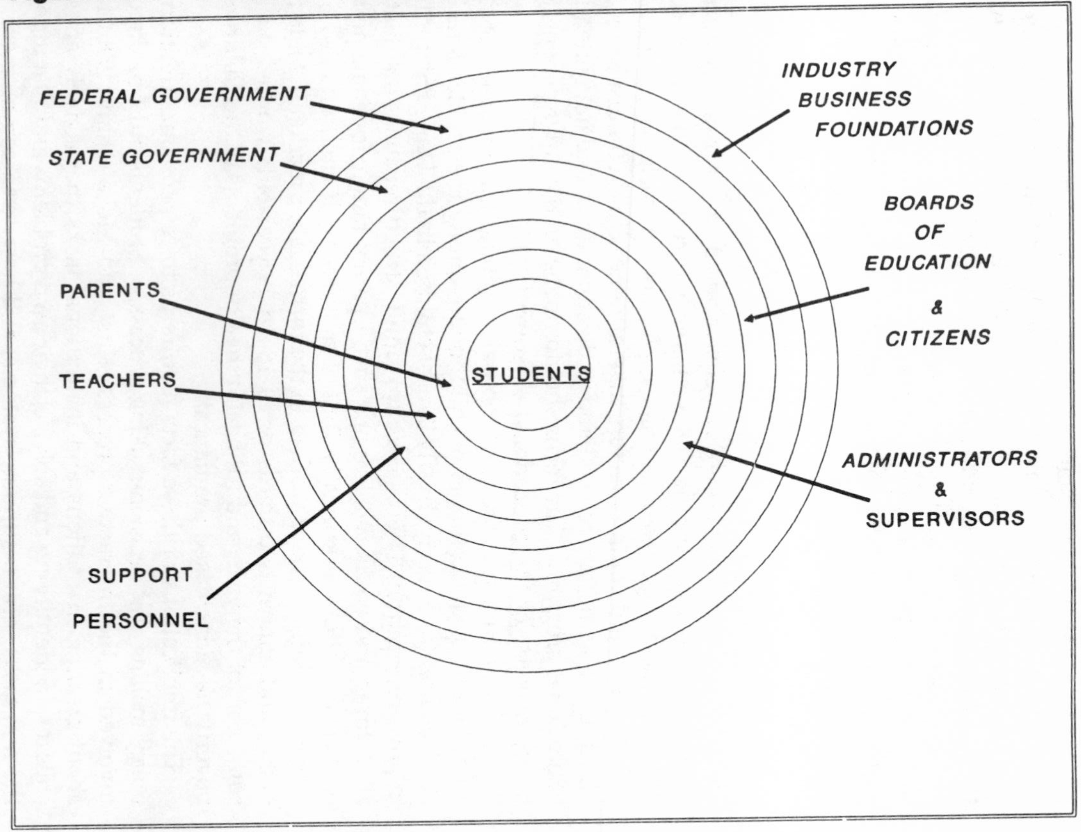

INDUSTRY
BUSINESS
FOUNDATIONS

BOARDS
OF
EDUCATION
&
CITIZENS

ADMINISTRATORS
&
SUPERVISORS

STUDENTS

FEDERAL GOVERNMENT

STATE GOVERNMENT

PARENTS

TEACHERS

SUPPORT
PERSONNEL

Parent involvement in schools has a long legacy, albeit hazy at times, controversial frequently, interfering occasionally, and nonexistent too often. Parent-teacher organizations and parent centers have existed for some time, and parents have been viewed as important "auxiliary support systems" for schools.

Recent developments have altered our views of parent involvement. Changes in family structures and the nature of the work force have caused parental involvement to take on different forms and functions. Because of the increased sensitivity of our nation to the advantages of educational systems in countries such as Japan, where the role of parents is a natural societal expectation, the importance of parent involvement is gaining greater currency.

Reed and Sautter (1990) focused on parent involvement in the Kappan Special Report on Children of Poverty. They indicated that barriers to full participation can be removed with training, encouragement, and resources that insure equal access. They found that parents can play a key role in many aspects of a school, providing a sense of community that can nurture as well as protect children.

Stevenson (cited in Reed & Sautter, 1990) found that, contrary to popular belief, black and Hispanic mothers were keenly interested in their children's education and wanted to be involved despite economic and social barriers to their doing so. The need to build new relationships with low-income parents in order to break the link between poverty and school failure was stressed by Davies (cited in Reed & Sautter, 1990).

In the past seven years the Fordham University/Community School Districts 4 and 10 Stay in School Partnership Program has been in operation in New York City. This is a collaborative program involving Fordham University's Graduate School of Education and Graduate School of Social Services with schools in CSD 4 in East Harlem, and CSD 10 in the Bronx. Activities were conducted which provided training, support, and encouragement for parents in various aspects of their roles. The program has resulted in increased parent involvement in general school activities and in stronger support for their children's education.

The boundary between the student and the parent in the Concentric Model is a permeable one. It is a matter of developing parents' attitudes, interests, skills, and so on. The boundary between parents and teachers is a less permeable one, but positive interaction is crucial. Careful attention will have to be given to developing relationships between parents and teachers. Parents need the support of teachers in their efforts to work with their children and to participate formally in the education process.

## THE FOCUS ON TEACHERS

It is a truism of organizational theory that the essence of an organization is determined by the quality of the primary functionaries. Ergo as teacher so the school. The quality of the teaching corps defines the quality of a school.

It is important that the work structure of teachers be such that they have an appropriate agenda, adequate resources, and the incentives to work effectively with students. Therefore, it is crucial that teachers have an appropriate role in decision-making processes affecting their work structures. They must be empowered.

Empowerment refers to making the boundaries that exist between teachers and the "upper levels" of the hierarchical organizational model more permeable. Teachers must be recognized as significant components in the human and social system of the school, and have the requisite power to influence decisions that affect students.

One of the major factors which prompted the teacher empowerment thrust was the reform movement of the 1980s. Corporate America expressed dissatisfaction with the quality of the work force being produced by schools. Major studies of schools were conducted and recommendations were made for significant changes in the total educational system.

Much of the reform literature of the early 1980s placed blame on teachers as a primary source of the problems with schools. If they could have done so, many writers would have waved a magic wand and removed the majority of teachers from schools. They would have replaced them with their concept of the best and brightest of society.

Later it became clear to the reformers that a major source of problems in schools rested with the conditions in which teachers were expected to function. Salary levels, job expectations, and work conditions were factors which drove the best and brightest teachers out of the field and which discouraged new candidates from entering teaching. In addition, alternative careers outside of the "traditionally accepted" fields for women reduced the pool of qualified teaching candidates. Efforts had to be made to make it more attractive for talented persons to remain in teaching and to enter the profession.

Teachers sought better pay and benefits, but they also pressed for one of the most important attributes of a professional, a strong role in decision-making processes. Rallis (1990) stated that empowering teachers, that is, giving them more control over decisions that affect their practice, is the goal of restructuring efforts. She equated empowerment with teacher professionalism. This is similar to what was done in the teacher militancy movement of the 1960s and 1970s which led to collective bargaining rights for teachers and other public employees in many states.

Darling-Hammond (1988) emphasized that professionalism seeks to heighten accountability by investing in knowledge and its responsible use. Knowledge—experiential, clinical, and research knowledge—gives the professional teachers the authority to control their own agendas.

In their historical perspective on teacher empowerment, Watts and McClure (1990) said that teacher leaders were not talking of educational reform as an abandonment of the bilateral decision making of collective bargaining in order to move to a different model. They called for the empowerment of teachers so that students could be se: ved more effectively.

The same authors stated that the bureaucratic model of school organizations was based on the assumption that teachers were minimally competent and required close inspection and supervision. They recommended that teachers and site administrators be placed at the center of the educational process with their students in order to obtain high-quality schools.

Rallis (1990) stated that the restructured schools need collaborative leadership through which a strong culture with shared values and beliefs is built. Similarly, Lieberman and Miller (1990) maintained that the role of teachers in school restructuring involves two behaviors: colleagueship and leadership. They stated that schools with strong cultures tend to celebrate collegiality, collaboration, risk taking, and experimentation; they value both individuality and community.

Teacher leaders do exist both in the context of informal organization and the formal entity of their associations. What is demanded within the context of the professional role of teaching is a different form and expanded concept of leadership. It is leadership that accepts responsibility fully and that initiates exchanges with all levels of the Concentric Model. It is eager to establish new relationships and to enhance old ones. The focus is on becoming a determinant force in making a positive difference in the success levels of the students.

## EFFECTS OF EMPOWERMENT ON OTHER ACTORS

The impact on the outer rings of the model are less clear at the present time. Concern should not be with such impact but rather on changes that must be made to facilitate the operations at the inner levels.

Statutes, policies, procedures, regulations, and other legal articles regulate the roles of administrators and the governmental rings of the Concentric Model for Restructure. Such items have been put into effect over an extended period of time. It will be necessary to alter them where they conflict with the new structure. Tradition should not be the basis for continuation of past practice. Recent executive, legislative, and judicial decisions at state levels give encouragement to the potential for responsiveness of bureaucracies to the need for change.

For the rings which include such entities as citizens, corporations, and foundations, empowerment of students, parents, and teachers provides an opportunity for greater awareness of actual needs at the operational levels. More effective evaluation of practices and greater accountability for outcomes may stimulate more external support for the school system.

## CLOSING COMMENTS

Many exciting ideas developed by experts on language, learning, and literacy were presented in this book. Their relevance to and appropriateness for particular settings have to be evaluated by school personnel. The present chapter's focus was on the dynamic interplay that must take place in the review processes. The need to make students the focus of the decision processes was stressed, and the critical need to restructure schools to make them more responsive to students' needs was presented.

The persons closest to the delivery of services must be involved in decision-making processes and they must be given appropriate power and responsibilities for selecting, implementing, and evaluating the literacy programs. Criteria for success must be defined in operational terms, and reliable and valid assessments must be made.

A dynamic, responsive system is essential for the success of literacy programs. The concepts underlying programs are complex, as are the needs of the students. The programs are being implemented in systems where it is impossible for persons at the top levels of the hierarchical order to identify all of the variables that will affect the programs, to respond to those that do, or to control their influence.

Persons working directly with the students, and, insofar as possible, the students themselves must be given the autonomy needed to function. They must be held accountable for making adjustments based on needs and on the levels of success in attaining program goals.

## REFERENCES

Baratta, A.N. (1990). The new literacy: A futures retrospective. In C. Hedley, J. Houtz, & A. Baratta (Eds.), *Cognition, curriculum and literacy* (pp. 215–223). Norwood, NJ: Ablex.

Darling-Hammond, L. (1988). An accountability and teacher professionalism. *American Educator, 12*(4), 8–13.

Duckworth, K. (1981). *Linking educational policy and management with student achievement.* Eugene, OR: Center for Educational Policy and Management, University of Oregon.

Kirst, M.W., & McLaughlin, M. (1990). Rethinking policy for children: Implications for educational administration. In B. Mitchell & L. Cunningham (Eds.), *Educational leadership and changing contexts of families, communities and schools* (Eighty-ninth Yearbook of the National Society for the Study of Education, part 2, pp. 69–90). Chicago: The University of Chicago Press.

Lieberman, A., & Miller, I. (1990, June). Restructuring schools: What matters and what works. *Phi Delta Kappan,* pp. 70–10, 759–764.

Rallis, S. (1990). Professional teachers and restructured schools: Leadership challenges. In P. Mitchell & L. Cunningham (Eds.), *Educational leadership and changing contexts of families, communities, and schools* (Eighty-ninth Yearbook of the National Society for the Study of Education, part 2, pp. 184–209). Chicago: The University of Chicago Press.

Reed, S., & Sautter, R.C. (1990, June). Children of poverty: The status of 12 million young Americans. *Phi Delta Kappan,* 71–10, K1–K12.

Watts, G.B., & McClure, R.M. (1990, June). Expanding the contract to revolutionize school renewal. *Phi Delta Kappan,* pp. 71–10, 765–774.

Westbury, I. (1990). Textbooks, textbook publishers, and the quality of schooling. In D.L. Elliot & G. Woodward (Eds.), *Textbooks and schooling in the United States.* (Eighty-ninth Yearbook of the National Society for the Study of Education, part 1, pp. 1–22). Chicago: The University of Chicago Press.

# Appendix

# Family Literacy Resources

## Robin Alinkofsky

### RESOURCES FOR LITERACY DEVELOPMENT IN A FAMILY SETTING

Most of the other chapters in this book deal with developing language and reading naturally. More specific resources that parents or teachers can utilize to develop literacy in interesting and fun ways are listed below. These materials are easily accessible in local libraries, bookstores, video stores, or computer stores.

One of the most highly recommended suggestions to help develop literacy is reading aloud to your child. When this suggestion is made to parents they often raise the question as to how they know what books to choose for their children. There are many resources that one can use to receive help in choosing books to read aloud.

The first resource is the children's librarian and/or classroom teacher. The second is books or videos that suggest books appropriate for different age/grade levels. Some examples of these include:

Brett, D. (1988). *Annie stories: A special kind of storytelling*. New York: Workman.
Copperman, P. (1986). *Taking books to heart: How to develop a love of reading in your child*. Reading, MA: Addison Wesley. [For parents of children ages 2–9.]
Fuller, D.W. (1988). *Video books kids love: A parent's easy guide to great books and shared reading*. Amherst, NY: Winward. [716/689-2157]
Hearne, B. (1990). *Choosing books for children: A commonsense guide* (rev. & expanded ed.). New York: Delacorte Press.
Kimmell, M.M., & Siegel, E. (1990). *For reading out loud! A guide to sharing books with children ages 5–15* (rev. and updated ed.). New York: Delacorte Press.

Korbin, B. (1988). *Eye openers! How to choose and use children's books about real people, places and things.* New York: Viking Penguin.

Landsberg, M. (1987). *Reading for the love of it: Best books for young readers.* New York: Prentice-Hall. [A guide to more than 400 great children's books.]

Lipson, E.R. (1988). *The New York Times parent's guide to the best books for children.* New York: Times Books (division of Random House).

Oppenheim, J., Brenner, B., & Boegehold, B.D. (1986). *Choosing books for kids: Choosing the right book for the right child at the right time.* New York: Ballantine Books. [Over 1,500 book reviews.]

Rudman, M.K., & Pearce, A.M. (1988). *For love of reading: A parent's guide to encouraging young readers from infancy through age 5.* Mount Vernon, NY: Consumer Union. [Features annotated bibliography for over 1,000 classic, award-winning, and contemporary children's books.]

Trelease, J. (1989). *Read aloud handbook.* New York: Viking Penguin.

Besides books and videos on choosing books, one can find guides to activities for children. The two most well known are Ruth Graves' (1987) *The R.I.F. Guide to Encouraging Young Readers* (a fun-filled activity book for parents and kids), Garden City, NY: Doubleday; and Peggy Kaye's (1984) *Games for Reading,* New York: Pantheon. There are also books that tell about places to take children in various cities. The following are examples from New York City: Bubbles Fisher's (1990) *Candy Apple New York for Kids* (2nd ed.), New York: Frommer/Prentice-Hall; and *Gulliver's Travels: A Kid's Guide to New York City* (1988), New York: Harcourt Brace Jovanovich, Inc. There are similar guides for other cities. There are also general books or pamphlets with ideas for parents. For example, there is a booklet that is based upon the report *Becoming a Nation of Readers* published in 1984 by the National Institute of Education, U.S. Department of Education, Washington, DC. This 1988 booklet is called *Becoming a Nation of Readers: What Parents Can Do* and is available through the Consumer Information Center, Pueblo, CO. A second source of pamphlets for parents is International Reading Association. Two examples include Silvern and Silvern's *Beginning Literacy and Your Child* (1990), and *Summer Reading Is Important.* Reading Is Fundamental (RIF) in Washington, DC has at least four brochures available for parents. The four titles are: *Building a Family Library, Family Storytelling, Summertime Reading,* and *Encouraging Young Writers.* Local libraries may have copies of some of these books or pamphlets for you to look over or borrow.

Another suggestion is to use books that have audio tapes or records accompanying them, such as *The Tale of Peter Rabbit* narrated by Meryl Streep published by Rabbit Ears Books. This allows children to read the book while they listen to it being read aloud without you as the parent having to read. This is particularly good for those parents who have reading difficulties themselves. One can also utilize children's magazines such as *Highlights for Children* or *Sesame Street* to develop literacy skills in an enjoyable way. A good resource that lists all the current children's magazines published is Donald R. Stoll's (1990) *Magazines for Children*, Newark, DE: International Reading Association.

Many experts including Jim Trelease and Marie Winn suggest doing away with television viewing. As a reading teacher I've suggested ways that parents can utilize television viewing to their advantage. It is suggested that they become aware of the educational programs that are available, such as *Sesame Street, Electric Company, Reading Rainbow,* and so on, and the public broadcast stations on which they appear. In some areas there may be three or more PBS stations that air these programs at different times of the day and week. Find out the days and times and have your children watch them. If they're in school at that time you can tape it on a VCR for later viewing. If you want to use programs on regular television stations, it is recommended that you watch the program with the children and then discuss the program after viewing it. You can also make the connection to books by choosing books that are about your children's favorite television characters; for example, there are a series of small books on the adventures of the Smurfs. Books like Steve and Ruth Bennett's (1991) *365 TV-Free Activities You Can Do With Your Child* (Bob Adams, Inc., Holbrook, MA), Susan K. Perry's (1990) *Playing Smart: A Parent's Guide to Enriching Offbeat Learning Activities for Ages 4–14* (Free Spirit Publishing, Inc., Minneapolis, MN), and Beatrice G. Davis's (1991) *On the Road to Reading: 101 Creative Activities for Beginning Readers* (Berrent Publications, Inc., Roslyn, NJ) all offer great ideas to develop literacy skills.

For those who have VCRs, one can find many educational videos to use with children. One can find classic children's stories, science videos, and videos that teach concepts such as numbers, alphabet, and so on. For example, *Dinosaurs* and *More Dinosaurs* by Midwich Entertainment, *Adventures in Dinosaurland* by Family Home Entertainment, *Dinosaurs! A Fun-Filled Trip Back in Time* by Golden Vision/Golden Books, *Romper Room and Friends* series by Playhouse Video, *Captain Kangaroo* by Brittanica Video, Sesame Street Home Video series, and *Jim Henson's Play Along Video* series like *Mother Goose's Stories* by Lorimar; Playskool also has a series of videos on a variety of topics.

A final suggestion deals with using the personal computer to develop literacy skills. One can find skills materials in foreign languages, social studies, science, mathematics, and language arts/reading. Linkword has foreign language programs in German, Spanish, French, and Russian, and Davidson has Word Attack Plus in Spanish and French. Broderbund has a series of social studies programs using a character called Carmen

Sandiego. This includes *Where in the US is Carmen Sandiego?*, *Where in the World Is Carmen Sandiego?*, *Where in Europe Is Carmen Sandiego?*, and *Where in Time Is Carmen Sandiego?* MECCA Software has a program on the wild frontier for ages 10 and up called *The Oregon Trail*. Vision Software has a program called *Alf's US Geography*. Brittanica has two programs: One is called *States and Traits*, and the other one is *European Nations and Locations*. Computeach has a program called *See the USA* for ages eight and up. PC Globe has two programs in this area: One is called *PC Globe* and the other is *PC USA*.

Dinosaurs are popular with children, and this topic taps social studies and science. Polarware has a program called *Dinosaurs Are Forever*. First Byte has a program called *Dinosaur Discovery Kit*. Interactive Learning has a program called *Dinosaur Dig* for grades 3–8. Maverick Software has one science program called *Discovering Chemistry*.

Programs in mathematics range from simple number recognition to algebra and geometry. Brittanica has *Math Maze* and *Trapazoid (Geometry)*. Maverick Software has one called *Discovering Numbers*. Davidson has *Math and Me*, *Algebra Blaster*, and *Math Blaster Mystery*. The Weekly Reader Sticky Bear series has four programs called *Numbers*, *Math*, *Math 2*, and *Word Problems*. Vision Software has a program called *ALF's Add and Subtract* and Learning Company has *Math Rabbit*.

In language arts/reading, there is again a wide range of materials. There are alphabet programs, writing programs, word attack/vocabulary programs, grammar programs, and comprehension programs. Maverick Software has a problem called *Discovering Alphabet*. Spinnaker has one called *Alphabet Zoo* for ages 3–7. Springboard has one called *Easy as ABC* for ages 3–6. Weekly Reader's Sticky Bear series has two programs called *ABC* and *Alphabet*. First Byte has a program that works on the alphabet and vocabulary called *First Letters and Words*.

There are a number of word processing or writing programs available. Learning Company has *Writer Rabbit* for ages 7–10 and *Children's Writing and Publishing Center* for ages 9 and up. Spinnaker has *Kids on Keys* for ages 4–9 and *Kidwriter* for ages 6–10. First Byte has *Kid Talk* (a reading and writing program for ages 5–12); There is also a program called *Bankstreet Writer* that is commonly used in school settings.

In the area of word attack/vocabulary development there were not that many programs available. Davidson has two programs called *Word Attack* and *Word Attack Plus*. CBS Interactive Learning has *Richard Scarry's Best Electronic Word Book Ever* and Vision Software has *ALF's World of Words*. The two programs on grammar found in the local computer stores were Davidson's *Grammar Gremlins* and Weekly Reader's Sticky Bear series *Parts of Speech*.

There are many programs to develop comprehension. Some samples include the following: Spinnaker's *Kindercomp* for ages 3–8; Computeach's *Stepping Stones I* for ages 2–4, *Stepping Stones II* for ages 5–7, and *Joshua's Reading Machine* for ages 4–7; Learning Company's *Reader Rabbit*; and Weekly Reader's Sticky Bear series has *Reading Comprehension.*

One can also find a number of interactive kind of story programs like Walt Disney's *Chase on Tom Sawyer's Island*, *Black Caulderon*, and *Matter-horn Screamer*; Computeach's *Once Upon a Story*; Origin's *Tangled Tales*; and Tom Snyder Productions *Flodd, the Bad Guy* (for ages 2–6).

Finally, there are games that can teach or reinforce literacy skills on the computer. Some of these games are based upon familiar board games, while others are based upon television game shows. Game Tek has programs called *Candy Land* for ages 3–6, *Go to the Head of the Class* for ages 8 and up, *Chutes and Ladders* for ages 4–7, *Wheel of Fortune Golden Edition*, *Jeopardy Fifth Anniversary Edition*, *Super Password*, *Double Dare*, and *Press Your Luck*. Share Data also puts out versions of *Jeopardy* and *Wheel of Fortune*. They also publish *Family Feud*, *Hollywood Squares*, and *Card Sharks*. Box Office puts out a program called *High Rollers*, and Electronic Arts puts out *Scrabble*. A version of *Scrabble* is also put out by Virgin Leisure Genius.

# Author Index

# Subject Index

## A

Approximations, 7
Assessment, 49–67
portfolios in, 52–63
developing a plan, 52–53
documenting literacy growth, 61–67
anecdotal records, 62
checklists and rating scales, 62
language inventories, 64
literacy folders, 63
procedures for gathering data, 53–63
analysis of performance samples, 55–63
oral miscue, 55–56
retelling of stories, 56359
writing samples, 59–61
observation, 53–55
problems with standardized tests, 50–53

## C

Cambourne's model of the conditions for learning, 5–7
approximations, 7
demonstration, 5
expectation, 6
immersion, 5
response, 7
responsibility, 6
use, 7
Conditions for learning, *see* Cambourne's model of the conditions for learning
Conventions of print, 120–124
Curriculum, writing across, 81–83

## E

Empowerment movement for new directions in literacy, 181–190
effects of, 187–188
restructuring the school, 182–183
Baratta concentric model for school restructure, 184

Empowerment movement (cont.)
parent focus within the, 184–185
student focus within the, 183
teacher focus within the, 186–187
theoretical framework for, 180–182
Duckworth's model, 181
Environments that promote literacy development, 167–177
creation of physical, 175–177
developmental model for teaching within, 171–173
language, thinking, and learning within, 169–171
natural language, 173–174
psycho-philosophical perspectives, 168–169
Environments that promote play, 44–47

## F

Family resources for literacy development, 190–194
Functions of language, 20–23

## H

Heuristic function of language, 22

## I

Imaginative function of language, 22
Information-processing theory, 13–17
Informative function of language, 22
Instrumental function of language, 21
Interactional function of language, 21
Intersubjectivity and language development, 20

## L

Language, 3–17
basic principles of natural language, 4–5
functions, 20–23
heuristic, 22
imaginative, 22